GOOD AS YOU

GOOD AS YOU

PAUL FLYNN

EBURY
PRESS

1 3 5 7 9 10 8 6 4 2

Ebury Press, an imprint of Ebury Publishing
20 Vauxhall Bridge Road
London SW1V 2SA

Ebury Press is part of the Penguin Random House group of companies
whose addresses can be found at global.penguinrandomhouse.com

Penguin
Random House
UK

First published by Ebury Press in 2017

www.penguin.co.uk

A CIP catalogue record for this book is available from the British Library

ISBN 978 1785032929

Song lyrics in order of appearance:
'It Ain't Necessarily So' by Bronski Beat (George and Ira Gershwin)
'Homosapien' by Pete Shelley (P. Shelley)
'Glad to Be Gay' by Tom Robinson Band (Tom Robinson)
'Karma Chameleon' by Culture Club (George O'Dowd, Jon Moss,
Mikey Craig, Roy Hay, Phil Pickett)
'I Should Be So Lucky' by Kylie Minogue (Mike Stock, Matt Aitken, Pete Waterman)
'Freedom! '90' by George Michael (George Michael)

Printed and bound in Great Britain by Clays Ltd, St Ives PLC

For Dave

CONTENTS

PROLOGUE

I was sitting in the basement of a coffee shop in Soho, London, waiting for a celebrated and garlanded rent boy from the parish. It was 2010, and Greek Pete had been the subject of a recent documentary film, following a year in his life. I was to interview him for the Dutch gay magazine *BUTT*. A Chinese man was slumped on the next table with a seeping paper cup of tea beside him, sleeping for the duration of what turned out to be a quietly riveting conversation.

I learned so much that afternoon, most alarmingly about how much it costs to have someone killed, a tale Pete told in relation to a friend of his in the same profession who was worried for his safety, as he had a famous MP as a client and his story looked like it was about to go public (it never did). Pete had not long since given up his life in prostitution and was thinking about returning to the education he'd abandoned when he started his career. He'd started reading philosophy again and was knee-deep in Plato's *Republic*, prompting something of an early-life crisis about the meaning of what he'd been doing, why and how it had all happened and what the consequences might turn out to be. 'Crisis' is probably the wrong word, actually. It was more of an evaluation. Pete was a deeply wise fellow. Young men who've seen a lot of life often are. 'Part of coming to terms with being gay,' he suggested at one point, 'is accepting that all your previous belief systems collapse. You are not accepted in normal, functioning society. So what is my function? I took that question and I ran with it.'

In the 45 years of my lifetime so far Britain has fluctuated between the wildest extremes of rejection and acceptance when it comes to gay men. We've fallen in and out of fashion like hemlines. One minute it was clobbering us over the head with truncheons in public lavatories, the next it was Nick Grimshaw waking up the nation on Radio 1, Gok Wan talking about frocks on Channel 4, national social-media mourning for Pete Burns, apologies to pensioners for putting them in prison and musicals about Alan Turing at the Royal Opera House. This being Britain, I suppose we were always going to take the wonky route.

I was having a drink with a straight couple I'm very fond of in 2014, the year it looked like the equal-marriage bill would pass through parliament, the last piece of statute to cement equality for gay men and women. One of them asked how I felt about it. Under a broad lens, of course, it felt brilliant. Why wouldn't it? Who wants to be unequal? But under a more microscopic glare it took me deep into the realms of a truth Pete hit on, one that I hadn't thought about for a while – that strange transition that happens in a gay man of my age's life, from feeling like an enemy of the state to being its friend. The thought lodged and I couldn't rid myself of it. How weird was it to have lived a short life with these odd parentheses wrapped around it? To have a life's experience right up to the point of becoming unquestionably middle-aged pivoting on the acceptance of people you're never likely to meet and the temperature they set toward your kind of folk in law?

Look, I've lived a pretty gay life. I went into the manic testosterone recesses of male post-pubescence in 1984, the same year 'Smalltown Boy' and 'Relax' came out, and I actually clocked the major acts of social significance in both songs. They're records I can't hear now without feeling like the boy I once was from the vantage point of being the man I never thought I'd properly be allowed to be.

I went to my first gay club at 16. I met the first gay man I knew dying of AIDS at 17. Not unrelatedly, that year was the last I ever said 'no' to the question 'are you gay?' I had my first boyfriend, not a secret, an actual one I told friends about, at 18. I read all six volumes of *Tales of the City* at 19, in between taking full advantage of the strange transition of my home city turning from Madchester to Gunchester to Gaychester. I had my first appropriate boyfriend at 20. I went on holiday with him to an eastern European capital city for the first time at 21. Because the sensation of being in love with someone of the same sex who I actually wanted to tell the world about felt so unequivocally ace and so completely alien, I behaved absolutely appallingly to him. I went to Trade for the first time at 23. At 24, I met an airline pilot in a club who took me to New York for the first time two weeks later. We danced at 4am in a dungeon close to the Chelsea Piers to Junior Vasquez playing an 18-minute, pots-and-pans remix of 'Get Your Hands Off My Man', just because we could.

By the age of 25 I had written my first feature for national gay magazine *Attitude*, about the filming of the first episode of *Queer As Folk*. I was 27 when the first gay man I knew to kill himself did so. I met my family's big musical hero Elton John at 30. I went to my first civil-partnership ceremony at 33. I got my first mortgage with a boyfriend that year, too. I interviewed the first Oscar-winning actor to play a gay role at 34. (It was Heath Ledger and he was absolutely amazing. I was offered ten minutes on the phone with him during the publicity run for *Brokeback Mountain* and I replaced the receiver an hour-and-a-half later).

I met Dave, the love of my life, at 36, walking up Upper Street, the site of Britain's first ever Gay Pride march. I met my first gay MP at 37, introduced to me by the gentlemanly Newport West Labour minister with whom I share a name, Paul Flynn, in a bar at the House of Commons. I went to my first gay bar in Beijing at 39. When I was 42, a really lovely vicar who was marrying our friend Polly offered his Wesleyan chapel for the purposes of gay marriage if Dave and I ever wanted to avail ourselves of his services.

Because life is life and you forget about all this business the minute it's happened, I hadn't realised what a shared and useful vantage point gay men had been sitting at to watch the changing perception of themselves by the establishment from the inside, on the right side of it all. I'd not realised how much I had actually felt that startling move from terror to tenderness. Feeling like the enemy, like you are feared for who you are, is almost as weird as the first time you hear 'homophobe' being shouted as a playground insult while walking past a schoolyard (Glasgow, 2006). You attune to so much small detail when you live with other people's presumptions of what you are, and forever fight hard to correct those misgivings.

I was on a job in New York the year after that conversation with my two friends, reading a story over breakfast in the *New York Times* Arts section about a book that had charted the progress in politics towards legal equality for LGBT people in America. I thought, You couldn't really do that in Britain. Because we are such a small, strange and marvellous place, successive governments tend to follow the lead of popular culture, not the other way round. I thought about the things that Britain is best at, our national obsessions – nightclubs, pop music, football, telly, magazines, even elevating rent boys to film stars – and started to see a tale of love and hate, pride and prejudice, a microcosmic and macrocosmic journey from 'Smalltown Boy' to same-sex marriage. All life (and death) looked like it was in there.

To keep *Good As You* a felt experience, I can only tell that story how I saw it unfold. There are as many different versions, timeframes and perspectives on the national run-around from fear to friendliness in our lives as there are LGBT people who've lived them. The British gay story is indivisible from the Great British gay culture. The more I look at it and the heroes it has produced, the greater that culture becomes to me. This monumental shift didn't occur because someone from above decided it would. Quite the reverse. Until I was 27 years old and a Labour government started affecting some genuine legal change, the state, schools, the Church and, in many people's cases, the family made being the person you are as wilfully difficult as they possibly could for no reason besides what the neighbours might say. Britain's big gay rollover happened because all of us made it happen, so that a little lad like Greek Pete coming of age in 2017 wouldn't have to think that accepting who he is would mean having to redraw his entire moral boundaries ever again. That's just the way it should be.

1. NATIONAL ANTHEMS

On 10 August 1984 I turned into a teenager. The kind of teenager I turned into was one who, each Sunday, would write down the charts in a stolen lined schoolbook from St Paul's, an all-boys Catholic high school in Manchester's crumbling garden suburb Wythenshawe. I was the first boy at the newsagent's two doors down from the chippy on the parade of shops on Wendover Road every alternate Wednesday, 45p in hand, ready for the new issue of *Smash Hits*. I told my mum I didn't want to join the Boy Scouts that year, firstly because I didn't want to join the Boy Scouts, and secondly – and most importantly – because the scouts clashed with the essential Thursday night double bill of *Top of the Pops* and *Fame*. We didn't yet have a video recorder, the exciting new machine that could change time and space on telly. All of that stuff, pop music, TV and the attendant cultural doors they opened into nightlife, fashion and art – everything that suburbia wasn't – seemed so monumentally important back then. It was not the sort of business you'd give up being in full knowledge of in order to learn how to tie knots, light fires or pitch tents with the added, unspoken potential undercurrent of being molested by a light-fingered Akela who hadn't reconciled his past with the thrilling reverberations of the modern world.

I suppose it was just a temporal accident that the year I turned teenage two pivotal gay figureheads appeared on *Top of the Pops* and the front cover of *Smash Hits*. But to a mind spiralling with the possibility of what life had to offer outside a grey, rainy world that pivoted on Saturday afternoons spent leafing through the vinyl at Wythenshawe library's record department, it felt exactly like magic. There was a point somewhere between the angry, sad falsetto of Jimmy Somerville and the mischievous sex of Holly Johnson that felt like a perfect distillation of a gay adult life. There were other figures seeming to support their contention in more clandestine terms, not yet ready to talk transparently about their differences. But the clues were all there. Because Holly and Jimmy were doing the talking for everyone, some amazing men acted as a fantastical supporting cast to the gay protagonists. There was Morrissey, the Smiths' singer, who opened his career with a record sleeve depicting a bare man's buttocks and a B-side called 'Handsome Devil'. Pet Shop Boys, whose first number one 'West End Girls' hid its light in plain sight on another B-side, 'A Man Could Get Arrested', a song about the lively gay cruising ground at London's Brompton Cemetery. There was Pete Burns, the gothic gob-on-a-stick who had turned the plaintive gender-bending prettiness of Boy George and Marilyn into something like a brilliant, brave nightmare and appeared all the more amazing for it. Here was Freddie Mercury doing the hoovering in a wig, moustache and patent leather miniskirt. Black Britain had the smooth posturing of Andy Polaris singing 'Love Is just a Great Pretender' and Imagination's Leee John gliding across the floor in a lamé jock strap. George Michael and Andrew Ridgeley parleyed something between friendship, brotherhood and unrequited love in Wham! With his Lady Diana hairdo and leather jacket it wasn't hard to figure out why George's guilty feet had no rhythm or what exactly the different corner was that he might eventually turn. Marc Almond was trailblazing an idea of self-invention and queerness that could shift from fragility to brutality in a couplet. Billy MacKenzie sang in a transcendent croon that brought Italian-opera levels of heartbreak to Thursdays. These were not figures at the margins of British culture. They were its home-grown stars.

Amid songs of men's pretence, desire, denial, corruption and complicity, 'Smalltown Boy' and 'Relax' rose straight to the top. Seeing first Holly Johnson batting a balloon back from his face and grinding his hips to 'Relax', then Jimmy Somerville's engagingly shy shuffle to 'Smalltown Boy' did something direct to me. It stopped me feeling alone. The reading materials and pictures in magazines only backed up what was perfectly obvious from their art. These were men who talked about the details of gay life with candour. They were unlocking doors. Within the loose narratives of both songs was everything I needed to shove me through the tricky terrain of pubescence in the often faltering knowledge that everything would probably turn out OK. That is how heroic meaningful pop music can be when it chimes at the right time with the right person.

At 12 years old in 1984 in south Manchester, I was used to hearing gay men being the butt of the joke. We couldn't have sex legally until 21. Homosexuality had become weirdly merged in the suburban mindset with the old bloke whose house you were told to stay away from and strangers opening doors and asking kids if they wanted a lift in a rusting Ford Cortina. The thought of marrying was unimaginable unless as a shoddy compromise to keep you in the closet. The advent of AIDS added a particularly crucifying new twist to the tale of homosexuality equalling a tragic end. The early choice from where I was sitting, before Jimmy Somerville and Holly Johnson offered a warm embrace from the TV screen, looked something like this: don't act on being gay and be unhappy, or act on it and end up beaten up, slagged off, laughed at and almost certainly dead.

Sometimes gay men becoming the butt of the joke was just because, yes, men who look and sound different can be funny, and sometimes just because British pop culture was in such a state of stilted infancy no one had worked out that, while often it's fun to be cruel, cruelty hurts. It has consequences. I grew up on the other side of the Arndale Centre from Bernard Manning's Embassy Club, a place that now feels like a Situationist joke but was part of the social climate in Manchester then whereby anything that was not white, straight and male was fodder to be torn apart. An imaginary line was drawn up between them and us, straight and gay. It didn't make any sense to me.

No one knew then that this predominant British culture was extinguishing itself and that a decisive move for gay men, from being enemies to friends of the state, was beginning at full pelt. Bronski Beat and Frankie Goes to Hollywood felt like its rallying cry. They were my first hints that men didn't have to stand passively watching the status quo, that we could fight back with intelligence, provocation and sincerity. *Top of the Pops* was teaching me the lessons a Catholic education couldn't.

When the idea of homosexuality is inherently ridiculous in culture, a dialogue forms in your little teenage brain. It says, OK, I get it: those older men that don't marry, that talk and walk funny, can't throw a ball properly and might do things that will send them straight to hell do seem to be a bit scared of life; those men like John Inman and Larry Grayson, even their executive predecessors, the *Carry On* elder statesmen Kenneth Williams and Charles Hawtrey, they're funny because they're different. But what if you feel a bit different, too? Do you just get used to the idea of being laughed at? Is that it?

To my 12-year-old mind Jimmy Somerville and Holly Johnson did not look queer at all. They didn't look fairyish, nancyish or anything like the punchline to an untold joke. They didn't seem punishable or there to be laughed at. Hitting the cranial hotspots scrambling at every identity issue in adolescence, they looked like the thing I least expected gay men to look like. They looked brave.

Telling the truth is a hard business. One of them would likely not have been enough. If these songs, three listens in and glistening already like national anthems, had occupied my brain space in isolation they might have represented an anchorless life raft. Perhaps if each one of Holly and Jimmy's alumni that kept their sexualities to themselves on *Top of the Pops* and in *Smash Hits* had come to be seen in their honest context rather than in the half-light of a closet door, well, that might have helped. But good pop fortune meant Holly and Jimmy arrived as a twin attack. They opened a conversation others wilfully shied away from, delivering the next generation, my generation, the full and complete confidence to be as good as you.

A Trip Round Liverpool

At 10am on Saturday 25 October 2014, Holly Johnson ordered a full English breakfast at the Hole in the Wall café in Liverpool. The singer was in high spirits. He swapped lively chatter with the waiter, a young, camp man who had yet to take off his coat for service. They exchanged glances in the way two gay men have grown accustomed to in twenty-first century Britain: an arch of the eyebrow that doubles as acknowledgement; a look that says 'I know what you got up to last night'. Likely, the young waiter didn't. Friday night had been a triumph for the singer. He played his first solo live show on home turf. At the Echo Arena he capitalised on the career promise that had suggested itself 30 years previously without ever quite coming to fruition. In 1984 Holly was part of a second wave of localised Liverpool pop hysteria, a countrywide moment that felt as if his five-piece gang Frankie Goes to Hollywood were the heirs apparent to Beatlemania. Perhaps the most astonishing detail of their rise was that the first Frankie single – the throbbing, emblematic, no-nonsense, million-selling number one 'Relax', a song that pulsed around the globe – was the sound of gay sex.

'For people of our generation, it was a big issue,' Holly says. 'For the first seven years of my life it was illegal to be gay. Now it's kind of a non-issue.' No single public figure stands up to the 30-year shift in British gay equality, from 1984 to 2014, with quite the poignant accuracy of Holly. It was as if, with 'Relax', he delivered British gay men their Big Bang theory or their Adam and Eve parable; in tandem with the old playground taunt, this time it really was the tale of Adam and Steve. Holly's life and work have traced the contours of the gay male transition in statute to legal parity with perfect, hard precision. In those 30 years he touched the highest highs and the traumatic lows of gay culture. Here, in Liverpool, his significance to the British gay graph played out transparently. As the hometown crowd moved as one to his fail-safe curtain call, the man who brought gay sex into the national living room in 1984 felt like its prodigal son and homecoming queen. It was hard not to see it as some kind of canonisation.

Satiated after eating, Holly left the Hole in the Wall and took a wander around some old haunts in the city. He walked up and down Bold Street and was stopped frequently in jolly recognition. He took a pit stop outside a local hairdresser's where the aproned owner wanted to share a special word about the previous night's engagement. He moved on past the Beatles incubation unit the Cavern Club, by the site of the old Probe Records toward Stanley Street, the home of the city's visible gay village. He delightedly pointed out the rainbow motif, the freedom flag for gay equality, etched into the street sign. 'It's the only one in Britain with it on, you know,' he noted.

Perhaps it was just coincidence that Holly's first solo date in Liverpool was in the year that Britain achieved complete legal equality for gay men. Perhaps higher powers were at work. He asked a cleaner coming out of a grand Victorian doorway whether this was the entrance to Jody's, the gay club whose walls had watched over his early rites of social passage and whose sound had seeped into his consciousness, forming the propulsive throb of 'Relax'. 'No, next door,' the silver-haired lady answered. She had a smile for the city's most infamous gay apostle.

'When I first came out onto the town in Liverpool,' he says, 'I came out as a gay person.' When he first arrived in the public consciousness he did it as a gay person, too. 'From 14 onwards I was going to gay places like the Lisbon and Jody's, seeing people, like Pete Burns, who were that little bit older than me. They had jobs at this hairdressing salon called A Cut Above the Rest. Jayne was the receptionist and Lynne was a hairdresser there.' Jayne Casey and Holly were in the band Big in Japan, which served as his punkier dress rehearsal for Frankie Goes to Hollywood. Lynne Burns was, astonishingly, Pete's wife. 'They were all employed and looked amazing. I looked up to them all because I was still a schoolboy.' Holly turned 14 in 1974: 'David Bowie was at the height of his fame. I went to see him at the Empire when he was Ziggy Stardust. I was wearing make-up and dying my hair and getting my head kicked in for doing it.' In the 30 years between his first number one record and first solo show on home turf, Holly Johnson has played out a tale befitting of the shifting sands of British gay culture. When Frankie first instructed the country to 'Relax', it was ready to do anything but.

William Johnson was born in Wavertree, Liverpool, in 1960, the son of a Catholic mother and Protestant father at a time when the difference mattered. 'My mother's family wouldn't go to her wedding at the Anglican church. It's hard to grasp now, living in this century, what it was like in the last one.' As an infant in the sixties he was schooled in a regimented religious doctrine that demonised homosexuality. 'I was a choir boy at St Mary's church. The American-style evangelists of Billy Graham would come to the local park and proselytise, and I went through the whole "a man may not lay with another man" idea of being gay. The torture of it, the guilt, growing up in Liverpool with a mixture of Catholic and Protestant religions, added to that macho guilt, football as religion, the whole spectrum of all of that. Religion pissed on its own chips, as far as I was concerned.'

Young William's God was instead anointed in the form of Andy Warhol. With his classmate Peter, who bore a passing enough resemblance to Bowie to get them both into an adult cinema on the London Road, he had his Damascene moment aged 14 watching the Warhol film *Trash*, then the scourge of polite society, inflaming the pages of the *Daily Mirror* on his mother's kitchen table. It ignited an intuitive spark in him for the power of meaningful outrage: 'The idea of controversy had an impression on me from being a young kid. It was the queerness of it, in every sense of the word. It seemed so exotic.'

In an unmarked personal baptism William renamed himself Holly, after Warhol's favourite transvestite Factory star, Holly Woodlawn. By the time he was in gainful employment with Frankie ten years later, Holly was sufficiently schooled in the high alchemy of the intellectual shock manoeuvre to practise as he preached. 'Ziggy Stardust and the Spiders from Mars was a template for something that scared the horses. It shook people's sensibilities up,' he remembers of Bowie putting his arm around guitarist Mick Ronson on *Top of the Pops*. In the interim, a new watermark had been set. 'It wasn't so easy after the Sex Pistols.'

Bow Wow Wow was Malcolm McLaren's second management charge, after the Sex Pistols, calculated to hit Middle England and produce outrage. Their tactical marketing gamble was sex, not anarchy, and singer Annabella Lwin, then under the age of consent, had appeared naked on Bow Wow Wow's first album cover. So Holly set himself a personal challenge: 'I had a vision in my head that Frankie had to be more than Bow Wow Wow. It had to be more than a young girl naked on a record cover. It had to be something even more extreme.' It had to look and feel like gay sex, a last taboo. 'That's when I called in the S&M, Tom of Finland, *Mad Max 2* look for Frankie.' As a fledgling art student who had abandoned his studies for pop stardom, Holly understood the arresting power of potent visual imagery.

Not long into its lifespan, a secondary party lent 'Relax' its first significant marketing boost to help it become one of the two gay national anthems to appear as if from nowhere in 1984. Sensing the genesis of the song's key depiction, Radio 1's breakfast show anchor, Mike Read, banned it on the grounds of lewdness. Mission accomplished. 'It's hormonal,' says Holly. 'It is its own sort of ejaculation, "Relax". Without actually saying anything. It was just the swagger of it. There'd been female orgasms on record before ... ' Jane Birkin and Serge Gainsbourg scored a hit with 'Je T'aime ... Moi Non Plus' in the sixties, while Donna Summer did so with 'Love to Love You Baby' in the seventies; both featured an oral climax from the respective female singers. The eighties was ripe for gender reversal. 'There'd never been a male orgasm in the charts before that.'

The populist sound of 1984 was a simple, audacious stroke of unequivocal, unapologetic gayness. 'It came without a political edge. It said: This is the way it is. And if you don't like it, so what? It didn't come saying we're fighting for the right to be this way. It didn't ask for permission. Political proselytising was not my style. "Relax" was one big fuck you.' Handily, the muscular physicality of 'Relax' had a political ally. 'Oh,' says Holly, 'I was hyper aware of it being the year of "Smalltown Boy", too.'

The Record Label Executive

In 1983 young music-business executive Colin Bell was handed the reins of the underperforming label London Records. Colin had earned himself talking-point status in the music industry during the tail end of the seventies as the only openly gay man in it. Everyone in the business knew about the personal and professional relationship between Elton John and his manager, John Reid, but its physical and emotional side was kept deftly from public view, a judicious decision made on the assumption that being out of the closet at that time would damage sales beyond commercial repair. Indeed, on Valentine's Day 1984, Elton married his recording engineer Renate Blauel in a ceremony in Sydney, an event that in retrospect looks mostly informed by the copious clouds of cocaine showered over it.

Colin Bell's tenure at the helm of London Records did not start well. 'For the first six months I hadn't a fucking clue what I was doing,' he recalls. 'I remember having a Christmas break and thinking, If I don't learn how to do this fucking job very quickly I'm going to get sacked.' One of his earliest signings was Seona Dancing, a late-doors new romantic outfit fronted by the young Ricky Gervais. The future comedy star was, he says, 'very camp in those days'. The roster of artists Colin inherited included Bananarama, three young women in whom he instantly isolated the potential to exploit a natural allegiance to the gay market, and at least one man he knew to be gay, Blancmange keyboard-player Stephen Luscombe. 'I never really talked to Stephen about sexuality. It was understood that you wouldn't back then. He was very quiet. He had a boyfriend and a very settled relationship, but he would not have felt comfortable talking about it. Nobody did then. For those who wanted to be in the closet I was a little bit *too* open.'

That Christmas, an invitation landed on his desk to see a new band play at the festive celebrations for the gay publishers Brilliance

Books. 'There'd been a photograph of them in *Capital Gay*,' he says. 'I'd picked up the magazine and it was captioned "Bronski Beat, gay group".' He recognised the three members of Bronski Beat – Jimmy Somerville, Steve Bronski, Larry Steinbachek – from a meeting he'd attended at the Ovalhouse, south London, held by Ken Livingstone, who was leader of the Greater London Council, to help found a pink arts festival for London.

Unable to attend the Brilliance Books party, Colin sent down an envoy from London Records' A&R department: 'He came in the next day and said, "You have to see this group. They are incredible. And gay." I was a bit shocked because I'd assumed they'd be lousy.' Colin went to see Bronski Beat support Tina Turner at the Venue, a converted cinema opposite Victoria Station. Turner was starting to enjoy her mid-life renaissance, coaxed out of voluntary musical retirement by another British three-piece electronic outfit, Heaven 17. 'We heard "Smalltown Boy" for the first time and said, "It's an absolute smash." I played the cassette of it on loop in the car on the way home. This was about as obvious as a pop hit could get. There was this extraordinary voice, this extraordinary lyric, extremely moving, a combination of high-energy music and a pop song. There is something about that simple riff when it starts; it's wistful, sad and yet a big dance song. We just had to sign this group.'

Because it was his story, too, Colin connected to the words of the song, the 'somewhere over the rainbow' story of gay everymen coming to the capital to escape the constrictive judgement of suburbia. 'Most other record companies would not get that,' he says. 'I understood the gay media. I understood the gay clubs. I was in it. Bronski Beat saw that. I saw that. I was the only person in the record industry who was steeped in it and could talk to them in that language. I felt that we could market them exactly as they were, without trying to change them, as three south London skinheads who were gay and had a political agenda, without any glamorisation, in contrast with anything and everything else that was around. And I was prepared to do that and to make a point of doing that. No other record company was.'

Colin Bell was born in Belfast and attended Manchester University as a drama student in the early seventies. Gay Manchester then was unrecognisable from the gay Manchester of now. 'There was a pub called Napoleons. There was a club called the Rembrandt. There was a gay sauna, and that was it. There was a tiny gay society at the university and it was so small that you hardly dared to go to the meetings in case anybody saw you. You felt pretty lonely. So people gravitated to London.' Ziggy Stardust and the Spiders from Mars had not had quite the effect on the young Colin Bell that it did on the teenage Holly Johnson. 'The impact of David Bowie saying he was bisexual was explosive on the one hand. On the other, it wasn't quite believable. You always had the sense that this was somebody exploiting the idea of bisexuality for commercial gain, which of course it was, because there was nothing gay about David Bowie and never had been.'

Colin Bell's gay pop epiphany, in which he recognised truthfulness and soul over aesthetics and artifice, was Elton John. During his gap year, Colin worked as a stage-door keeper at Manchester University. 'Elton John came and did some concerts, and I think that's what turned me on to the music industry. I watched these concerts and my mind was blown. I thought, What the fuck is this? Genius talent. Of course, they were not publicly gay.'

It was a position he understood back then. 'Conventional wisdom in the music industry until Bronski Beat and Frankie Goes to Hollywood was, really, you have to keep it a secret. You couldn't be openly gay or it would damage your career forever. That wisdom lasted right through until 1984.'

Bronski Beat was not Colin Bell's first experience of handling gay pop stars who were out; he had already had his dress rehearsal for how to take a song like 'Smalltown Boy' to market unadorned. In 1976, Colin was introduced to another young performer, Tom Robinson: 'I had read an interview with the only openly gay musician I happened to have heard of, which was him, and I said, "You must be Tom Robinson in Café Society?" He was incredibly flattered because no one had ever recognised him before.'

Mutual friends of the pair assumed that Tom and Colin would become lovers. 'We tried on the first night and it lasted about five seconds before we collapsed into giggles. We went to bed and neither of us could or wanted to do it. Immediately after, we sat up all night talking.' At the time Colin Bell was living with Carolyn Eadie. Michael Portillo was then her boyfriend, not yet her husband. The future Tory Party leadership candidate was a trusted part of Colin's seventies London circle, one that mostly revolved around the Villiers Street gay nightclub Heaven. 'There were extraordinary people around. You wouldn't get this in London now, but it was where everybody interesting and gay went, all the time. Michael had his dalliances too, but was never gay. I admired him for talking about them publicly. But yes, Caroline was in the flat at the time of Tom and me, probably in the next room.'

Rather than becoming lovers, Colin took on the role of Tom's manager. Tom had experienced a similar awakening to Holly Johnson on seeing the Sex Pistols. Tom and Colin would argue into the small hours about the quality of the band, with Tom insisting that they would become as big as the Beatles and Bell stating that their songs were simply incomparable. Tom Robinson saw in the Pistols a door creaking open. 'He left Café Society and wanted to put together a new group that would be a politically orientated, openly gay punk group.' Colin became convinced of Tom's star potential after hearing him play two songs, '2-4-6-8 Motorway' and its more contentious cousin 'Glad to Be Gay'.

'Everyone leaves Tom Robinson out of the story,' says Holly Johnson on the subject of the pop cultural road to British gay equality. For Colin Bell, the omission is impossible. 'The thing about managing Tom was that he gave you no option about being open about your sexuality,' he says. Ironically, it was the 'Glad to Be Gay' author's homosexuality that was the thornier issue than his manager's. 'Tom was conflicted about his sexuality at that time and I think always was. It was part of the reason he was a little bit more extreme. It was almost to compensate. In his case, being gay was partly rebellion against a very conventional family background. I didn't have any of that. I was absolutely gay. No question about it.'

Colin Bell tried to get Tom signed as a gay punk act to the sound of repeatedly closing doors. Then Janet Street-Porter booked him for a show. 'We went on, did "Glad to Be Gay", and the next day every record company in London wanted to sign us,' says Colin. 'Glad to Be Gay' was never allowed to be an A-side. 'It would have been unimaginable to hear it played on the radio at that time. But it was an incredibly exciting period because Tom was the only gay artist around.'

The Tom Robinson Band had fleeting international significance. They went to America, where they played 'Glad to Be Gay' at the march on Washington for Harvey Milk, the San Francisco mayor who did more to change gay politics on a transatlantic political stage than anyone prior or since. 'We met Allen Ginsberg there. There were extraordinary experiences.' Robinson was later booed off a Gay Pride stage in London by a militant wing of the Gay Liberation Front when it was revealed that he was dating the woman he would go on to marry.

If his whistle had been whetted for a gay pop act to break through to the mainstream, Colin Bell was circumspect enough to recognise the tension of the times Bronski Beat, his next assignees, found themselves in. As a press officer at Phonogram Records in the early eighties he was charged with the marketing of a young electronic pop duo by the name of Soft Cell. 'Marc Almond was 500 per cent in the closet,' he says of the brittle, compelling frontman that would go on to number among the greatest British pop performers and songwriters of his age. 'It wasn't even a conversation. You couldn't say to him, Are you gay? Marc exemplified many of the artists of the eighties. Within themselves, I don't think they were ready to come out, let alone take all the risks of being public about it.'

In early eighties pop-marketing terminology, being gay was still considered to be the love that dare not speak its name. 'He would sometimes come in with a hunky boyfriend,' Colin says of Marc Almond. 'I was sitting in my office once, and there was a bag on the floor with a tube of KY Jelly at the top of it. I don't know what I was supposed to think.' He would try to persuade Marc to do interviews in the gay press, with *Gay Times* or *Gay News*. 'Not a chance. There was terrible anger between Soft Cell and the record company. There was a famous incident where they came in and smashed up all the gold discs in one of the offices.' Colin Bell's association with Soft Cell reached a tragicomic peak when a senior executive called his office to task the press officer with a new job. 'I was sent down to *Top of the Pops* to try to make Soft Cell look more butch. I remember the managing director saying you're the only one that can do it. Because I'm gay? Right.'

The fractious nature of dealing with the public issue of sexuality was not going to rear its head with Bronski Beat. 'If you felt like it was going to have an effect on your life, if you wanted to be a musician and an artist and being openly gay was going to stop you reaching your potential, I personally felt people had the right to make that decision for themselves. Bronski Beat nailed themselves to the mast from the start and you had to admire that. There were risks.'

'Smalltown Boy' was released in June 1984. Colin, Jimmy, Larry and Steve personally escorted a 12-inch disc to Heaven, the pulsating seat of London gay disco bacchanalia, to hear it played for the first time to its native audience. The Saturday night DJ Ian Levine spun the record twice, in succession. 'It was maybe one of the most exciting nights we had, just hearing that record on a Saturday night in that place. Levine must have been aware of it and we must have set it up with him.' Its first play on Radio 1 was by the DJ Peter Powell, who doubled his support of the group by airing the video on *Oxford Road Show*, the Friday night pop portal beamed out of the BBC studios on Oxford Road, Manchester.

The video for 'Smalltown Boy' was directed by Bernard Rose, who six months earlier had done the same on the video for 'Relax'. He was effectively charged with visualising the outer and inner lives of British gay men in 1984. 'The first video storyboard for "Smalltown Boy" was about somebody cottaging and being beaten up,' says Colin. He took an aggregate of the power of an openly gay pop act in 1984 against how far the elasticity of public acceptance would stretch: 'That, we couldn't get away with. We had to do it another way. And we came up with the idea of replacing the toilet with a swimming pool. We implied the beating up but didn't show it. So it could be a lonely boy who got beaten up in the big city by some rough types. There were his three mates, and what kind of relationship they had was all implied.' He recognised a similar collusion and blurring of the lines in the way that 'Relax' was marketed. 'We were aware that you had to be able to read music this transparent in two ways. You had to be able to see it for what it was, but you had to be able to explain it another way. It's all about drawing people in and allowing them to ignore it if they want to. The thing about "Relax" was that, although we can say it was about gay sexuality, it also was just about male sexuality. You could read it two ways.'

'Smalltown Boy' gathered popularity momentum with a speed that came as a surprise even to Colin Bell: 'The record just exploded.

You couldn't stop it. Straight up the charts, and worldwide, except for America where we nearly broke it but didn't quite. We got it to number 40 in the charts there and then Madonna invited Bronski Beat to open for her on her Virgin tour. Jimmy wouldn't do it. He didn't like Madonna. That was the start of the break-up of the band because Larry and Steve, who were less political and wanted the music career, wanted to tour with her.' In the event, 'Smalltown Boy' reached number three in the British charts. It was held off number one, in a sublime retrospective moment of British gay social history, by Wham!'s 'Wake Me Up Before You Go-Go' and Frankie Goes to Hollywood's 'Two Tribes'. According to Colin, Jimmy Somerville's primary opposition to Madonna was one thing: 'Overt heterosexuality.'

Top of the Pops

For men of a certain age and persuasion in 1984, getting to open the door of your first *Top of the Pops* dressing room at the BBC's Broadcasting House represented the pinnacle of suburban ambition. It was the golden carriage clock your parents had spent a lifetime toiling toward in factories, shipyards, hospitals, schools, mines, typing pools, shops, hotels and faceless office blocks. Pop was the other way: the great, glamorous working-class get-out clause. With certainty, purpose and vanity, the pouters, preeners and perverts claimed pop as their own that year.

George Orwell was wrong about 1984. Public surveillance was still in its infancy. The digital age felt like something even the popular technology programme *Tomorrow's World* could not cook up. *Big Brother* wouldn't steal the crown from *Top of the Pops* as TV's definitive national youth portal for another 15 years. The realities of screen culture for at least half an hour every week would have made Orwell blush. *Top of the Pops* in 1984 was the church of

the big gay pop dream. It was the place to show off and show out,
a stage of totemic personal significance. For the aspiring pop star
with something to say for himself, a wardrobe to wow with, a pose
to strike, a gong to bang and a song to sing, being on *Top of the Pops*
meant he'd made it.

Being introduced by a bloke off Radio 1 with a blond tint
and pastel leisurewear while surrounded by screaming teenage
girls under neon strip-lighting, miming to a backing track with
your buddies, worrying about what to wear and going out to lap
up the affirmation and adulation afterwards? This was it. For the
generation that had sat in their living rooms in the drizzly back
end of nowhere thrilling to the heroes that passed through their
telly every Thursday at 7.30pm, stepping into the footsteps of their
forebears was the first moment in turning from loser to legend.

For the gay wing of this thrilling postmodern cabal, both in and
out of the closet, it was about divesting your evident otherness of its
shame and turning it into a talking point. In the 17 years since the
Sexual Offences Act was drafted, legalising male homosexuality in
England and Wales, a generation had come boldly of age, refusing
to be cowed by the conventional understanding of how the Great
British angry young man dressed and spoke, at which angle his wrist
pivoted and, more fundamentally, what he got up to in bed. These
men had discovered the muscle and flounce of disco, heard Bowie
flirt with bisexuality, lived through punk and steel-plated themselves
to the first five years of Margaret Thatcher's government.

'Jimmy didn't like us back then,' says Holly Johnson about
Jimmy Somerville. 'But no one liked anyone. Boy George wrote
to *Sounds* newspaper saying we gave gay people a bad name, while
he was still saying that he'd rather have a cup of tea than sex. We'd
be in the same green room at Tyne Tees Television in Newcastle
to perform on *The Tube*: Bronski Beat on one side and us on the
other. Getting daggers. I refused to engage with Morrissey when he

hung around me at *Top of the Pops* with his hearing aid in, because we were *it*, I'm afraid.'

'We were very aware of Boy George,' says Colin Bell, 'because George was having hits at the same time as Bronski Beat and they were eyeing each other warily. I think George was rather in awe of Jimmy, and Jimmy rather despised George. I remember going to the cinema with Bronski Beat one night to see some film, and Marilyn and George were two rows behind us and each group was almost yelling abuse at each other. It was most bizarre. There were jealousies involved.'

It may just have been serendipity that the two national anthems of the UK gay experience were released barely six months apart. Perhaps it was lucky timing that they got in the year before the Band Aid behemoth changed pop stars forever, turning them surreptitiously from heroes to role models and divesting them of the urge to fight one another for supremacy, and instead dumping them all in this together. But Frankie Goes to Hollywood's 'Relax' and Bronski Beat's 'Smalltown Boy' presented a satisfactory solution to rendering both the loins and emotions of gay men for full public display. Britain could not understand the interior and exterior life of a properly unprecedented generation before it had been shown it. One had the brains, the other the brawn. These simple three-minute pop songs flung a door wide open, without apology. Watching all of this play out from a south Manchester sofa at the age of 12 could not have been any more scintillating.

A Letter and a Scoop

At London Records one of Colin Bell's first jobs was to take the visiting San Francisco superstar and bellwether of American gay counterculture Sylvester on a promotional tour for his sensational new single, 'Do You Wanna Funk'. Sylvester was ground zero for global gay culture, embodying every beautiful, soulful strand of otherness that would come to be explored by the eighties pop canon. There was something in the voice of the maestro that felt unleashed, unhinged and connected to the cerebral cortex of gayness. Sylvester had pounded through with his liberation anthem '(You Make Me Feel) Mighty Real', but his canon was dotted with every shade on the disco, soul, electro and gospel spectrum and acted as a gateway drug into mythological avenues of the American gay experience. He connected to Harvey Milk's citywide revolution and martyrdom in San Francisco, through his producer Patrick Cowley to the glorious hedonism going on at the EndUp nightclub, and to the old performance art troupe the Cockettes, who would come to cast a long shadow over the cabaret wing of Britain's alternative gay culture.

'There's a very sad story about that trip, actually,' Colin recalls now. 'Sylvester came over to do some shows, and I got this terribly sad letter from some guy who had slept with one of Sylvester's entourage in Newcastle. He had contracted HIV and was asking if I could put him in touch with him. Awful. Because, of course, it was all over San Francisco. I thought, Oh my God. I put him in touch directly and didn't get involved. What could you do?'

In May 1984, five months after 'Relax' and one before 'Smalltown Boy', the US Secretary of State for Health Margaret Heckler announced the identification of the virus responsible for AIDS. 'As soon as I saw the letter I understood the sadness and significance of it,' says Colin. 'Do You Wanna Funk', another unequivocal ode to gay sex, was written and produced by Patrick Cowley, a former band member of Sylvester's and an early fatality during the US AIDS pandemic. Tim McKenna, Sylvester's manager, is remembered in Joshua Gamson's comprehensive biography of the singer *Fabulous Sylvester* as pushing the artist in a wheelchair through his last Lesbian & Gay Freedom Day Parade in San

Francisco in 1988. McKenna held aloft a banner reading 'People Living with AIDS'. The singer died later that year.

Delighted with the number one public reception to his debut solo album *Blast* and with Frankie now a maniacal memory captured in pop posterity, Holly Johnson was offered his first solo tour of the UK in 1989. 'But I knew instinctively that there was something wrong, so I didn't accept the offer,' he says. 'I had swollen glands, which in retrospect would have been a symptom. I was diagnosed and became really ill in October 1991.' Sixteen months later Holly conducted an interview with Alan Jackson for *The Times* about his illness. Aware that his health was about to become public knowledge and with his own ideas as to where and whom the rumours could be sourced back to, he decided to take full ownership of his health issues, despite still believing that this was his death sentence.

Tabloid Britain had other ideas. 'Piers Morgan stole the interview from the system of News International and gazumped Alan,' he says. 'He got the scoop in the *Sun* on the Thursday and totally sensationalised the piece. Alan Jackson, the copyright holder of the article, was, via the Press Complaints Commission, granted some sort of compensation and Piers Morgan was labelled with the use of non bona fide journalistic practices by them.' This was not the way it was meant to play out. 'It was a big drama, that whole time. I was on the front cover. I don't know how they headlined it. It was really negative. They used a quote about my being part of a hedonistic gay generation. It was not the angle that I wanted it to come out in. Alan Jackson had written quite a different piece, but they'd taken out quotes to make it as sensational as possible.'

'I have never forgiven him for it,' he says of Morgan, 'because it resulted in my parents being door-stepped, three days before I had warned them that the story was going to break, at that time when HIV was a high-stigma illness. Can you imagine how painful and torturous it was for them to be doorstepped in Liverpool? It was an evil thing to do, in my opinion. It had evil results, anyway.'

Both parents had kindly reactions to Holly's status: 'We'd had difficulties before, me and my dad, but because of his ill health and mine we had common ground suddenly, towards the end of his life. Something to talk about that unified us in a bizarre way.' He heard about his father's death from his long-term boyfriend and manager Wolfgang Kuhle on returning from the singer Kirsty MacColl's funeral. 'I came home and Wolfgang had been telephoned to say that he died of a stroke in the kitchen with the tap running when he was about to make a cup of tea. That was quite a day.'

Not long after the Alan Jackson interview, Holly released his autobiography, *A Bone in My Flute*. 'I ended the book with the diagnosis because I couldn't face writing the next chapter at the time.' The launch party for the book was held at the Ivy Club in Covent Garden. The joke was that it was to be an audience with Holly at the Ivy. 'Bob Geldof and Paula Yates turned up for two minutes, did one circuit of the room and left.' There was another unexpected guest. 'Jimmy Somerville appeared,' he says. Nine years since 'Relax' and 'Smalltown Boy', this was one RSVP Holly had not expected to be returned. 'I was gobsmacked.' Jimmy presented Holly with a gift, a handbag. 'There was a card in the handbag and it said "I thought it was a very brave thing to do and I don't know whether I would have been so brave". That was a very touching moment for me.'

The initial reactions to Holly's diagnosis were equally warm elsewhere. Then, in the promotional preamble to his 1999 album *Soulstream*, he had to sharply accustom himself to backlash. 'I'm quite an emotional, sensitive person, and when things don't go your way in the music industry it can be soul-destroying. After the positive reaction to me having come out as HIV-positive, I remember reading somewhere in the back section of *The Face*, it said, "Well, actually, we don't have to pretend to like Holly Johnson's work just because he's HIV-positive." That one really took the biscuit.' What hurt most about the comment was the context Holly understood was wrapped around it. '*The Face* was supposedly quite a progressive magazine with a well-known stylist, Ray Petri, who had died from HIV infection. I remember that Ray Petri did actually have trouble in some quarters of the fashion press, and a fund was set up among his friends to help him out at one point. I also remember from my own experience, in summer 1989, when I was about to work with *Aladdin Sane* make-up legend Pierre La Roche on a video, the director rang ahead to ask if I minded that Pierre was HIV-positive. Those kind of things really happened. It was exhausting. There were a couple of people who didn't want to book me for their shows. Maybe they just didn't want a gay man with HIV. Who knows? There were all kinds of things like that.'

In 2001, Holly decided to silently excuse himself from the pop playground. 'It took so much out of me, being ill for ten years. I still didn't believe, even though combination therapy had made me loads better, it would be forever. You get like that when you've been ill. You think that nothing is forever. I watched the aeroplanes go into the twin towers on TV and made the decision that I'd been cogitating on and went back to art college.'

A Trip to the BBC

For political pop savants Bronski Beat, the dream of a trip to *Top of the Pops* quickly became something more bespoke than their peers'. It wasn't about the adoration or the sales. It certainly wasn't about the teenage girls. None of them are quite sure which of the three gay men was the first to discover the added masculine thrills going on behind locked doors, graffitied walls and through diligently poked-out glory holes in the basement gents lavatories at Broadcasting House. It hardly mattered. If Bronski Beat had arrived with a radical, melodious new slant on questioning the establishment, with the specific intention of striving towards the unimaginable goal of complete gay equality, here was a sign that *Top of the Pops* might be the best place to achieve it: the BBC's very own cottage.

Bronski Beat made full and frequent use of the resource with each successive visit. It was their private joke. They delighted in sharing with one another which BBC executive's shoes from underneath the cubicle divides they could match to faces as they sidled down the most hallowed corridors of British media power. 'Correct,' says Colin Bell. 'Absolutely correct. I never found it myself. But yes, they used to come and tell me the stories of the cottage down there. Jimmy, of course, used to take his bicycle on tour with the Communards and ride off to various towns, famously, disappearing off before or after soundchecks. He was rampant, absolutely unstoppable.'

Jimmy Somerville grew up in the depressed Glasgow district of Ruchill; Steve Bronski is from five miles down the road in Castlemilk. Seventies working-class Glasgow was not the open-armed place it is today to its gay brothers. The 1967 Sexual Offences Act did not include Scotland. Sex between two men was not decriminalised until 1980. The first known Scottish gay-rights lobby group, the Scottish Minorities Group, met in leader Ian Dunn's parents' house in Glasgow for the first time in 1969, with six men in attendance. Dunn organised a Glasgow social called the Cobweb, Scotland's first ever gay disco, as late as 1976. In the late seventies Jimmy and Steve had to go to London to live complete adult lives outside of criminality. Jimmy's father was scared to watch his son's first *Top of the Pops* appearance in case he came on 'in a dress, like Boy George'.

Jimmy, Steve and Larry Steinbachek were not pop stars by inclination. They were part of a gung-ho, DIY group of gay men squatting in south London with one foot on the dance floor at Heaven and the other marching with the Socialist Workers Party, the Young Communist League, miners' strike support groups, anti-racist coalitions and the Gay Liberation Front. Across Britain, these last bastions of old socialism were tabloidised under the mocking nickname the Loony Left. When you'd run away from home with everything you owned in a little flight case on account of your sexuality, they looked like the only people speaking any sense.

On *Top of the Pops*, Bronski Beat came on like a three-strong coalition of the previous 17 years' worth of British gay activism, set to song. The follow-up single to 'Smalltown Boy', 'Why?', concerned homophobic hate crimes, which were escalating throughout the country as gay men started to demand equality, loudly.

The third single from Bronski Beat's audacious debut album, *The Age of Consent*, was a cover of the George and Ira Gershwin standard 'It Ain't Necessarily So', 'specifically because George Gershwin was a gay man and that lyric "things that you're liable/ to read in the bible/It ain't necessarily so". Funnily enough, that was the song that really sold the album in massive terms. The other two set it up.' Colin Bell was aware of the sea change washing over British pop culture in 1984, crystallised by the success of 'Relax' and 'Smalltown Boy': 'There was a curious dislocation between people knowing somebody was gay and what they thought about them. It didn't matter a fuck.' The UK was beginning to relax. 'You would find little girls going to Bronski Beat concerts, and whether the penny dropped and they would realise Jimmy was gay or not didn't even seem to come into it. Likewise, with Tom Robinson. He had arguably more straight fans than gay. Straight people were seeing these gay people, in Tom's case, as the boy next door. He wasn't some flamboyant queen. Suddenly, you could relate to him. That's just a normal bloke. The three skinheads in Bronski Beat were skinheads. The fact that they were gay, although it was there in the lyrics, didn't seem to bother the audience. I think the record labels thought this would be a problem. It never occurred to me because I was of that generation, and with Tom we'd already taken that risk and I knew it wasn't an issue.'

Bronski Beat's success was a turnaround for the fortunes of London Records. 'In a career in the music business you work on an awful lot of shit records,' says Colin. 'And I did. Terrible records, often hits. "Smalltown Boy" I would have to say, for me, is probably the most important record I ever put out. You're in a certain place, at a certain time, and it's just an extension of your personality. I wasn't really a music person. I was a gay person who happened to be in the music industry at the right time.'

Because Jimmy Somerville didn't speak to Holly Johnson backstage at TV shows, he never got to tell him about the action-packed toilet in the basement of the BBC's Broadcasting House. 'No,' says Holly Johnson, laughing. 'See, what a twat, keeping that to himself? He could've tipped us the wink.'

The Power of Love

In 2014 we didn't just see the first ever Holly Johnson solo tour of the UK – the tour that in the early nineties he never quite dared imagine would happen – reach an explosive climax in Liverpool. We saw Jimmy Somerville, too, climb reluctantly back into the spotlight after a protracted hiatus. The surprise British film hit of the summer was *Pride*, a feel-good story about a gay protest group set up to raise funds for the striking miners in 1984. It was a fictional retelling of the story of Mark Ashton, the Northern Irish friend of Jimmy's who was the subject of his eye-watering ballad 'For a Friend', the song that sits alongside Pet Shop Boys' 'Being Boring' and Boy George's 'Il Adore' in coming as close as anyone has got to scoring a British national HIV anthem.

In a pivotal scene in the film based on real events, Ashton puts on a benefit concert, Pits and Perverts, in honour of the Welsh community his protest group has been fundraising for. Shot in shadow, an actor playing Somerville can be seen singing Bronski Beat's 'Why?' from behind. At the film's London premiere, Jimmy Somerville was coaxed from semi-retirement back on stage to sing it.

At the climax of his show in Liverpool's Echo Arena, the smile on Holly Johnson's face was discernible as he sang the couplet 'love is danger, love is pleasure' in tandem with the capacity crowd during the moving crescendo of 'The Power of Love'. In that moment, no couplet could have hoped to consolidate the shift in perception of British gay men between 1984 and 2014 with more clarity.

2. TEATIME TV SPECIAL

The Missing Love Story

As a 15-year-old schoolboy by now tentatively starting to picture a future, I found myself looking for examples of gay men who were happily coupled. There appeared to be none in my branch of south Manchester suburbia, where even the hairdressers had wives and the firewomen husbands. I actively looked for stories of gay relationships and found Joe Orton's *Diaries* and Andrew Holleran's *Dancer from the Dance* in the bookshop, and *My Beautiful Laundrette* and *Another Country* at the cinema. I picked up a cheap paperback biography of east London gangland kingpin Ronald Kray in a charity shop. I found what looked like the template for all these posh boys and their bits of rough in the Merchant Ivory adaptation of E.M. Forster's *Maurice*. In one and all, gay relationships appeared either to end in death, doom or disaster. Good luck with that.

As was customary with Manchester teenagers of the eighties, I'd long since been handed the family copy of *Devil's Disciples*, written by journalist Robert Wilson about the Moors murders. In it, I'd learned that Ian Brady picked up one of his victims, 17-year-old Edward Evans, in a cruising spot at a Manchester train station. That hardly helped. Evans was a grimly notorious ghost on our street, often talked about as a neighbour had worked alongside him briefly at a hat shop in Ardwick. He was, in some respects, the closest I got to an actual gay man in my peripheral vision: not just dead, but murdered and dumped in a bathroom.

These were the years that predated Elton and David, George and Kenny, Gilbert and George, Colin and Justin, Tom and Dustin. The gay love story did not yet come publicly with a happy ending. The only gay male couple entrenched in British culture was the irreverent, scallywag sixties playwright Joe Orton and his neurotic lover Kenneth Halliwell, whom he teased to their deaths. Bound up in toilet sex, high art and criminality, theirs was another cross-class relationship – the scholarly gentleman and the oik – albeit one that ended with Halliwell bludgeoning his partner to death with a hammer in their Islington bedsit before taking a fistful of pills to end his own life.

Being gay had started to look like rather a dangerous business by the time Colin and Barry strode into *EastEnders*. They constituted the programme's singular reprieve. I squirmed on the settee as I watched the interplay between two men who seemed to exist as a counterweight to all the other fictional and real gay relationships I'd schooled myself in, and I liked the way that squirm felt.

The Ballad of Colin and Barry

When professional acting started to dry up for him, as it does for many whose fame fuse burns bright and fast in the glare of soap-opera stardom, Gary Hailes took the Knowledge to become a London cabbie. It was the 1990s, a decade after he had become one of the most recognisable faces in the national living room.

Gary, who is straight, will always be known as one half of the first gay couple featured on prime-time British TV, Colin and Barry in *EastEnders*. As a double act, Colin and Barry wore the voguish air of Pet Shop Boys' aesthetic drama, the smart one and the scruff – easily readable archetypes from within gay culture in 1986. They looked like the businessman and his bit of trade, an unusual, unforeseen piece of casting for prime-time TV. Yet there was tenderness to them. Colin, the older, well-turned-out, erudite, genial, wine-sipping graphic designer, probably enjoyed the opera; Barry, the winking barrow boy in his leather jacket supping a pint at the Queen Vic, probably knew his way around a dartboard. Somehow it worked. Colin entered Albert Square weeks before he came crashing off his pushbike, smitten, after spotting Barry on his market stall. Their effect on the British psyche was as immediate.

'I was going for a casting in the West End the other day,' says Gary Hailes now. 'It was pissing down with rain and some guy came up to me and said, "I've just got to shake your hand. You're the reason I came out." That was it.' I sometimes wonder whether he was mine, too. Gentlemen of a certain age do this often with Gary, 30 years after he was pecked on the forehead by his fictional boyfriend in what was quickly deemed a national outrage. In the pre-digital age, this was the power of the television set. It could change lives.

When he got his cab licence, Gary didn't give up performing altogether. His agent will call from time to time with the opportunity to film a pilot episode of a progamme. Friends shooting corporate videos chuck him the occasional bundle to help out. To his delight, Gary is heavily involved with UK Garrison, the non-profit initiative that travels around the UK dressed as Star Wars characters, raising money for charity.

In a galaxy not so far away – in Southampton, in fact, in the spring of 2015 – Gary was playing a Storm Trooper at an event with UK Garrison when he spotted a familiar face in the crowd. He asked his girlfriend, a relationship that stretches back to his fleeting time spent playing one of the most prominent gay men in Britain, if she'd mind taking a picture with a hero he'd acquired at the time. 'I saw Jimmy Somerville and just had to ask for one,' he says. 'I believe he, much more than anyone, stood up against prejudice, and he did it in such a way that he really did not give a shit if it fucked his career or even his life. He believed in it and that was all that mattered.'

The more Gary got to learn about living as an openly gay man in eighties Britain through playing one on *EastEnders*, the more his esteem for Somerville grew. 'It was so clear just from watching him. So many other people would have this protective thing going on, where you could see behind the eyes, Well, I've still got to pay the bills and I can't be too risky. Whereas Jimmy Somerville just seemed so principled. It was all from the heart, not the head. I remember seeing him on the news once, being carried away by police, and thinking, God, that could ruin his career. You could see him thinking, Who cares? What he was doing was using that platform, that talent and celebrity he had for something good. I admired him so much when I was playing Barry. He became this ultimate hero to me.'

Not above flirting with a table leg, Jimmy gave the admiring Storm Trooper asking for a photo a wink, unaware of which near neighbour of British gay pop culture was behind the mask. 'He said, "Oh, you're about the right height, I could date you." He's fucking tiny. He makes me look tall, and I'm five-foot six.' Gary can give as good as he gets. 'I said to him, "That's the best offer I've had all day." All I was thinking was, I have the utmost respect for you, as a man. When I look back at "Smalltown Boy" through the eyes of Barry, and as someone who has a certain amount of understanding of what the journey of that song is about, I see a true hero.'

Gary Hailes was born and raised in the north London manors of Highbury and Archway. He got a taste for the spotlight as a primary-school kid and was offered a place at the Anna Scher Theatre in Angel, Islington, for drama night-classes. He says that his friends didn't consider it a particularly poofy thing to do: 'Theatre certainly would've been, but TV was a little bit different. That was a bit cooler.' Within five weeks at Anna Scher, at the age of 11, he was cast in his first show. His peers at the drama school included actor/director Dexter Fletcher, *Birds of a Feather*'s Linda Robson and Pauline Quirke, *EastEnders*' Gillian Taylforth and her sister, Kim.

Gary paints a picture of a school that was disciplined but marked by a class-blind liberalism that felt new to him. It caught him at a good age, prepubescence, when meeting and associating with gay people was not an issue. By 17, he had his own coming out to do. He had to tell his parents he intended to pack in his full-time job as a postman to take a role on *Grange Hill*, the revolutionary BBC school drama. *Grange Hill* was the brainchild of Phil Redmond, the visionary Liverpudlian television producer who first put a gay man in a British soap opera, beating *EastEnders* to it with *Brookside*'s local drip, Gordon Collins, declaring himself gay in 1985.

'I fucking hated it,' Gary says of the postal service. 'With a passion. It just wasn't for me. I got the phone call to say I'd got *Grange Hill*, went home and told my mum and dad and I just got this barrage of, "Are you kidding? You're 17 and you've got a pension!" What 17-year-old gives a shit about a pension? They were like, "You're seriously going to give it up for this pipe dream?" For them that was the pinnacle, a job for life, 17 to 65 all mapped out, marriage ahead, 2.4 kids, a pension and then die. That was the closest I got to coming out. And I've never regretted it.'

Anna Scher's broader off-stage sociological education passed through to the corridors of *Grange Hill*. 'One guy that I met there, Roy, one of the dressers, he was gay and he was one of the funniest guys you could ever meet. It was never about, Oh, he's gay. That was never a thought. It was just, Oh, he's a great bloke. So I'd never had a problem with it, which meant that later, discovering the kind of prejudices that there were out there? Oh, fuck.'

As a teenager, Gary was part of a small north London rockabilly coterie, in thrall to James Dean, Elvis Presley and their punkier local progeny. The boys hung around Camden. Affiliates included David Scarboro, the actor originally cast as Mark Fowler on *EastEnders*, and Mark Savage, who played *Grange Hill*'s resident hard-nut Gripper Stebson. Filming *Grange Hill* was split between a school in Fulham and the BBC's Elstree Studios. 'We'd go to work and there would be *Top of the Pops, Blake's 7* or *Doctor Who* filming at the same time. Your mates were on other shows. It was brilliant.'

Gary first met the two giant guiding hands behind *EastEnders*, Tony Holland and Julia Smith, while filming a kids' TV show in Cardiff. They asked him to audition for the part of Mark Fowler. 'Every ship needs a captain,' he says. 'Julia was very much the captain of that ship. Tony was much more sort of louche, shall we say; he was freer and light.' Gary auditioned for a five-episode cameo and was gutted not to get it, before a producer took him aside to tell him Tony had another part in mind that he'd like to hold Gary back for.

The call to audition for Barry came one Monday morning while he was working at a telephone research centre off Regent Street popular with young actors before they got their first big jobs and with older actors out of work. In nine months' employment, enough time to think that he might never act again, Gary had worked his way up to being a supervisor. The *EastEnders* audition was to be held on Friday. 'It was a really nervous week. A really odd week.'

He was told no more than that the part was for a young gay man. 'That was as much as I was allowed to know about Barry.' A new *EastEnders* casting was treated by Julia and Tony like a state secret, such was the out-of-the-box success of the first flagship BBC soap. 'I don't tend to get nervous for auditions but, in a positive way, this one was kind of different. It wasn't because it was a gay part, more because I hadn't been working for a long time.'

On the Friday he turned up at Union House, one of two sets of BBC office suites on Shepherd's Bush Green. 'I went in and saw Tony and Julia. They asked if I watched *EastEnders* and if I knew who Michael was.' Michael Cashman had already been introduced to life on Albert Square as Colin, Barry's soon-to-be screen boyfriend. 'At this point it hadn't been revealed that Michael's character was gay. But I think it was obvious, to be quite frank, from the way they were shooting him. They just hadn't gone, Ta-da, he's gay! yet.'

Julia and Tony had specific instructions on how they wanted Barry played. 'They told me they wanted to portray real people that just happened to be gay. They didn't want stylised gay characters. They wanted him to be played, for want of a better word, straight.' He says that older gay British screen archetypes like limp-wristed comics Larry Grayson and John Inman were mentioned only implicitly and never by name.

There had been similar instructions for the writers working on scenes for Colin and Barry. 'There were conversations during the script meetings,' says Juliet Ace, one of Julia and Tony's preferred early writers for the soap. 'As writers we were all conscious of the fact that we were not going to be portraying them as stereotypical gay men, that these were two people first – ordinary people doing ordinary work, one a professional, one not – and that their sexuality should be incidental. They were not introduced with fanfares. It was a romantic affair. When I was writing for them I just wanted them to be two people who were in love with each other.'

When the *EastEnders* writing factory began operating in earnest, Tony Holland was not big on giving notes. 'But he did say to me,' says Bill Lyons, Tony's closest writing hand on the crew, 'they know they're gay so they're not going to spend their lives discussing it. These are not their problems. They're not thinking about addressing their nature every day. They're more concerned about, you know, you've been an arsehole over this. There's a difference between writing that and writing, Oh, you've been a gay arsehole over this.'

Gary's audition scene, one of the first Barry would appear in, saw him receiving a massage from Colin, demarking the relationship as physical from the start. Tony read Michael Cashman's lines. 'I didn't add anything to it,' says Gary. 'I didn't draw attention to who he was or what he was, and just read it as it was written. It's just playing a scene with someone you're in love with. That's it, no distinction.'

The producers liked what they saw and told Gary to come back in an hour and a half. He spent the time wandering round Shepherd's Bush. 'My head was all over the place,' he says. 'It was a big show. There was a certain amount of pressure.' From the start, *EastEnders* would regularly get viewing figures of around 20 million, an unimaginable total in the multi-channel age. The Christmas 1986 episode was watched by 30.1 million Britons. *EastEnders* was water-cooler TV before anyone knew what a water cooler was. Yet despite its size, it retained the local flavour of genuine multicultural communities. Tony Holland would take bus journeys around London as market research for his television darling, to see which storylines were connecting with the audience and which characters were being gossiped about, and reframe the show in accordance with what he overheard.

Gary returned at 4.30pm. He saw a young fellow actor leaving the audition room and gave him a nod. He read for Julia and Tony once again. 'They said, "OK, we need to think about this but we want to discuss a few things with you first."' Gary had never had caveats put on a part before.

For Tony Holland, the casting of Colin and Barry was a personal pet project that had begun gestating properly in his mind a decade earlier, during a spell as an in-house producer at Thames TV. He wasn't about to throw his actors under a bus for being the face of it. As Gary puts it: 'They said, "This role will be quite controversial, potentially will have a big, negative effect on your private and personal life, it will be talked about a lot and will affect you in a lot of ways."'

(This conversation would be echoed 15 years later when the great influx of real-life soap characters began auditioning to star in *Big Brother*, shifting the gay conversation with it from fiction to reality: You may want to be famous before it happens; afterwards could be another story. You will not necessarily be known as the person you recognise yourself to be.)

'They said, "Before you make any big decisions, you need to spend some time discussing this with your family and think about it long and hard." They were really careful. But I'd already thought about it. Like fuck am I going to turn that down.'

Gary had an evening class at Anna Scher that night. He smoked a packet of ten Benson & Hedges during the short journey from Archway to Angel. At one point he was so excited about the potential professional tangent his life was about to head off in that he had to jump off the bus to walk off the adrenaline. Scher's partner, Charles, greeted him in the corridor. 'He's a very tall, slim man, really business-like, very straight, calm and to the point. He didn't get emotional about anything, good or bad.' He offered Gary an unusual welcome, most out of character. 'As I walked in he came running up singing the theme to *EastEnders*.' Tony Holland had phoned Anna to offer Gary the part. 'Tony had reiterated to her that before I accepted, I needed to consider the consequences of it for my life. Anna said, "Have you got any thoughts on that?" And I said, "Yeah, I'll do the job."'

He reasoned it thus: 'I'm an actor. You don't have to murder someone to play a murderer, so you don't have to be gay to play a gay man. You can understand it and get into the psyche of it. It's all about understanding people, understanding emotions.' The only times he had previously heard actors getting these stiff instructional caveats on what might happen to their lives after accepting a role was when they were auditioning to play a paedophile. 'Which, to be honest, should have given me an idea of how some people thought about gay people back then.'

There were concerns closer to home. He dutifully explained to his parents that he was about to play half of *EastEnders*' first gay couple and that the producers had warned him there may be unexpected consequences from it. 'My mum was OK but my dad was not so OK.' He advised Gary against taking the role. 'It was a different time. My dad wasn't a man of many words. He just said, "I wouldn't do that if I were you."'

For Gary Hailes, a north London boy who could handle himself socially and had a working knowledge of gay London life and plenty of professional associates to show him round it ('They let you in free to Heaven on Thursday nights if you had an Equity card'), none of this made any real sense. 'I didn't know it at the time, but with hindsight I can make that parallel of how far we've come, of just how negative being gay was seen to be back then. I spoke to Charles and said, "I'm going to do it. It's fine. I have no issue with it at all."'

The horse emerged out of the trap. 'I had no concept, if I'm being honest, of what was to come. But I didn't really care either. At 20 you can't be as aware as you are at 30, 40 or 50 because life is a matter of experience and I wasn't experienced. There was nobody before Elvis Presley. There was no role model for what he did, so if he got fat and took drugs, there was nobody before him to look at and say, "Oh, they fucked that up." And this is the closest I'll ever get to being compared to Elvis, but it was the same for Colin and Barry.' They had no antecedents. The north London rockabilly was headed onto uncharted turf. 'There wasn't anything that had gone before us so we couldn't compare our path to anyone and say, "Oh yeah, we need to do it this way." I guess if I was to look back at my time in *EastEnders*, the word I would use most to describe myself would be naïve.'

The Unlikely Lad

Bill Lyons got a call from his best friend, Tony Holland, at the start of 1976, asking if he'd be interested in writing the pilot script for a sitcom idea he had. Holland was employed as a producer by Thames TV at the time and was a vocal fan of 1960s Newcastle-set comedy two-hander *The Likely Lads*, not long since revived as *Whatever Happened to the Likely Lads?*, a big hit for the BBC.

Holland's idea, fleshed out in some detail, was for *The Unlikely Lads*, a sitcom with another central pair of male characters – one middle-class gay man living with his younger, working-class boyfriend. Legal homosexuality was less than ten years old in the UK. The central tension was to reside around their class differences, not their sexuality. Bill Lyons was a scriptwriter with a strong reputation, a close professional allegiance to Holland and full faith in his friend's ability to cook up the unthinkable; his interest had been piqued.

He'd heard Tony Holland's criticism of gay men on TV often enough to know what this fresh idea meant to his friend: 'He would always say, "Why can't they ever be funny? You fight to get something through, but it always has to be a big, serious issue. When you have a gay doctor and a gay detective, then you've got equality, when they aren't there just to be gay. Then it doesn't matter, because they're just playing a part and they're not representing a community."'

Bill Lyons used to meet Tony Holland in the Salisbury pub, a favourite of West End theatricals in the mid-sixties. Lyons was working as an assistant stage manager, while Holland was performing as Wallace Eaton's sparring partner at the Piccadilly Theatre's production of *Instant Marriage*. Bill had taken the first read-through for the play. Tony had already brokered his way into television, writing for the police drama *Z Cars*, where he was introduced to Julia Smith. They went on to work on the popular hospital drama *Angels* together, with he as script editor and she as producer.

Tony and Julia were no-nonsense, nose-to-the-grindstone telly pros, a formidable partnership. Bill can recall her walking onto set on *Angels* with a tissue to smear off make-up that had been applied to turn actresses playing nurses into starlets. They both liked to keep fiction close to reality. Their attention to detail was unparalleled. 'She was volatile, he was volatile,' Bill notes. They were as feared as they were respected. 'To be fair, none of us were easy people.' Tony Holland said early into his professional relationship with Julia, 'Bill, you and I have the dreams. She makes them happen.'

Throughout his life on the stage and in television, there was no question of Tony Holland not being out. 'One just took it for granted,' says Juliet Ace. 'He was overtly gay in his behaviour and it wasn't a big deal.' She says that if you'd been through repertory theatre at the time, 'you'd seen everything. Within my group, gay men were always accepted, regardless of legality. I wasn't aware of anyone at the BBC who would have had a problem with that.'

'When I first met him it was illegal and that never bothered him,' says Bill Lyons. There was a mutual understanding between his friends about Tony's leisure habits. 'There were parts of his life that were quite separate. He used to be off down Holland Walk or whatever, and I'd just leave him to it. That was his life.' Tony was an exuberant bon viveur, infectious and loyal company. He was

Bill's best man at his wedding. 'Tone was also a very heavy drinker,' notes Bill, adding that creative sessions in the wine bar opposite the *EastEnders* office could often run up to ten hours long.

By 1976, Tony had sensed a prevailing wind across the TV networks in the wake of the successful airing of *The Naked Civil Servant* the previous December. It starred John Hurt on startling form as Quentin Crisp in a television film of Crisp's peerless memoir. 'He thought that was great,' says Bill. 'But Tony's whole thing, which you need to know, was popular drama. He wanted gay characters as part of popular drama, the same as anybody else. In a strange way, it's almost how black characters were being written at the time, too. They felt token and were always there to be about black issues. It was never about them being a part of the drama. That was Tony's big thing. So he said we could do a fantastic, funny show which would be like *The Likely Lads* with a twist. The younger one was a plumber. It was the clash of cultures that was the point of it, not their sexuality. They were send-ups not of gay people, but of the British class system.'

Tony Holland is remembered with heart-warming fondness by those who were closest to him. 'The thing about Tone was, he was crushingly honest as a human being,' says Bill. 'No side, no bullshit, just crushingly honest.' He was famously generous. Juliet Ace talks about a party at her house when he gave her daughter his coat. He bought a fancy Cartier watch during *EastEnders*' speedy ascendency and insisted Juliet take it as it looked better on her than him. Bill Lyons remembers a time when a junior accountant at the BBC questioned Tony's expenses chitty. 'He said, "Do you think I'm fiddling my expenses?" The guy said, "No, no, no, I just don't quite understand it." And Tony tore up his expenses and said, "Fine, I won't have them." That's just the way he was. He had no interest in money, even though he earned a vast amount throughout his life, a lot of which he gave away.'

Bill wrote a half-hour script for *The Unlikely Lads*, which he still keeps sequestered in his west London attic. 'It was just a comedy drama about a working-class guy and a posh boy and their lives,' he says. 'It was very funny.' Tony was delighted with it and took it to his natural first port of call, Verity Lambert, the head of drama at Thames Television. Lambert, the first producer of *Doctor Who*, was both commissioner and producer of *The Naked Civil Servant*. 'She answered him with the classic phrase, which I have forgiven her for now, "We've done our bit for gays with *The Naked Civil Servant*."' Tony was sanguine about the rejection, telling Bill that it may have been ahead of its time.

The idea was parcelled at the back of Tony's mind until he and Julia Smith were charged with bringing to life the first BBC soap opera. The seedlings of *The Unlikely Lads* turned into Colin and Barry. *EastEnders* was ordained by BBC director general Michael Grade to rival the ITV counterparts *Coronation Street*, *Emmerdale Farm* and *Crossroads*. Grade understood Tony and Julia's clever, populist touch for drama and put them in charge.

Juliet Ace bumped into Julia and Tony in the reception of the BBC's other Shepherd's Bush offices, Threshold House, in 1984. The pair had returned from Lanzarote, where they'd produced a document of everything *EastEnders* would become. Juliet offered a bumbling apology for an episode of their latest hit, *The District Nurse*, she'd written for the pair which had received a poor review. 'I was terrified of them at first,' she says. 'They said, "Oh, nonsense." They didn't look at reviews; they liked ratings. Tony looked at Julia and said, "Shall we give her one of these?" and handed over the bible of *EastEnders*.' They took Juliet for dinner. When she returned home, she stayed up most of the night reading it. 'I just could not put it down,' she says. 'Tony was always very good at stories.'

'From the start,' Bill Lyons says, 'Tony definitely wanted gay characters in it. His big idea for *EastEnders* was that he wanted to put Thatcher's Britain on screen. We got crucified by the *Daily Mail* for that, but it wasn't ever party political. It was about what was going on in the country, a reflection of the times.' Julia had second thoughts about introducing gay men on Albert Square from the start. 'I don't want to be unkind to her, because she did make dreams happen and she was probably right, but Julia was much more careful and pragmatic about what we could get away with. Tony was cross because he wanted to make this happen earlier. If he wanted to do something, he wanted to do it. He didn't care if it was the right time. He never cared.'

EastEnders' characters were drawn largely from Tony Holland's sprawling Essex family. The grand matriarch Lou Beale and her children Pauline and Pete were named after his aunt and cousins. When it came to crafting Colin and Barry, it's tempting to see a conflagration of Holland's own character. Bill Lyons remembers their conception differently. After his tenure at Thames TV in the mid-seventies, Tony Holland was hospitalised with a burst stomach ulcer. 'It was a very serious situation,' says Bill. 'Thames, to their eternal shame, wouldn't renew his contract while he was in hospital. He was clearly not going to be all right.' He went to live with Bill for a while in Devon: 'I nursed him back to health. He came back to London and he couldn't get a job for love nor money. He said to me, "Well, if I can't be in television, I shall be the best barman in the world."'

Holland took a pub job in Northfields, west London. 'A lot of people dropped him because he wasn't important anymore.' Ever the producer, he began to germinate another idea for a TV drama. 'He said to me, "I think there's a great show in a pub," and talked about doing a show called *Relief Couple*, about a married man and woman who go from pub to pub as relief managers. Essentially, it was Den and Angie Watts. The BBC turned it down, which I thought was fascinating.'

Early *EastEnders* blossomed thanks to Den and Angie: the fragile couple, the philanderer and the love-fool, the dictator and the alcoholic. The Fowlers were supposed to be the central family, but when Tony heard on public transport how much Den and Angie were being talked about, he shifted the dramatic emphasis of the show onto the landlord and landlady of the Queen Vic. Theirs was a story closer to his heart.

'At the beginning,' says Bill Lyons, 'I was the only person who knew who Angie was based on. Tony asked me, "Who do you think she is?" And nobody got it apart from me. I said, "It's you, Tony." It so obviously was.'

The Transposed Gay Voice

Telling gay men's stories through female characters has dramatic precedents from long before Angie Watts twizzled round to pour her first vodka and tonic in the Queen Vic. Granada TV employee Tony Warren – the founding father of British soap opera and an openly gay man – wrote the first 13 episodes of *Coronation Street*, which launched in 1960, after getting the green light from Harry Elton at Granada for an idea he'd had on a train journey about putting ordinary people on TV.

Warren talked about the voices of the brassy, no-nonsense women of Weatherfield being direct invocations of the gay men he heard in the New Union, the gay pub he frequented on what would soon become Manchester's other iconic address, Canal Street. The tradition goes back further still, to the masterful American dramatist Tennessee Williams fashioning coruscating treatises on the gay condition, pre-legalisation, through the mouths of his most famous anti-heroines, Blanche DuBois in *A Streetcar Named Desire* and Maggie in *Cat on a Hot Tin Roof*.

'They say there'd never been a gay character in *Coronation Street* before,' says Antony Cotton, the actor who as Sean Tully on *Corrie* is now the longest-standing, most-enduring gay character in British soap opera. 'Well, there had. But it had just been Hilda Ogden and Elsie Tanner. You don't get any gayer than Ena Sharples. But the *Coronation Street* writers had to write them as camp women. When Tony Warren was inventing these characters he was thinking of all the drag queens from Paddy's Goose and the New Union.'

Cotton was taken for dinner early into his *Corrie* life by Warren, just after his casting in 2003. 'He talked about the history of who those people were on the show. That's what I used to absorb from him. I would do and say things, little ad-libs that came from stories of Tony's. He'd never say, "There was this girl called Sharon." It was always "one-eyed Sharon". In 1960 Tony couldn't write one-eyed Winny from Paddy's Goose because you weren't allowed to.' *Coronation Street* debuted seven years before the legalisation of homosexuality in England and Wales.

'They famously say that Tony Warren came along and translated all his gay male voices into women,' says Russell T Davies, the writer of Channel 4's flagship nineties gay drama *Queer as Folk*. Though it was the temporal bellwether of the blossoming of gay acceptance, *Queer as Folk* held strong to traditions heralded in early *Coronation Street*, unearthing similarly folkloric truisms around Manchester's central gay strip. 'The women, the mothers, the kitchens, the socials, the cobbled streets – Tony Warren was looking at his own TV and saying, "Why aren't I there?" Which is a huge step towards putting us on the TV screen. You wouldn't have got to Gordon Collins on *Brookside* without all that.' It was exactly the motivation that led to Davies scripting *Queer as Folk*.

Brookside creator Phil Redmond is not a gay man. 'But Phil you can also look on as another radical,' says Davies. 'Again, someone who looked at television and wanted to put things on screen that were not visible. But in a sense, and this is not to take anything away from Phil, anyone inventing a Channel 4 soap opera in the eighties would have had to include a gay character. That was Channel 4's remit. He's the opposite of Tony Warren in one sense. Tony was determined to do his work within the system.'

Bill Lyons can see obvious differences between Phil Redmond and *EastEnders'* Tony Holland. 'Actually, *Brookie* was much better earlier on, but it went down a path that Tony didn't want to go down, in the way that it was much more heightened drama. Tone never wanted to do that. I've worked with Phil and I know the difference. Phil has a vision; Tone has a vision and then he hands it over. Phil has a definite idea of what he wants, and if he could, he'd write it all himself, whereas Tone was more inclusive; he wants you to bring something to the table.'

Despite the specificity of their vision, neither Tony Warren nor Tony Holland ran dictatorships. 'It's very interesting that the two most successful British soaps have been created by gay men,' says Bill Lyons. 'Soap opera has changed now, but I think it's because they both created very matriarchal societies. The way soap has gone now is finger-of-fate stuff. It is incidents. Things happen and that creates the story. Both the beginnings of *Corrie* and the beginnings of *EastEnders* were character-based. Those characters created a world.'

Those female characters fed straight back into the tongues of gay men. Ena Sharples and Elsie Tanner would feed back into the vernacular of the exact gay men on which they were based, at the warming local hostelries around Manchester's nascent little gay village. A tradition of picking up tart lines of social observation is one of the traditions that still traces gay culture, whether it be from the pen of arch Mancunian humourist and social satirist Victoria Wood, or the fictional inventions of Caroline Aherne and Julia Davis.

Bill Lyons and Tony Holland were schooled under the hugely influential BBC television producer Betty Willingale. 'A wonderful, wonderful woman,' says Lyons. 'She taught you that when you have a character you ask three questions of them: who is this person, what do they want and how are they going to get it?' For Colin and Barry this was easy: Colin was a successful man looking for love; Barry, a happy-go-lucky market trader looking for self-improvement. 'They don't actually have to get there, but what is the path they're going down? All of the *EastEnders* characters I worked on with Tony, we would answer those questions about.'

Prior to work on *EastEnders*, Holland and Lyons had been on a three-month Transactional Analysis course, the psychology programme that deals with adult, parent and child patterns of discourse and disagreement in relationships. 'It fed into how we did characters,' says Lyons. It found its perfect genesis in Colin and Barry. Gay in this instance was mesmerisingly new, based on patterns of behaviour rather than sexual proclivity.

Gary Hailes had experience of working with Phil Redmond on *Grange Hill*, where Redmond brought teenage pregnancy, drug use and racism into the teatime television conversation for kids. 'Phil Redmond was a smart guy, still is,' he says. 'He found a gap in the market for real teenagers. Up until then you had *Just William* and that type of posh schoolboy that didn't mean anything to any of us actually watching TV. There wasn't anything comparable to *Grange Hill*. It was gritty. It almost started a new way of talking to teenagers and school kids.'

'I don't think he did it consciously for a second,' says Russell T Davies of Tony Warren's groundbreaking early artistic achievements on *Coronation Street*, 'but he did do a phenomenal job to create the soap opera, creating an entire tone of voice. That demotic, working-class voice with a lot of camp and a lot of comedy, he created from that very first scene of Elsie Tanner walking into the corner shop. That's not just a great scene. It's a template for the next 60 years of drama. Astonishing.'

Tony Warren underpins much more of television writing than just his immediate influence on the soap operas that followed in

Coronation Street's momentous wake. 'People who claim to hate *Coronation Street* write in those patterns,' says Davies, 'unaware that they've picked it up from this man. It comes from other places as well – from comedians, from people like Alan Bennett – but to put it on prime-time TV and to make it a success, that was all Tony Warren. They were his codes.'

Warren unleashed a gay sensibility across the national television palette that caused seismic shockwaves. 'I think he's absolutely brilliant,' says Davies. 'It's that outsider, that person who doesn't quite fit in. There's a strong, unique man. There's an outlier. By being an outsider he wanted to drag television over to the outsiders.' He was not the only gay man to prove wildly influential in his particular TV field. Echoes of Russell Harty's pre-eminence on the eighties chat-show circuit could be felt heavily later in the rise of more openly gay hosts Graham Norton, Alan Carr and Paul O'Grady. The indelible imprint of the riotous comedian Kenny Everett can be seen through the character comedy of *Little Britain*'s Matt Lucas and David Walliams, and the more absurdist *The League of Gentlemen*. Russell Brand can often feel like a character scripted by Everett, some barely plausible, proselytising, messianic political naysayer. For one reason or another, British TV has become a place indebted to the voices of gay men. Tonys Warren and Holland were just two of the most effective.

Tony Warren never got to cast a gay role for his creation while he was directly involved in *Coronation Street*. 'There was a dubious wig-seller at one point in the seventies,' says Antony Cotton, 'but no, it was never said out loud.' He had to fight for his right to get his gay voice heard on heartland television. 'In those days, if you were going to work in television and you were gay, you had to be three times as good as anyone else,' Warren told the *Guardian*'s TV editor Gareth McLean in 2010. 'The first *Coronation Street* writing team contained some of the biggest homophobes I've ever met. I remember getting to my feet in a story conference and saying, "Gentlemen, I have sat here for two-and-a-half hours and listened to three poof jokes, a storyline dismissed as poofy and an actor described as useless for us as he's a poof. As a matter of fact, he isn't. But I would point out that I am one, and without a poof none of you would be in work today.""

A Straight Hate Crime

When he began filming *EastEnders*, Gary Hailes lived on Fairbridge Road in Archway. Each morning, as he left to take the trip up to Elstree Studios for filming, he would nod hello to the builders working on scaffolding across the road from his house. They often exchanged pleasantries. Why wouldn't they?

Filming on the most successful show on television was initially daunting, but Gary takes pains to point out how accommodating his co-star Michael Cashman was at easing him through the process. 'He was helping me with it all,' says Gary. 'Michael was a really good teacher, helper, supporter, friend and fellow actor, from day one.'

As a man who made no secret of his sexuality, Cashman was the needle in the haystack of British actors at the time. He was known to Tony Holland long before *EastEnders* and was always intended to be his first port of call for a gay male role on the show. Bill Lyons's relationship with the actor went back further still, to when they were both child actors and Cashman played the lead in an early West End revival of *Oliver!*

An actor driven more by the political than the dramatic consequences of playing half of the first gay couple in a British soap, Cashman went into politics after *EastEnders*. He has served as a Labour MEP, is one of the founding members of the gay rights campaigning group Stonewall and, as of 2014, now sits in the House of Lords.

Bill Lyons says Cashman was held in high esteem by Tony Holland. But they fought. 'I think in terms of gay politics,' Lyons says. 'That was the crunch that Tone always got cross about. Michael would often say to Tone, "Oh, I don't think we're representing gay people properly," and Tone would say to him, "You are *not* representing gay people. You are playing a character." He was a good actor but he was very, very earnest. Gary just got on with it.' The intensity and speed of soap-opera production doesn't allow pause for pontificating. Lyons says the actors are often hired on the basis that they'll operate by Noël Coward's old motto: 'Say the words and don't fall over the furniture.' Gary was the fun half of the partnership. 'But Michael brought a certain gravitas to it that you might not have got with anyone else,' says Lyons.

Gary filmed for eight weeks before his first episode aired on a Monday evening. No amount of warnings from Tony and Julia at his audition could have prepared him for the greeting from his friendly neighbourhood builders the next day: 'As I came out the door – and I still remember this now – they shouted "Fucking poofter", "Shitstabber", "Queer". I was like, What the fuck? These people that I'd been speaking to every day? This is how it's going to be?' He didn't hurry away, scared, but stood his ground before walking to the tube. 'I was just really in shock. Looking back on it, it's almost funny. But at the time I was truly shocked. Still now, I can't believe that ten minutes of TV could have that profound emotional effect on these guys, who clearly had been talking about it before I came out. Like, Did you see that fucking geezer last night? What's that all about? And we've been fucking talking to him?'

There were some positive reactions to the introduction of Barry. Gary's fan mail would split equally into three camps. The first from gay men thanking him for the portrayal and representation; the second from religious zealots complaining about it; the third from a particular type of woman of a certain age 'who wanted to straighten me out'. Did he ever? 'No, I didn't. I used to send a photo and say thank you very much, something polite.' His aunt would help with responses.

After their initial outburst, the builders blanked Gary for the duration of their stay. By now he could rationalise some of their behaviour toward him. 'I think what was so frightening about *EastEnders* – and I use that word because I think that's what it was – was that the two gay characters were quite real. They were like the people you sit in the pub with. They could be your mate or your brother or your son, and that's what was frightening about it to some people.' He understood that it was not the builders' collective response to Barry that mattered, but a British culture of embedded homophobia which allowed them their abusive response.

There was more to come. The press reaction to Colin and Barry built heat from the outset. It was not the infamously horrified 'EastBenders' banner daubed across the front-page of the *Sun* after Colin and Barry first kissed that struck Gary the most. He could forgive the tabloids' leading telly reviewer Garry Bushell his acidic response to Colin and Barry as a man employed to be an emblem of his times. It was another front page that really got to the actors. 'I remember Michael and I laughing in horror at a front page of the *Daily Star* around the time of the kiss, which was a little picture of Michael and me in the corner and the word SCUM written in massive letters. That was all the front page of the *Daily Star* was that day. What the fuck? Are you kidding me?'

'With Colin and Barry you inevitably have to talk about EastBenders,' says Russell T Davies, 'because that's a very good headline. It is a very good joke, actually. But it becomes part of the language. It comes to define the eighties and the newspapers don't define the way we think. It's a trick they pulled on us to imagine that they do.' Davies's memory of the arrival of Colin and Barry, which he watched while living in south Wales, was somewhat different: 'I remember these characters coming along and everyone just waiting for them. With Colin, we were just dying for him to come out of the closet. There was one scene very early on where he started to talk about an ex-lover in the Queen Vic and me and all my friends were hooting with laughter.' The gender was unspecified. 'I don't even mean my gay friends, I'm talking about my sisters and their friends. There was a great energy to welcome these characters.'

Davies points out that Colin and Barry were not even the first gay characters on the show. That glory went to Ruth Lyons. 'She was a social worker,' he says, 'only in it for a few episodes. Dr Legg had to explain to Pauline that she was a lesbian. That was in its first year. Not to be radical or to be different, just to include people that weren't normally seen on screen. We were all just nodding away. It became a game of who would turn out to be gay. Will it be Wicksy? Will it be Lofty? And then in comes Colin, and of course it's going to be Colin. It wasn't about people being shocked and shouting, "EastBenders!" It was just as much people saying, "Please bring us this."'

There were complaints after the kiss. 'Maybe people complained,' says Davies. 'I think in those days it would've been about 400 people, which is fine. The sad thing is that those 400 people have set the memory of those times. They've established what apparently was the status quo. It wasn't. It was very successful. Ratings kept on going through the roof. I loved what they did with the kiss. That's when we were all apparently up in arms and cross about it, that harmless kiss. But it's all just a game, isn't it? It's just part of the nonsense, that game the newspapers are still playing to this day in some shape or form. What I remember was simply how unmissable it was to have a gay character in a soap opera. It meant that I would watch every single episode with Colin and Barry in it.'

Of the complainants themselves, of viewing families that were actually horrified by the sight of one man kissing another whom he loves on the forehead, Davies is equally forthright about how history can so easily be rewritten. 'I'm beginning to realise as I get older that you look at a homophobic family and there's always something more that's wrong with it. It's not the gay people that have the problem. Every family that's homophobic, they blame it all on us, but when you peel it back there's something wrong already there. Of course there is.'

This observation that if you're homophobic, there is something genuinely wrong with you, is rarely noted. 'But it always becomes our problem,' continues Davies. 'It's always us that have to explain ourselves or defend ourselves. We have to stand up for this or defend that. No! It's nothing to do with us. We're just getting on with our lives. Where are you getting all that hate from? What is wrong with you?' That is the question.

The problem with a media storm brewing, however reflective of its time it may or may not be, is that someone will catch the fallout of hate being propagated by authority voices. Gary Hailes says that he and Michael Cashman would sometimes joke to one another about the fact that Gary, a straight man, was taking the brunt of Britain's unvoiced homophobia while closeted members of the entertainment industry – pop stars who wouldn't say they were gay, actors who kept schtum because they felt it might diminish their suitability for roles in the future – would get lauded for their subtle deceptions. With the media, Gary was too young to care: 'I made a fairly conscious decision early not to give a shit.'

Others took more notice. 'I had a couple of incidents,' Gary notes, wildly underplaying the direct effect Barry had on his life. The first is certainly the funnier of the two. One day he was walking down the bread aisle of Sainsbury's on Borehamwood high street, near the *EastEnders* studios, when a woman caught his eye, recognising him. 'This old lady chased me around with a French stick because I'd been nasty to Colin, running around shouting, "You don't take any notice of him!" She really meant it, as well.'

The second was less amusing. He pulled up at a petrol station in Swiss Cottage in north London late one night after filming, paid for his fuel and returned to his car. A man approached the vehicle, ranting and raving homophobic abuse, clearly drunk. 'I made the mistake of engaging with him. It was a mistake, but bear in mind I was 21.' He estimated to the police later that the man was aged somewhere between 35 to 40 years of age. 'The window was open and I said, "Why don't you fucking grow up?"'

He pulled out of the petrol station and stopped at traffic lights when he saw the man coming towards him once more. 'He was screaming abuse at me, pissed up. It was kind of scary. I thought, I don't need this shit, so I did the window up. He came up and tapped on the window. I didn't even look. But what I didn't do was lock the door, so he opened the door and got in. He was grabbing my throat. I was carrying a lot more weight then – I was kind of chunky – and I was arched over the centre point of the car with him on top, with his hands literally round my throat. Of course, on top of that the car started to move as it was still in gear, so I started down the A41.' The car swerved and just missed a lamp post before he could put his foot on the brake. 'On the driver's side you couldn't get out. Somehow I managed to get my foot on his chest and push him up. He swung and took a chunk out of my eye, caught it with his nail.'

A further tussle ensued. They both ended up out of the car. 'By this point, I'd gone. I wasn't Gary anymore. I wasn't a human being anymore. Red mist, call it what you like, but I had gone. I was not a rational person. I hit him so hard in the face. He moaned something about "poofters". That was the trigger. I opened the boot because I had a crowbar in there, a tyre iron. He walked off and said, "You poofs, you're all the same," and I pulled this thing back and I was aiming – and I would've killed him, I would've split his skull in half – but the girl who I had been following in the car had realised that I was no longer following her and came back to find out where I was. She took my arms and said, "Stop, stop."' The man made his escape and Gary flagged down a police van to explain what had happened.

Gary Hailes is a man who can find positives in most situations. After a period of reflection, he reconciled himself to what had happened: the homophobic attack of a heterosexual man ignited by a gay character on a soap opera. 'I write it off now. From my point of view, I always try to find an up, and do you know what I thought? I must be a fucking award-winning actor at playing gay because, for whatever reason, he hated gay people and he really hated me. He'd bought that. That's what he believed. So as far as I'm concerned, great, I did a good job. Him being an arsehole, I can't control.'

Over the 30 years since he stepped onto Albert Square, Barry comes back to haunt Gary in ways he could never have foreseen at the time. Not all are good. The first job he was seriously considered for after leaving *EastEnders* was as presenter of a Saturday morning kids' TV show. 'I was told by the producer that she wanted me to do the show but had been told I couldn't because of the controversial homosexual past of the people I'd played on TV.' The ultimate irony was that the job went to an actual gay man. 'He was just in the closet.'

Some repercussions feel nice. A teacher friend recently told him that the scene in which he explains to the elderly, fag-smoking grand dame of Albert Square's launderette, Dot Cotton, about his relationship with Colin is regularly used to educate on homophobic behaviour in schools. 'It's just so cool that they use that to educate about tolerance,' Gary says. 'And how times have changed.'

The Weatherfield One

In a scene redolent of one of Sean Tully's interchanges with his *in loco parentis* landlady Eileen Grimshaw on *Coronation Street*, Antony Cotton came out to his mother when he was 17. It was the early nineties, seven years after the arrival of Colin and Barry on prime-time telly. 'She fell on the floor and pretended – which I didn't know at the time – to cry. I remember being stood over her and the first thought in my head was, This is the worst thing that's ever happened to me. She was on the floor by the breakfast bar stools and then she started smiling. She said, "Oh, of course I knew." I asked her since when and she said, "When you were about three."' She went on to regale Antony with a story of his infant self twirling through a rail of frocks in Manchester department store Kendals. 'She said, "Come away, those are for grown women, they aren't for you. They're for big girls." And apparently I said, "When I grow up will I wear dresses like these?"'

Antony was a child actor at the Oldham Theatre Workshop, very much the northern mirror to Gary Hailes's experience at Anna Scher. He didn't get on with regular school – 'I had a problem with authority. Still do' – and says attending his alternative alma mater gave him 'the best years of my life'. He, too, was part of an illustrious peer group that included actresses Marsha Thomason, Gemma Wardle, Lisa Riley and Anna Friel, who was famously one half of *Brookside*'s first lesbian couple in the early nineties.

Antony Cotton had built up a strong stage and screen portfolio by the time he left school at 18. Castings became more problematic as he grew into gay adulthood. Parts for men of his particular countenance resolutely refused to appear. 'There was a time when every job I ever went for either I got it or Kieran O'Brien or William Ash got it. I'd had a good run of it. Then I got to an age where if there was a part in *Heartbeat* it would be for a thug who robs the corner shop. It got to that stage when I wasn't getting the work because there was always going to be a bigger lad for the part, like Chris Coghill or Kieran.'

Cotton was working bar shifts at the svelte second-wave Canal Street bar Velvet in the late nineties when he heard that Russell T

Davies had begun casting a drama about gay life in Manchester for Channel 4. 'I was like, I really have got to get this job.'

The part of Alexander in *Queer as Folk* had originally been written with Davies's best friend, Phil Collinson, in mind. 'I always thought it would be nice to get some proper gay people in there, but that didn't feel possible,' says Davies. 'I can remember exactly Antony walking through the door. Never seen him before, never heard of him. He came in and it was the audition of a lifetime.' Cotton regaled Davies and his producer, Nicola Schindler, with tales of working behind the bar at Velvet. 'Such a gift. I said, "That's him!" There's an out gay man in the cast, brilliant. He was such a laugh and such good company on that show, too.' Davies says it was Cotton who predicted the success of *Queer as Folk* earliest. 'He was ahead of all of us at the time.'

Cotton got the call to say he'd been cast as Alexander in the middle of working a daytime shift at the bar: 'At that time it was just two scenes and my agent said, "Oh, I've got some other news for you. You're in it all – there's eight episodes." I said to my boss Mark, "Sorry, I know it's mid-service but I'm fucking off to get drunk. I've got a job!" Mark, God love him, went, "Go on, off you go."' Things turned out OK for Phil Collinson, too; he gave up acting and went on to find massive success as the producer of the revival of the *Doctor Who* franchise with Davies.

Post-*Queer as Folk*, the doors for Antony began opening, moving him conspicuously up a professional gear. In the wake of the drama's popularity and notoriety the parts started to appear. The show had a palpable effect on casting gay men in mainstream drama. He presented a regular feature on the era-defining Channel 4 morning show *The Big Breakfast*, called the Pink Pound. He was cast in perennial gay favourite *Absolutely Fabulous*, and for the stage in Pet Shop Boys' musical *Closer to Heaven*, where he met his great friend Jonathan Harvey, now a regular *Coronation*

Street writer and the author of so many of Sean Tully's memorably crisp lines.

It was a full 17 years after the exit of Colin and Barry from *EastEnders* that *Coronation Street* finally cast a gay man. Todd Grimshaw, played by Bruno Langley, was the first, and once the doors opened, the show compensated quickly for any tardiness. Antony Cotton quickly entered as Sean Tully, answering a flat-share notice in the corner shop. Antony is a tenacious, funny and gifted man, the absolute product of Manchester, the city that spawned him. He's as slim as a whippet and sharp as a blade, as useful an emblem of self-made northern achievement as any of the city's more lauded pop stars or footballers. If anybody would care to tot up the sums, as Sean Tully he is perhaps the most visible gay man per view per capita in Britain of the last decade, possibly of all time. Unlike Gary Hailes's, his fame fuse has burnt hard and long.

Sean's major usefulness on *Corrie* is as a decorative, quick-witted chorus figure, an emotional pointer for viewers. 'Unusually for a *Coronation Street* character,' says Antony, 'Sean doesn't have any enemies. He's witty and that's the armour that he's had to have all his life to stop someone having a pop at him. He's always gone in first.' Because he works in the knicker factory, Underworld, the local pub, the Rovers Return, and lives with his surrogate family the Grimshaws at number 5, the former house of Elsie Tanner ('That always gives me a shiver'), he is a continuity resource that spreads across hours of *Corrie* screen time, still one of the most-watched TV shows in the country.

His *Coronation Street* arrival is a lesson in consummately Antony Cotton audacity. When he bumped into the show's casting director June West during the interval of a play at Manchester's Royal Exchange Theatre in 2002, she asked him why he'd never done *Corrie*. 'I said, "Because you've never asked me." And she said, "Oh, it doesn't really work like that." I'd never auditioned for

Coronation Street because it would break my heart if I didn't get it.' On the way home I decided to act on impulse and do something about it.'

He wrote new executive producer Tony Wood a card: 'Dear Tony, welcome to Weatherfield. You've never had a homosexual on *Coronation Street*. If you ever want one then I'm the man to play him. I've got my own house, my own car, I don't do drugs and, best of all, I'm cheap. Come on, Tony, you know you want to. Best of luck, Antony Cotton.'

Given how much Canal Street had embedded itself as the gay capital of Britain by the time Sean Tully arrived in Weatherfield, Antony isn't quite sure why it took *Coronation Street* so long to cast its first gay characters. 'I think in some transient universe, the *Coronation Street*/Weatherfield version of Canal Street had been shown in *Queer as Folk*,' he notes. The Grimshaws were introduced under the direct influence of the great matriarch Hazel Tyler in *Queer as Folk*. 'Tony Wood said he cast Antony Cotton because he wanted Eileen Grimshaw's house to be like Hazel's house,' says Russell T Davies. 'You still can see to this day, there she is with her gay lodgers and ragtag family of passers-by.'

Unlike Colin and Barry on *EastEnders*, Sean Tully's reception in the press was warm. The country was thawing to gay representation. The actions of Tony Blair's New Labour administration reflected the shift. The age of consent had been equalised, bringing it down from 21 to 16; the ban on gays joining the military had been lifted; Clause 28, which stopped councils spending money on anything perceived to promote a gay lifestyle, was repealed.

Cotton expected a six-month tenure on *Coronation Street*, maximum. 'I'm an actor and I was used to being peripatetic, schlepping round with my bag on my shoulder to do the next thing, scripts in one hand, duffle bag over shoulder. I thought, Six months in Manchester? That's heaven. And then it turned into something else.' It is now almost unimaginable to picture a *Coronation Street* without Sean Tully on it. 'Sean is a character,' he says, 'that is so fundamentally *Coronation Street*. I'm playing Tony Warren. I'm playing who he was in his twenties, a gobby, wiry, smart, quick-witted gay man. That's basically who he was and basically who Sean is.'

While straight Britain had warmed to Sean Tully, a groundswell of criticism was directed at him from within the gay world. 'I knew it would polarise the gay community,' he says wearily. 'I expected all that stuff, the backlash – he's put the cause back 20 years, all of it. I expected all of it and it was a load of bollocks. I understand why the gay community had an issue with it. Actually, no, I don't understand. But I could see where it came from.' As gay men started appearing with regularity on the small screen, as our stories began to be heard by the mass market, the gay community was free to argue among itself on what they did and didn't want to see. Largely, that would be something that was real but not too real, a fantasy universe in which every gay man is that little bit better-looking, that little straighter-acting than may be the reality. It coincided with a further noticeable sociological shift in British maleness. 'It's because of the metrosexualisation of the wider world,' says Cotton. 'As straight men's gayness comes up a little bit, gay men want theirs to lower so the two meet somewhere in the middle. That's fine if that's what you want, but stop telling other people what they can and can't be.' He thinks it masks a deeper truth. 'You go down Old Compton Street or Canal Street and you will hear at any point 500 Seans. And each and every one of them would have you believe that they're not like that.'

When very vocal criticisms started hitting Cotton from inside the gay world, he turned to his good friend Sir Ian McKellen for advice on how to cope with it. Cotton and McKellen had met at the end of the nineties, at a dinner for Stonewall, and quickly hit it off. 'Whenever I get myself wound up or in a certain situation I think, What would McKellen say? More often than not it would be nothing.' He once shared with Antony an actor's truism that steel-plated him to criticism. 'He said, "Antony, what anybody else thinks of you is none of your business." It was the most profound thing. If that man there doesn't like you, he's allowed not to like you.'

His fan mail was comforting in the face of accusations of gay stereotyping: 'Boys of 16 would write to me and say, "I can see myself on screen now. At last."' In his time on the *Street* Antony has earned himself a National Television Award and a Stonewall Award, neatly framing his gift to British culture. He's an emblem of his times, a character that reminds the northern suburbs that men like Martin Platt and Kevin Webster, Christians like Emily Bishop and (obviously) brassy barmaids of the Liz McDonald ilk would not blanche at sharing a drink and enjoying casual conversation with a gay man like Sean Tully in the twenty-first century.

Antony accepted his National Television Award at the Royal Albert Hall. He took his mum. 'I was able to say thanks to her, thanks to ITV for putting on this character at 7.30 in the evening, cheers me dears and here's to queers.' He gratefully received his Stonewall Award at the Victoria and Albert Museum. 'My whole speech was nothing to do with me,' he says. 'It was for all the camp, the femme, the sissies, all of the people that marched at Stonewall, the very people that those awards take their name from. They were the people that were rioting in the streets. They were the people that changed history. The straight-acting ones couldn't do the hard work because they couldn't be seen. The sissies had to do it all.'

The Cabbie's Coincidence

Tony Holland and Julia Smith left *EastEnders* in 1989. They had nursed their baby to successful school years and were ready to go. Tony decamped to Dublin to create a blueprint for the Irish soap

Fair City, and he kept his finger in TV production. The effect of their leaving on *EastEnders* from the viewers' perspective took a while to become clear and can't be divorced from the aggressive ratings battles that began in the multi-channel age, starting in the mid-nineties. There were immediate after-effects that Bill Lyons can't imagine Tony ever having stood for, not least of all giving the HIV storyline to a straight character, Mark Fowler, the part Gary Hailes had originally auditioned for.

'I thought that was one of the dullest fucking storylines in history,' says Lyons. 'A great wasted opportunity, too. I guess the point is that at that time gay characters were virgin territory and people were feeling around for what they could and couldn't do with them pre-watershed. It was interminable, though. It just went on for bloody ever.' He notes that even if Tony Holland had agreed the story, he wouldn't have stood for it rolling on like that: 'He had his finger on the pulse of what people were interested in more than anybody I've ever worked with. People got bored of that story.'

In 1991 Holland and Smith were lured back to the BBC to see if lightning could strike twice with the ambitious new Mediterranean soap opera *Eldorado*. 'It was a disaster, start to finish,' says Lyons. 'Shouldn't have been, but it was.'

'Awful,' agrees Juliet Ace. Both writers worked on the show and could see its effects first-hand on the once untouchable super-producers. 'It killed Julia and nearly saw off Tony,' says Ace.

Bill Lyons has his own ideas about what went wrong with the show, a short-lived project that cost the BBC millions and earned the corporation some of its most stinging criticism. 'You shouldn't piss on people's dreams,' he says. 'A lot of people at that time did want to move to Spain. They don't want to hear the problems with it.'

Tony Holland was not used to failure. '*Eldorado* hit him so hard. He had such a wonderful track record. That was a walking disaster.' He took scant solace in the small triumphs of the show. 'We did some good gay storylines in that, actually. The original document was "Little Britain", which has been used elsewhere now but hadn't at the time, and what Tone was interested in writing was about those certain parts of Spain that are more English than England. They're clinging to that identity abroad and that's what he wanted to write about. Then it was out of his hands, and it became what he described as "Euro-porridge". People from all sorts of countries started putting money into the show, so it had to have Swedish characters or whatever. Disaster.'

After *Eldorado*, Tony Holland found work abroad. He worked in Sweden on a flagship drama for a while. 'Then,' says Juliet Ace, 'it all got too much and he deteriorated. It was very sad, really. A lot of his friends abandoned him. I cared about him very, very much.' She does not think Holland was proud of *EastEnders* per se. 'I don't think that would ever come into the equation with him. It was a part of him. And he always, always expected the best of himself. It was quite a natural thing to happen, that things should go well and be appreciated, which is why when he didn't have proper control on *Eldorado* he would not have been proud. The work was eating and breathing and everything else to him, I think.'

Ever the drinker, ever the bon viveur, Holland was admitted to hospital in 2008 with a broken leg. 'He seemed to be getting better,' says Ace, 'and then he contracted MRSA.' She was with him at the end. 'We spent most of the day with him, and then finally they said they were going to turn the machine off. His heart must have been very strong. We went in there while they did that and it took a long time for him to stop breathing on his own. He looked lovely. Beautiful, in fact.'

Tony Holland's story is a soap opera of its own. His influence in casting the first gay couple in a soap can be felt everywhere in the genre. *The Archers* was the first soap to get a civil partnership. Sean Tully was joined by his boyfriend Marcus, resident

Coronation Street lesbians Sophie and Sian, Gail's dad Ted, a local vicar, Audrey's transvestite boyfriend and the re-emerging Todd Grimshaw in a cast that led the august *Evening Standard* art critic Brian Sewell to pen a piece for the *Daily Mail* in 2011 asking: 'What have they done to *Corrie?*' *Emmerdale* has brokered one power-lesbian in a business suit, one suicidal gay youngster and his boyfriend, and several less incendiary, long-running gay characters. Phil Redmond's Channel 4 follow-up to *Brookside*, *Hollyoaks*, would barely exist without its prominent gay cast and storylines. It even lets them kiss properly. In *EastEnders*, the gay men and women have hit with varying degrees of success, asking questions about homosexuality and religion, family, petty crime, homicide and masculinity. Tony Holland flung British soap opera's closet doors wide open. They stayed that way.

Gary Hailes had not been thinking about *EastEnders* for a while when he was driving his black cab up Tottenham Court Road in central London one stormy winter night in 2013, nearly three decades since he was cast as Barry on the show. 'This man puts his hand out, I wind down the window and he tells me the name of a fancy restaurant.' He recognised the voice.

A couple of well-dressed gentlemen got into the back: Michael Cashman and his partner. 'We haven't seen each other for a good while,' says Hailes, 'and as I'm driving I can't even remember where he's asked to go because my brain is all over the place. But that's his voice. Definitely. I made some jokey comment about how soon you forget things. He said, "I know you from the East End, don't I?" I was like, "Well, yeah, sort of." And then Michael twigs.'

The first gay lovers on British prime-time TV reminisced over the course of their journey about the past and where their lives had taken them since. They agreed on one thing that night, that if the time came again and they were offered the parts of Colin and Barry, for better or worse they would jump at them head-first.

Gary Hailes says that, even knowing what he knows now about how events would transpire, he would take the part of Barry Clarke again in a heartbeat: 'Oh, I'd still do it. Absolutely. Wouldn't even think about it. I'm not changing anything. Because it was a brilliant time and, who knows, I could still be working at a telephone exchange. How many people can say that something they did 30 years ago is still being talked about now and feels like it has a little part to play in history?'

3. CAPITAL CITY

Work Experience

I was sent to see a careers officer in the last year of school. She was a plain woman sitting behind a wilting pot plant with a haircut too sharp for her face. She said, 'What do you want to do when you leave school?' I said, 'I'd like to be the editor of *Smash Hits*, please.' The likelihood of my learning the necessary skillsets in the three remaining months before being flung into the wider world clearly gave her some pause for thought. After some polite expectation-management she gave me an address for local newspaper the *Wythenshawe World* and suggested I asked them about apprenticeships. It wasn't anything I was interested in so I screwed it up and threw it in a rubbish bin outside the room.

A year later I was at sixth form college in Rusholme, geographically and emotionally closer to the heart of Manchester. A kindly, wise A Level English literature teacher plucked a copy of the collected plays of Tennessee Williams from her desk and instructed the class that two of them would constitute the week's reading. She prefaced the plays, *The Glass Menagerie* and *A Streetcar Named Desire*, with an unusual little eulogy to their importance. 'I probably shouldn't be teaching you this, by law,' she explained, while talking about the central theme of the first play. The hero, Tom Wingfield, is a troubled, shy, poetic sort. Clearly, he is gay, though the word is never used. Williams writes him sadly but sympathetically.

For a teacher at a northern Catholic educational establishment, mentioning the political climate around teaching the text constituted a small but significant act of rebellion. It wasn't the first time I'd heard somebody allude to Clause 28, the Thatcher government's divisive bill to ban 'the promotion of homosexuality' in the classroom, but it was certainly the most personally appropriate. The teacher taught the text sensitively, without caution, a heroic little act of personal approbation at a government's involvement in the personal development of students she clearly cared a great deal for. Manchester in the 1980s was a great place to come of age.

Those hours learning about Williams and how he had drawn upon much of his own experience with the characters of Tom Wingfield and *Streetcar*'s Blanche DuBois were pivotal moments, when life and art coalesced as one. We sat and watched the film of *Streetcar*, with Marlon Brando as Blanche's nemesis, Stanley Kowalski. Nobody had ever looked more arresting to me. During a break in the smoker's common room, a classmate asked if I'd like to go to the Number One club that night. I knew of the Number One already. It was the only gay club in the city that people from the Haçienda went to. I hopped along for the ride.

Back at college, the work-experience question came up again. I wrote a polite letter to Mike Hill, the editor of the Manchester magazine *City Life*, suspecting it would come to nothing. A month later I was working there, making tea, listening to local gossip, finding out the finer machinations of how musicians, actors, local celebrities and politicians made the transition from person to page, and how best to bring them to life and honour their tales.

Those few weeks were magical for two reasons. Firstly, they satisfied a love of magazines I'd nurtured since childhood. I have an older brother and sister who did their extracurricular learning on the glossy pages of these fantastical editorial worlds, full of fashion, nightlife, sophisticated pop music and art. I picked up the vernacular initially out of curiosity, and then by instinct. I learned about Comme des Garçons and New Order, the Blitz club and Afrika Bambaataa. There were few details of these carefully curated kingdoms I didn't love. They spoke of escaping suburbia, embracing differences, being the person you wanted to be.

The second reason had more to do with the person I knew I was becoming. Sequestered in the corner of the *City Life* office, up a New York-style industrial lift shaft at 1 Stevenson Square, was a two-man operation working from one desk to print *City Life*'s sister magazine, *Gay Life*. I must have seen it on the shelf at some point in a newsagent's. I must have noticed. But I hadn't realised that these publications were housed under one roof. The deputy editor, Nick Delves, took me to see Prince's *Sign o' the Times* film at a press screening. I wrote a review of it. It wasn't a big thing. It felt enormous.

Turning 17 in central Manchester in 1988 was not just a piece of demographic good fortune on account of the thrilling cultural life in the city at the time. It was a year that gay culture and Mancunian nous began to form indivisible bonds. A short, confident man called Chris Payne edited *Gay Life*. From his desk at the corner of the *City Life* office he was helping the North West Campaign for Lesbian and Gay Equality (NWCLGE) in their endeavours to crush Clause 28 by street-level activist force.

While I was in the office, a protest gig was organised for the No Clause 28 initiative, headlined by local heroes James and supported by emerging stars the Stone Roses. It was just one of a series of events that echoed what I'd heard in the classroom – that if you try to shut down a voice it will come back to haunt you in a manner louder and more considered than your prohibitionist, backward-thinking bill can ever attempt to suppress. It will do it with wit, style and humour, because draconian laws invite smart modern answers. They are open goals.

On 20 February 1988 a rally through the centre of Manchester organised by the NWCLGE turned the city upside down in its relationship with gay men. It was the start of Manchester becoming Britain's unofficial capital city of Gay. Nothing makes me prouder of my home city than thinking about the shift that happened from 1988 to 98, a useful microcosm for what would happen with gay men in the rest of the country. When a demographic has taken the one giant leap from being enemies to friends of a city in a ten-year handover, it is a whisper away from doing the same in the state.

Let the Light In

Peter Dalton was educated at St Bede's College, an impressively forbidding building at the Alexandra Park junction of Princess Road, the thoroughfare that cuts south Manchester in two. The school housed a brigade of young boys primed and headed for greatness – a junior division of the great northern powerhouse. As Manchester's most prestigious Catholic school, however, sex education was not a priority in the early eighties. 'It wasn't on any kind of curriculum,' says Dalton. 'The kind of sex education we got was really quite bizarre. We had the biology teacher's version, then we got the priest's version, and we were supposed to put the two together to work out what was going on.'

The possibility that any of the youngsters might turn out gay was not so much the love that dare not speak its name as the intimacy it's easier to pretend does not exist. 'It wasn't even mentioned or discussed.' Yet behind the façade, the establishment was not quite the bastion of moral rectitude it appeared. In 2013 the school's former chaplain and head of religious education, Father William Green appeared in Manchester Crown Court to plead guilty to 27 counts of sexual assault on boys under his moral guidance at the school, dating back to Dalton's tenure. The boys were between 11 and 15. A further assault on an eight-year-old at a school where he had taught before arriving at Bede's was taken into account on sentencing. 'He was my form master for a year,' says Dalton. 'I wasn't aware of that when I was at school. Nothing happened to me. But in hindsight, when I started thinking about things like school camps, well, it didn't really stack up too well.'

Another incident stung him hard. Peter's school-friend Damien was the first person he knew to talk openly about being gay. Damien left St Bede's before sixth form and, freed from heavyweight academic expectation and repressed Catholic double-standards, he began hanging around gay bars and clubs in the city, telling tales of excitement in the city's clandestine basements. Manchester may have been a decade away from having its gay village christened at the start of the eighties, but the pre-village gay community already had a thriving underground afterhours scene. There was the Stuffed Olives club, tucked behind the fancy strip of King Street shops, Hero's off John Dalton Street, Manhattan on Spring Gardens, the leather club Rockies on the old site of the venerable northern soul club the Twisted Wheel, and High Society on Princess Street. The Manchester Polytechnic student disco at Aytoun Street ran a busy alternative gay night on Fridays. The Haçienda's in-house promoter Paul Cons had attempted the impossible, to house Gay Mondays at the club. John Waters's irrepressible drag heroine Divine appeared, as did former Buzzcocks singer Pete Shelley, the local hero who had written Manchester's more diffident take on a 'Glad to Be Gay', 'Ever Fallen in Love (With Someone You Shouldn't've)' and was then promoting the less equivocal 'Homosapien' ('I'm a shy boy/ You're a coy boy/And you know we're homosapien, too'). 'If you look at footage of it now,' says Cons, 'there are two-dozen men stood around in overcoats. It was, shall we say, a bit ahead of its time?'

Gay pubs the New Union, New York New York, the Rembrandt, Paddy's Goose and Napoleons serviced the square half-mile now known as the village, an axis that congregated around the intersection of Bloom and Sackville Streets. Men looking for fetish-wear, amyl nitrate and imported Hi-NRG music were serviced in a little outpost called Clone Zone, run by Les Cockell, the Hero's and Rockies DJ with the fulsome moustache and encyclopaedic dance-music knowledge. Les played the northern counterpart to Ian Levine soundtracking gay London at Heaven. Both had been schooled well and hard in the speed-fuelled northern soul circuit. They knew exactly how to make men move.

One of the pre-village gay pubs in Manchester achieved local-legend status through the rumour mill. According to who you did or didn't listen to for music-industry gossip in the eighties, the Thompsons Arms gay bar near Chorlton Street bus station was the place referenced in the Smiths' ode to the loneliness of men looking for love 'How Soon Is Now?'

Damien would tell Peter Dalton about these places, quite unaware that some years down the line his friend would be partially responsible for a complete turnaround in perception of gay Manchester. He mentioned bumping into a music teacher from St Bede's during his nightlife adventures. 'The teacher had a word with him,' says Dalton, 'and told him not to say anything because it could get him sacked.' The news of the teacher's night-time proclivities made it to school under crueller circumstances when he tested HIV-positive and was admitted to the first Manchester AIDS ward at the Monsall wing of North Manchester General Hospital. 'Before he died there was a real witch-hunt.' This was the other prevailing climate of Manchester classrooms of the eighties when it came to homosexuality: fear and suspicion. 'It was wrong on so many levels.

The mother of one of the boys at school was a nurse at Monsall and she was involved in his treatment. First, she outed him, and then she demanded that he was removed from the school. Unthinkable. These things were happening before I'd even come out.'

Peter tentatively began coming to terms with his sexuality at Liverpool University, where he studied French. He arrived at University with the intention of joining the army. 'My best friend at Bede's was an army kid. I spent quite a lot of time with him, on holidays and stuff. I was really outdoorsy.' He did two years with the Officers' Training Corps before the realities of the ban on gays in the military hit. 'That's when I sacked that one off.' He became more interested in his life as a gay man. Liverpool was perhaps a little too close to home to start dabbling in the underworld, but when he took his third year out in Paris the doors of personal liberation inched open: 'I went out a few times in Paris, then told my friends over there and they weren't bothered. That gave me that little bit of confidence when I came back to Manchester.'

Peter's first experience of gay nightlife was epic, continental, chic and sexy. He visited Le Queen on the Champs-Élysées, the gay night at La Locomotive, next door to the Moulin Rouge in Pigalle, and the eye-popping sleaze scenes at Le Trap on Rue Jacob, not far from the apartment he rented. 'Now, that was an education.' He strolled through Le Marais, traditionally Paris's gay district, wowed by the openness of the café culture that saw gay people transposed from the only gay existence he knew of – those nocturnal northern underworlds in Liverpool and Manchester – to chic daytime leisure pursuits. 'There were gay bars and clubs in Paris,' he says, 'but you didn't really need to go in them because gay people were everywhere; men and women walking their dogs, doing their shopping and getting a coffee and just living their lives. I think that was the first time I started to feel genuinely comfortable about being gay.'

Something deeper registered. 'I thought, OK, I'll come home and tell everybody at some point about this.' He wasn't sure how or when. 'Hanging out in the bars in Paris, in Beaubourg around the Pompidou Centre, I remember thinking, Wouldn't it be great if we had a bar like this in Manchester? There wasn't anything that wasn't branded massively as a gay place where you could just sit outside, have a coffee and a pastry and read the papers.' The nearest Manchester got to unapologetic gay culture on the daytime street was the six-foot neon Statue of Liberty outline on the New York New York pub, with its one raised hand limp at the wrist.

A gay bar that broke with old tradition and threw back the shame-intimating curtains to physically and metaphorically let in the light? Peter Dalton returned from Paris in the summer of 1988, Manchester's pivotal summer of love, with a vague plan brewing. Two years later, with the scent of Paris still lingering on his collar, the ecstatic chaos of Madchester its homespun backcloth, the newfound confidence of a university degree, all thoughts of joining the army now a distant memory, Dalton became the architect of a new kind of gay life in Manchester, opening the first glass-fronted gay bar in the country, Manto.

The Clause 28 March

Chris Payne arrived in Manchester in 1982, another young man with early army ambitions. The son of a military historian father, as a teenager in west London he had joined the 2nd Field Regiment of the Royal Artillery. He first looked up the word 'homosexuality' in a book on Greek history at the age of ten. He failed his second entry interview to Sandhurst and wound up in the North West to study history and politics at Salford University. His student years were split between running an Army Cadet corps for the local scallies and at bars in the emerging gay village. 'I'd been dabbling in London. I'd always been happy and comfortable in my sexuality,' he says. 'The New York New York and the Thompsons Arms were my social life in Manchester. I'd go to the Thompsons in uniform sometimes.' It would raise the occasional eyebrow.

His sexuality was not a secret among his young charges. 'I wasn't out to the other adult instructors, but all the cadets knew and didn't give a monkey's.' Rough-and-tumble kids in Salford joined up the dots and couldn't care less that Mr Payne was gay. 'I'd get just as dirty as they would, running around in mud, fighting, teaching them. I wasn't a caricatured gay man, and often in working-class communities back then, much more so than among the middle classes, people would judge you on who you are, not what you are.' This organic pecking order of democratic socialising was one that would come to define first Manchester's musical dominance of the late eighties, when the Stone Roses' Ian Brown famously declared, 'It's not where you're from, it's where you're at.' The mantra trickled down into Manchester's relationship with a blossoming gay community ready to step out from the shadows.

Payne is a community-minded man by nature. He enjoys the cut and thrust of local politics and had watched with impressed admiration a major shift in emphasis at Manchester City Council in May 1984. Local councillor and leader of the city centre sub-committee Pat Karney and council leader Graham Stringer led an internal Labour coup in the council to oust the right-wing Labour old guard and bring into power a modern, left-of-centre, socially liberal political leadership for Manchester that was both progressive and pragmatic. Karney is a gay man, and Stringer one of the city's key straight figures at a pivotal moment for gay life. It's tempting in retrospect to see some comparison in the way they moved the city with purpose into fresh terrain to the straight/gay political double act of Tony Blair and Peter Mandelson and what they would later achieve for gay rights in the country. But Karney and Stringer were tough-talking local zealots. Theirs was ambitious street-level politics, in love with local geography, possibility and change.

'Part of the contrast,' says Payne, on this new way of running a city council, 'was that they were pragmatic and modern, and not dogmatic and sectarian, as Militant were in Liverpool. It was a tale of two cities in the 1980s.' He points out that the official opposition in Manchester, the Lib Dems, were led by an out gay man and included a number of out gay councillors. 'This meant that though Labour and the Lib Dems battled for votes and support across the city, on LGBT issues and HIV and AIDS issues there was cross-party support.' The city stood as persuasive symbolic opposition to Mrs Thatcher throughout her time in power. Its politicians and people seemed to sing broadly from the same hymn sheet.

After university Payne became involved with the Campaign for Press and Broadcasting Freedom, concentrating on how gay men and lesbians were portrayed in the media. He schooled himself well in the rhetorical power of gay Manchester's two distinct, specific and notorious enemies at the time: the city's evangelical Christian chief of police James Anderton and his primary, if unofficial newspaper mouthpiece, *Manchester Evening News* columnist Andrew Grimes, 'who almost every week would find a way of attacking lesbians or gay men, particularly if it linked back to an initiative by Anderton.'

This was the culture of the day. Ray Mills and Garry Bushell were scripting the same anti-gay missives on a national level at the *Sun*, primed by their editors and proprietors and disguised by bluff language as the voice of the common man. For emerging gay men in Manchester, when attacks came from those who were neighbours and supposed to be looking after their wellbeing and safety, they felt more personal. Anderton trumped everyone in the catcalls to demonise gay men during the AIDS crisis when he famously declared that gay men were 'swimming in a cesspit of their own making', a slogan that became a rallying cry for the extreme

Christian right and strangely energising for the growing number of local council initiatives and right-minded, appalled Mancunians that were watching with interest piqued as Manchester's primacy on the gay UK map began taking nervous shape. 'Being a born again Christian,' says Payne, 'Anderton's belief system was very robust, and he brought that into his position. He would have seen it as his moral duty to clean up Manchester.'

He said so himself, whenever given a microphone. James Anderton was an equal-opportunities player when it came to policing the city's sexual behaviour. It wasn't just gay sex he disliked so much. He had built up a habit of police procedures that included raiding local sex shops, gay and straight, and swooping into newsagents to divest them of top-shelf materials. He banned a book of page 3 girls from being sold in WHSmith. He was immortalised in song in the Happy Mondays' banging rave-era anthem 'God's Cop' and was one of the few police chiefs to find support from both the feminist movement and Mary Whitehouse's anti-pornography league. His pedigree was of strong, efficient, authoritarian policing. He'd contained two marches of the National Front through Manchester city centre in the late seventies and presided over the roughshod manhandling of the Moss Side riots of 1981.

He had strong national allies. The *Sun* was quick to get behind his alarming zero-tolerance talk on AIDS. After he posited on a local radio interview, 'Why do homosexuals freely engage in sodomy and other obnoxious sexual practices knowing the dangers involved?' the *Sun* responded with, 'What Britain needs is more men like Anderton and fewer gay terrorists holding the decent members of society to ransom.' Many investigating officers in the Manchester constabulary of the eighties have less-than-fond memories of Anderton, and recall being positioned in the roofs of public conveniences directly above the stalls, watching for hours on end as men urinated in the hope of finally securing a conviction.

Thatcher quashed an investigation into Anderton as he revived a nineteenth-century law to ban 'licentious dancing' between two or more people of the same sex, a dictate that reached peak efficacy when he raided the Mineshaft, in the basement of Rockies leather club. Local lawyer Robert Meaton was there that night, and the incident prompted him into action. He used his decisive legal mind to help men fight cases in court about their right to engage with one another, flipping Anderton's interpretation of the law back on itself. The late Meaton would eventually become chairman of the Village Charity, long after Anderton had been unseated.

There are two stories every gay man and lesbian who remembers his iron policing rod over Manchester during the eighties will tell you about Anderton. The first is the 'swimming in a cesspit of their own making' quote. The second is that his daughter came out as a lesbian in the nineties, less than a decade later, a poetic twist that provided a satisfactory analogy for just how devastatingly institutional homophobia can spill into the homes and private lives of its most voluble practitioners; of how damaging genuine homophobia is not just to society, but to local communities, splitting families asunder; how antithetical it is to that central Christian tenet of loving your neighbour as yourself. 'You can't choose your parents,' notes Payne.

Chris Payne was methodical during his work for the Campaign for Press and Broadcasting Freedom, documenting and monitoring the representation of gay people over Manchester's local news media: 'Things that now would be unusual but then were everyday, detrimental homophobic attacks and characterisations of lesbians and gay men, referred to as "sick" or "perverted" or "weird". It was about challenging how we were set up for ridicule. All sorts of people around the UK were doing all sorts of work on this.' Andrew Grimes in the *Manchester Evening News* and his war on the 'right-on' culture at Manchester City Council became a recurrent bête noir for the charity. 'You could see who it appealed to and why.' These columnists were supposed to represent the voice of their readers.

Yet, in a way, it was Anderton who pushed the powerful force of his opponents into direct action, lending their cause previously unseen urgency. Without his lunatic addresses might the city not have been galvanised into action? 'There are a confluence of events that help to put Manchester on the map and make it a very different city in terms of its LGBT history, first compared to London, and secondly against other regional cities,' says Payne.

The confluence of events Chris Payne talks about is geographic, demographic and, at a deeper level, esoteric – spiritual, even. Manchester's useful positioning on the UK's transport network played directly into its eventual gay communion. 'Manchester sits along the M62 corridor. An hour away on one side, you're in Liverpool, an hour away the other, you're in Leeds and Sheffield, further on to Hull. You drop down 45 minutes and you're in Stoke, up 45 minutes and you have the whole Lancashire belt, Burnley, Accrington, Blackburn, Preston. All of that can come in quickly on the M62 and M60, an easily accessible motorway network that makes Manchester very specific. It makes it a hub.' If there aren't enough of one minority in small towns, cities and villages to represent a confident visible majority, they have to come together to form one. Manchester was handily enough positioned to become a gay and lesbian youth club in the eighties for anyone north of Watford.

Manchester has form for proving itself as a 'can-do' city, over and over. 'That's how Manchester perceives itself and the gay scene could ride off the back of that, as well as benefiting from Manchester pushing itself forward to compete with other European cities,' says Payne. It is a city particularly good at bouncing back from adversity. 'It bid for two Olympic Games and didn't get them, but actually it gets the Commonwealth Games. An IRA bomb goes off and, after the emergency services have dealt with the aftermath, a competition is announced to rebuild Manchester. It's a renaissance city.'

There may just be something in the water. 'It's strong-minded, strong-willed and independent. It has a history of being radical, being independent, standing on its own two feet. With my marketing head on I go back to product, place, people, price and promotion to assess Manchester's village and where Manchester is in terms of selling itself. So Manchester as a scene is big enough to attract the biggest names and businesses, but it isn't as big as London, which people can feel isolated in, in a series of mini-villages that don't always connect.'

Manchester is a small enough place to hear them all talk at once and yet big enough to facilitate real, effective engagement on a common cause. It is a city of gobshites and polemicists, of personal publicists and poetic mavericks. It is blessed and occasionally cursed with mercurial levels of city pride. 'The emergence of the gay village all sits,' says Payne, 'in a wider position of where Manchester was in the mid- to late-eighties, under a Labour administration that was willing to work with the Conservative government if it was willing to promote Manchester.'

The city's student population regenerates the city every September, a new demographic at entry level of their serious, independent thinking. 'The fact that Manchester has a very strong, vibrant student population,' says Payne, 'the largest in Europe both then and now, means that every year Manchester is reborn, with tens of thousands of new people living in the city. It's continually refreshed.' It's continually, visibly young in a way a city as prohibitively expensive as London can never be. 'Within that there are lesbian, gay, bisexual, transgender, curious, what we would now describe as metrosexual and polysexual people. Manchester gives space to them all. This builds conversations about human rights, women's rights, rights for people of colour, a whole range of progressive issues. So there is a wellspring of support there that was particularly strong in the eighties, archetypally so. It's a backbone to what everyone's doing.'

All of it coalesced on 20 February 1988 with a march through the city centre supported by the already thriving underground gay world of the city and facilitated by a cleverly pragmatic city council – and policed by James Anderton's force. The No Clause 28 rally saw over 20,000 demonstrators emerge from the sidelines and stomp down Market Street, towards Albert Square. This was a historic act, constituting a record number of protestors drawn to the city, and a symbolic one, too, with the council handing over the civic reins to the gay and lesbian community. 'Just to be able to have the event in Albert Square and to be inside the town hall,' says Payne. 'You were looking out and down on the square and watching it fill up. It really was magical. There are famous shots from that day, aerial views of Albert Square just full of protestors. The energy that gives people is quite incredible.'

Peter Dalton was thrilled by what he saw. 'You could see the first seeds of that change,' he says. 'All sorts of things happened on that day in Manchester.' He had more pressing concerns, however. 'I was more worried about who was going to see me.' Would a *Granada Reports* camera crew catch him on film, inadvertently outing him to his Catholic family? 'Just that. I wanted to be there but I didn't want anyone who knew me to see me. I think that was the start of everything snowballing for me.'

The demonstration looked like the end of one era of gay Manchester and the beginning of another. Spotting familiar faces from the gay village was like playing a local game of pin the tail on the donkey. Graham Stinger made his triumphant speech: 'First of all, on behalf of the Manchester Labour Party and the City Council I'd like to welcome everybody from outside Manchester to Manchester and say what a wonderful and magnificent demonstration this is.' The crowd roared. 'This is the largest national demonstration there has been in Manchester in the last 20 years and we are very proud of it … We're told by the police that there are 12–15,000 people here, though given the police aren't the most numerate people we're still counting.' Another roar. 'We think there are about 20,000 people.'

By now the crowd was cheering like the terraces at Old Trafford and Maine Road football grounds, the regular soundtrack to Saturday afternoons in two corners of the city. 'People at the moment in this country are very concerned about health and about civil rights, and we shouldn't make the mistake of thinking that Clause 28, the attacks in the national media and the press on gays and lesbians are disassociated. The real project that the Conservatives are on is to destroy public service, to destroy local democracy and to place the power into the hands of those people and those organisations with most money. The reason Clause 28 has been introduced is to divert attention from their real project: to scapegoat, victimise and create a new second-class citizen. Manchester City Council and the Labour Party in Manchester are not prepared to be used to help create second-class citizens in this city or anywhere else.'

Stringer left the stage for Tom Robinson to sing 'Glad to Be Gay'. The crowd sang back as one, 'Sing if you're glad to be gay, sing if you're happy that way', the city's first, collective, unifying good-as-you moment. Sir Ian McKellen, the marvellous Lancashire-born-and-bred actor, then just plain old Ian McKellen, delivered a speech to give proceedings his personal touch: 'I'm here because I'm one of millions of normal homosexuals who are affected by this new law. Clause 28 is designed, in part, to keep us in our place. But it didn't work with me. We must be out and about in the streets of Manchester. We must be out and about in the media. We must be out and about in pubs and clubs and in the classroom, talking about homosexuality, encouraging our friends and families to think about homosexuality and, in fact, in that sense, promote homosexuality. Until this whole country realises, as we do, this Clause 28 is, in itself, to coin a phrase, "an unnatural act".'

McKellen stepped down to introduce Michael Cashman, who had moved on from playing Colin in *EastEnders* and was now at the start of his serious political career. 'I'm here because I'm proud,' said Cashman, clenching his fist to the air. 'Gay men and women are ordinary men and women made extraordinary by society's focus on what we do in bed. As ordinary men and women we demand the same rights, no more, no less, the same rights as other ordinary, civilised human beings. There's been a lot of talk about the money that is spent to "promote" homosexuality. Even Saatchi & Saatchi couldn't sell it for us. In a civilised society it shouldn't be necessary to spend money to promote equality. Because that's all we want. Equality. Nothing more. Finally, I want to leave you with this. They can round us up. They can gas us. They can shoot us. They can do whatever they like with us, but they will never annihilate us, because so long as a man and woman procreate, so homosexuality will exist. And we will never surrender.'

By now the scenes in Albert Square looked something like the work of Harvey Milk during his galvanising work for gay rights in America. Cashman handed over the microphone to fellow soap opera alumnus Sue Johnston, then playing matriarch Sheila Grant on *Brookside*. 'I'd not intended to speak,' she said. 'I'm not very good without a script. But when I first heard about Clause 28, I thought about Hitler's burning of the books. And we all know what happened there. It must not happen here.' Later, at a Never Going Underground concert at the Free Trade Hall, one of a series in support of the rally, Jimmy Somerville took to the stage to sing 'There's More to Love than Boy Meets Girl'. McKellen followed the Communards on stage to tell the hollering crowd that the first time he was in the building was to see a Cliff Richard concert, leaving the audience to draw their own conclusions about what that might say about past gay visibility in Britain.

All this so school kids like me could read a Tennessee Williams play? 'The party went well on into the night,' says Chris Payne.

'We'd enlisted all the bars and clubs. They had all got extra licences which the council had granted. What we did was invite all these people to our city, to demonstrate and to have a great time.'

The city's emerging nightlife had a part to play. 'It was political but it was with a purpose, and there was the party element. We made sure people actually enjoyed themselves. Suddenly, all these people that had come together and had never been to Manchester before thought, This is all right here, we'll come back again. That helps create impetus. We didn't stop there. In 1989 we did Love Rights, then followed that on with Liberation 91, all things continually in opposition to Clause 28 and then spreading out to fight for the equalisation of the age of consent. We just kept the momentum up. Off that, you get the fact that entrepreneurs will come in.' The time was approaching for Peter Dalton to put into action the ideas he'd begun forming in Paris.

'Things rub off on each other,' says Payne. 'This is a transformational moment for Manchester and a transformational moment for wider gay culture. I'm not saying that Manto couldn't have happened without the Clause 28 march, but it helped. This is also Manchester that is consumed by itself as "Madchester". It's the summer of love and ecstasy from 1988 onwards. It is that party atmosphere. It is The Haçienda and FAC 51. It is T-shirts that say "On the Sixth Day … God Created Manchester". Manchester is acutely about a sense of its own place, and within that the lesbian and gay community is able to bloom and blossom and grow because there is a fertile and sympathetic environment. It's all about coming out of the shadows and into the sunshine.'

Unity House

Peter Dalton's first job out of university was with the big north-western wing of brewery Bass, as a trainee account manager/salesman. 'I just wanted to avail myself of every possible bit of training,' he says. 'I was getting it all out of them, which was pretty callous really because I never intended to stay.' His dream of opening a new kind of gay bar in Manchester had taken a propulsive surge after the opening of two smart straight venues at which he could see a growing population of young, cool, gay Mancunians. First was Dry Bar on Oldham Street, the drinkers-and-thinkers outpost of the Haçienda, shaped with sleek grace and post-modernist adventure by the infamous nightclub's interior designer, Ben Kelly. The second was the Cornerhouse cinema, art gallery and bar on the corner of Oxford and Whitworth Streets.

'The trendy gay crowd were all there, right from the start,' says Dalton. 'Even though Dry wasn't a gay place I felt instantly comfortable in there. It was never a case that we wanted to replicate it. It was just the idea of putting a heavy design aesthetic into a bar.' He'd heard on the brewery-industry grapevine that Whitbread brewers had put a lot of money into Dry Bar and the Haçienda, as its popularity went supernova in the post-88 summer-of-love rush. He approached an area manager: 'I said, "I don't know where this is going but I've got this idea and I'll be looking for a brewery to supply it." I had to put it in terms that the brewery would understand. I just said my generation, the young generation of gay people, don't want what's on offer and I want to do a gay version of Dry Bar. It was a way for them to understand it. He said they would be interested in putting some money in.'

Peter Dalton had no gay allies in the brewery industry, and he wasn't out at work. 'Oh no, not at all. Back then, it was a macho profession. Every lunchtime would be two or three pints. You had to have a liver test every six months if you were key personnel. You were encouraged to drink because that was the business. But at the same time you'd have a liver test to make sure you weren't overdoing it. I didn't feel comfortable enough to be out there.' The initial burst of interest from Whitbread was enough for Peter to begin a property search. 'Not all in the gay village, by any means,' he says. He found a disused railway arch on Whitworth Street, in strolling distance from both the Cornerhouse and the alternative arts space Greenroom, which housed a more performance-art inclined and often noticeably gay clientele. He looked at the huge Minto & Turner disused warehouse building near Shena Simon College and a small venue in the more rarefied end of town at St Ann's Square, near Henry's wine bar, where the ritzier young professional gay element would do their drinking in the late eighties.

Key to his belief that a young demographic big enough to fill a smart, cool, design-savvy gay bar in Manchester existed was the monumental turnaround at the Number One club, a small box tucked behind Bootle Street police station, near the rear entrance to Central Library. The club was the most obvious answer to the question, 'What does Manchester's summer of love mean to gay people?'

'I went in Christmas 1987,' says Dalton, 'when I was staying at home for the holidays, back from Paris, and then again when I came back in the summer of 1988, after the whole summer of love thing had happened. When I was in there at Christmas the staff were wearing lycra shorts, there was a VIP area up the back, Patrick the doorman was dressed up in a suit and the owner, Geoff Bibby, was fussing around. When I came back the carpets had been ripped up, the whole place was dripping with sweat, full of smoke and everyone was going mental on ecstasy. I absolutely loved it. Oh my God, what happened to this place? It was magically important.' The Number One developed a religious sense of devotion among smart Manchester clubbers, gay and straight alike.

In the summer of 1987, Number One club DJ Tim Lennox had started carefully slotting Chicago house music drawn from the US city's gay subculture at the Warehouse nightclub in Boystown into the more traditional gay soundtrack of Hi-NRG and pop music. By 1988, Tim was playing fully inventive and immersive house sets on

Friday and Saturday nights at the Number One. He was buying his records from the same selective Manchester vendors and attracting the same devotional support as local club heroes Graeme Park and Mike Pickering at the Haçienda or the 808 State boys, Darren Partington and Andy Barker, at the Thunderdome on Oldham Road. Lennox is the great unsung hero of gay Manchester, still ripe to bring a misty eye to followers who doted on his intuitive reading of a specific dancefloor at a specific time. The crowd would frequently queue to buy cassette tapes at the end of the night for £5 off Ian Bushell, the lighting tech sat next to him in a sweat-drenched local nightclub freed from the prying eye of the national press who had all descended on Manchester that summer, to get up close and see what a youth culture like acid house could do to a city.

In 1989 Peter Dalton found his venue on Canal Street. Fittingly, perhaps too fittingly before purchase, it was called Unity House, a neat compound of what had happened within Manchester's gay community the year before and the music that was facilitating it. 'Perfect, I know,' he says. Unity House was a crumbling, beautiful Art Deco wreck situated next door to Tony Warren's old stomping ground, the New Union. 'Unity House just came into my sights and it was my eureka moment,' says Dalton. 'Oh my God, that's the building. It really was that.' He found the owners of the building, the dynamic young architectural practice Benedict Smith Associates by phoning British Gas and blagging a name. The more Peter looked into the building, the more perfect it seemed. It had started life as a boilermakers union and was later the site on which the Transport and General Workers' Union was founded in Manchester. The industrial buildings of Canal Street at the time were largely home to upscale design practices, another captive audience for his bar. Benedict Smith Associates had hoped to transform the building into a signature office suite, but the woman he was dealing with at the practice told him that things had started to go awry. 'A few things had happened and a couple of their big retainer jobs had gone. It was 1989, interest rates were 15 per cent, there was a recession going on and people were struggling.' He made a suggestion to her. 'I said, "If you were to sell it and we gave you free rein to do the design for the bar, how does that sound?" She said, "I think we could have a deal." That's when I started to get really excited.'

Dalton only had one specification for the design of the bar, that it must have a full glass front. 'We didn't want the kind of gay bar where the trap door opens and someone peers out to see whether you could come in. We wanted a glass front where we could all see out as much as everybody could see in. We were there to see and be seen. That was the only bit of the brief we gave the architects.' But the possibility of his dream bar turning into reality hit a stumbling block: Whitbread pulled out as backer. 'I was a bit naïve thinking the brewery would just cough up the money. After a couple of meetings with them I realised that wasn't going to be the case. I was a bit despondent. It was only because I was young and naïve, really, that I kept going.'

The second half of the Manto duo stepped in. On the dancefloor of the Number One, Peter bumped into an old acquaintance, Carol Ainscow. He'd known Carol's girlfriend Theresa since he was at St Bede's, when two of her brothers were his schoolmates. He'd worked for Theresa one Christmas at her market stall in Harpurhey, north Manchester, when he was 15 and met Carol for the first time then. 'I was scared to death of her at first,' he says. 'She was Theresa's very successful businesswoman girlfriend.'

Carol had made her money in the North West property boom of the eighties. 'She bought a really beautiful building in Bolton that was rundown and turned it into a rest home. The logical next move was to do a nursing home, one step up the care scale. She was making money.' When they met on the Number One dancefloor, Dalton was still in his first proper job. 'Financially, I didn't know anything. But she seemed to be doing well. She was driving a nice car, had a nice house, not crazy grand, but she was buying this house in France for £10,000, which she'd asked me to help out with translating documents, so it was all a bit of a wow to me.' Carol wasn't necessarily happy in her work. 'She didn't like what she was doing because it was a bit morbid. The thing with care homes is that people do die all the time. She said it was a good business but it wasn't what she really wanted to be doing.' Peter mentioned the Unity House building to her and his recently thwarted plans for it. 'She could totally tap into what I was talking about. She was really canny and she said, "I'll back you."'

Looking back, Peter isn't quite sure why she made the decision. 'I realised very early on what a debt of gratitude I had to her. There's no way it would've happened without her.' Their relationship didn't come without some initial complications. 'It made me quite nervous, too. She was backing someone who was 23 at the time we had the conversation. If you asked me now, at 48, to back a 23-year-old to open a bar in the gay village there's no way I'd do it. I'd probably laugh in your face. But she'd seen me grow up. She'd seen me go through uni and then use my graduate job to learn a new set of skills, and she knew I was serious.' Peter Dalton was a diligent young man, smart, liked and intelligent, who tapped directly into the swirling chaos of a city changing its perception of itself. 'I think that's how she saw me. It wasn't like I was a dizzy scene queen out every night.'

Work began in earnest on Manto in the summer of 1990. Honouring their promise, Benedict Smith Associates demolished the frontage of Unity House and inserted plate-glass windows on either side of the steel entrance and across the front of the first floor. Peter interviewed for staff at the Northern Counties housing association flat he shared with his boyfriend in India House, one of three buildings in Manchester city centre you could live in at the time. From the start he had a specific idea of building a Manto family, beginning with his staff and expanding out. 'I didn't necessarily want people with loads of experience. I just wanted people who could buy into what we wanted to do. I wasn't bothered whether they were gay. I wanted a mixture of ages, sexes, sexualities and experience. I still call them the Class of 1990.'

The name Manto was a compound of 'Manchester' and 'today', given extra figurative meaning through its Greek mythological history. 'Manto was the lover of Apollo and she was a prostitute. At the time, Canal Street was a sleazy red light area.' The celebration of the city as a sex-positive home for the dispossessed was registered early, with some local wag painting over the 'C' and 'S' on the Canal Street signs to rename it 'anal treet', a witticism that endured into local legend. The acquisition of Unity House cost Peter and Carol £120,000. Just prior to the bar opening, Peter signed over the tenancy of his flat at India House, a building buzzing with the good, the bad and the ugly of Manchester's world-conquering music business and the closest Madchester ever got to having its own Chelsea Hotel. The tenancy went to Peter's friend Louise Jones and her then boyfriend, Inspiral Carpets' young guitar tech Noel Gallagher. When Manto first opened, it had an unusual postman. 'For the first few weeks after I'd moved out of India House,' says Dalton, 'Noel used to come into the bar and give me the mail each morning.' Liam Walsh is another unsung figure in gay Manchester's development. As a radio plugger at the independent music promotions agency Red Alert, he would look after talent staying in the city, taking them to places young Manchester was choosing to hang out in. Manto would become the first cross-pollinating gay bar on his one-man promotional tour of the city's nightlife.

If you peel back the layers of any of Manchester's key cultural institutions, there is always a gay man somewhere lurking at a pivotal point in the story. 'There were a lot of gay men in influential positions at Piccadilly Key 103,' says Chris Payne of the hugely popular local radio station. The model agency Nemesis, which was owned by music manager and former casting agent Nigel Martin-Smith, moved into quarters at the back of Albert Square after Martin-Smith had his first pop hit with Damian's cover of *The Rocky Horror Show* song 'Time Warp' in 1989. When *Gay Life* magazine wound down in 1989, Chris Payne started a new gay publication, *Scene Out*, from an office below the management of Inspiral Carpets and James, at the bottom of Rochdale Road. 'That's how we got James to support a No Clause 28 gig,' he says.

There were esoteric links between the local music scene and gay culture, too. The Smiths' debut album featured a still from Andy Warhol's seminal film *Trash* on the jacket, of hustler Joe Dallesandro masturbating, cropped from the chest up. When the Happy Mondays first looked like becoming an unlikely breakthrough mainstream success, the casting for their 'Wrote for Luck' video, shot at Legends, extended its search for ecstasy-addled young ravers at Konspiracy, the Thunderdome, the Haçienda and the folk ripping up the dance-floor at the Number One club. New Order found their sound on a Factory Records trip to New York that they'd spent mostly in the gay clubs Paradise Garage, Danceteria and Area. 'A song like "Blue Monday" is just Ian Levine, really,' says Peter Dalton. The band could've saved themselves the airfare by visiting Les Cockell's counter at Clone Zone, where his impeccable taste in Hi-NRG was on full, if low-lit display. A useful bricolage of links between straight and gay Manchester was being built, conjoining the city's glossy shop-front faces and gleeful foot soldiers.

Every Manchester nightlife venture sat in the spectacular shadow thrown out by the Haçienda. Perhaps the most important link between Manchester's prominence on the cultural world stage and its gay community at the close of the eighties and start of the nineties was the impressive figure of Paul Cons at the club. Like

Chris Payne, Cons had arrived in the early eighties to study in Manchester, from his family home in Pinner. Unlike Payne, he was in thrall to the gender-bending look of the moment in the capital, a more adventurous, theatrical strand of emerging gay culture. 'I was working a sort of Boy George androgyny look when I arrived,' he says. He'd begun his gay life in Manchester at the Aytoun Street student gay night. 'At Hero's and Stuffed Olives you'd only hear Hi–NRG, but at Aytoun Street they'd play Siouxsie and the Banshees and the Smiths.'

Cons was a committed political zealot and attended all the demos and protests expected of a young Manchester University student. 'I got arrested at one and was called a "poof" by a police officer. They threatened to take me to Risley Remand Centre for the weekend until the NUS stepped in and, ironically, a local Tory councillor got me released.' His first involvement with the Haçienda was promoting a Lesbians and Gays Support the Miners benefit concert, featuring the Communards, the Redskins and 'Homosapien'-era Pete Shelley. He began Gay Mondays in 1984. 'We were lucky if we got 60 people through the door,' he says. The Haçienda capacity was 1,800.

The Haçienda would have had its part to play in invigorating gay Manchester with or without Cons's involvement. He was the cherry on its cake. 'I think it was known to everyone in the Haçienda and Factory offices at the time that Tony Wilson's dad was gay,' he notes. Wilson, the irrepressible founder of Factory Records and co-owner of the Haçienda, was known to Manchester primarily as a local newsreader. 'Tony and Lucy Meacock,' says Chris Payne of the dandy entrepreneur and his *Granada Reports* co-host, 'were useful allies, always.' He remembers an episode of *Granada Upfront*, presented by Wilson, when Payne was invited on with a member of the religious right, a visiting reverend from London, to debate the setting up of a local street-level police initiative in the early days of the village. 'I had 15 minutes up against him. He said something about me not getting into Heaven, and I said, "Yes, the queue's huge and it costs you £10 once you get there." His whole argument was about the evil things we do and I said, "So are you going to arrest me, then? Are you going to send me to jail?" It was about taking that on, one person at a time. But the fact was that we had people like Tony Wilson and Lucy Meacock on our side. They were giving us that outlet.'

The downstairs bar at the Haçienda was called the Gay Traitor. A huge picture of Anthony Blunt, the Cambridge art historian who spied for the Soviet Union, was hung above it. The other two bars, Kim Philby and Hicks, were named after his fellow spies. Paul Cons was brought on board in 1986 to look after promotions at the club. He found a note on his desk from the outgoing Ellie Gray saying, 'Would you jump in my grave this fast?' before being dispensed on a fact-finding mission to New York. 'It was the last golden age of New York clubbing, of Area and Pyramid.' He returned and set up two nights, first the student Thursday, the Temperance Club, with a crucifix logo painted in the Haçienda's signature yellow-and-black bollard stripes, designed by the young graphics team of Glenn Routledge and Brendan O'Brien, who worked at the Haçienda café, part of the swell of the venue's gay staff. Glenn and Brendan would later set up Manchester's notorious semi-legal after-hours gay party Strangeways.

On Wednesdays, Paul Cons tried to circumnavigate his desire for a gay night at the Haçienda by throwing one without branding it gay. Zumbar was a template for what was to come later, with the night punctuated by fashion shows thrown by the local couturiers at Geese and Richard Crème, the first people to bring John Richmond, John Galliano, Comme des Garçons and Issey Miyake to the city. Zumbar was a favourite with the staff at Vidal Sassoon hairdressers on King Street, another noticeable gay stronghold at the more chic

end of the city. After Zumbar closed, Cons's great early *coup d'état*
was Hot, the Wednesday night which officially christened ecstasy
as the drug of choice for a new era of bold, confident Mancunians
and kicked off the summer of love. 'It was absolutely brilliant, right
from the start,' he says.

By the early nineties, Cons had one employee that would further
cement gay links between Manchester institutions. 'Do you know how
I used to get into the Haçienda?' says *Corrie* actor Antony Cotton.
'Me and my friend Michelle Kelly got Cons's phone number. We
used to phone up and say, "Hi, it's Jason and Candy from Granada
Studios' costume department," so we could get on the guest list and
we wouldn't get IDed. We were 14-year-old school kids.' Both Kelly
and Cotton ended up working for Paul Cons. 'Can you imagine
me and Michelle answering phones for an actual business? We'd go
through the guest list, put all our friends on it, hand it in and Cons,
the twat, would write £5 next to them all after we'd said they were
getting in for free. They'd get there and have to pay a fiver. Cons
said, "We are supposed to be running a business."'

The doors of Manto opened in December 1990: new decade,
new city, new gay life. 'Right from the start we got attention,' says
Peter Dalton. 'Andy Spinoza, who wrote Mr Manchester's Diary
in the *Manchester Evening News*, was there from the start. He was
very supportive.' When the tapes from Tim Lennox at the Number
One started playing, the staff started serving and the tills started
ringing, Manto quickly elevated from the diary pages to a news item
under Spinoza's guidance. 'He made a new kind of bar coming to
the city into news. Straight away that was validation that we were
onto something. If the newspapers care about it, we must be doing
something that's interesting. You don't get page 3 or 5 features if
you're opening a wine bar because it's just another bar. Right from
the start it was a news item and it didn't go away as one. There was
always something that put it back into the paper.'

The national reporting of Manto, a gay bar that had beaten London to the chase with its glass front, was less auspicious, until the journalist Simon Fanshawe arrived and christened the city 'Gaychester' in the pages of the *Independent*. 'That was just after Gunchester,' notes Paul Cons, who, when the Haçienda closed down during the summer of 1990 due to gang violence and shootings, had suggested turning it into a completely gay club. 'That didn't go down well.' The pink fringes at Factory only stretched so far.

'Gaychester wasn't something that happened as part of a masterplan,' says Peter Dalton. 'It was an accident because the Hac had closed down. Manchester was moody; people wanted to come to gay places because they felt safe there.' The first summer of Manto, 1991, was Gaychester's very own summer of love.

Cons's request to turn the Haçienda gay was the beginnings of the night that would become enshrined as the godfather of Manchester gay nights. Flesh at the Haçienda was held on the first Wednesday of the month from 1991 to 96. Like Peter Dalton and Carol Ainscow, Cons formed a strong partnership with lesbian activist Lucy Scher to promote the night. 'What was so astonishing about Flesh,' says Cons, 'wasn't that people were getting dressed up in all their finery, that 2,000 people were traveling from all over the country to come to it and that everyone, pretty much, was off their heads on ecstasy there. It was that all that was happening on a Wednesday night.'

Tim Lennox was the headline DJ, finally ascending to his rightful spot in the spaceship DJ booth suspended over the Haçienda dance-floor. A flurry of DJs emerged in his wake. Grimsby-born, formerly Leeds-based Dave Kendrick moved to the city to join in the fun, and became Dalton's new flatmate and the first resident at Manto before taking the warm-up spot for Lennox. Kath McDermott, the trusted hand at Piccadilly Records and ardent lesbian and gay rights activist, was gifted the most prestigious turntables in town. Matt Ryan, the handsome face so many Mancunians knew from working the shop floor at the French clothes shop Chipie, off St Ann's Square, and boyfriend of Antony Cotton's buddy Michelle Kelly, had his turn. Paulette Constable brought her unique, fiery glamour and instinctive feel for New York house music to the basement Gay Traitor bar.

Cons and Scher famously booked Take That to play at Flesh. 'We gave them 50 quid for it.' Jason Orange and Robbie Williams were regulars when they were back home. When their manager, Nigel Martin-Smith, saw the roof being raised at 4am as Tim Lennox played his final song of the night, the full 10-and-a-half minute version of Dan Hartman's 'Relight My Fire', he took his young boyband charges off to record their own version and instructed the video director to bring something of Flesh's incendiary energy to the video. The lunatics had truly taken over the asylum.

'When we brought up the London club Kinky Gerlinky to play on the second birthday party,' says Paul Cons, 'I swear Manchester has never, before or since, looked more glamorous. The first night of Hot and the first night of Flesh are without doubt my favourite ever nights at the Haçienda.' The Flesh flyer promised 'Serious Pleasure for Dykes and Queers', reclaiming the catcalling names of the past. It made good on its promise. Before long, straight men were having to kiss their male friends, lubricated by their socially disinhibiting ecstasy intake, to gain entrance. It had started to look less like a nightclub, more like a portion of the country questioning its sexuality.

The stars started rotating through the doors at Manto. 'We had Take That, Paula Yates, Helen Mirren and Robbie Coltrane when they were filming at Granada,' says Dalton. There is a whole scene in one of Mirren's best episodes of *Prime Suspect* filmed in the bar. Graham Stringer and Pat Karney were regulars from the city council. The *Corrie* cast drank Japanese beer there, and Granada shot a pivotal *Coronation Street* episode of Des Barnes's affair in the bar. 'Janet Street-Porter was filming *Reportage* at the BBC building on

Oxford Road at the time, and for a while it seemed like all her staff were gay and Manto regulars. Liam Walsh was important in bringing people down and crossing it over.' Watching the success of Flesh, noting the closure of the Number One and seeing the throngs swing through the doors of Manto left Peter Dalton and Carol Ainscow hungry for a club to add to their burgeoning gay empire.

In January 1993, Carol saw a story on the front page of the *Manchester Evening News* and took it to show Peter. Tony Wilson's Factory Records had gone bankrupt. 'She threw it down on the desk in the office and said, "Have you seen the news?" I said "I know, sad, isn't it?" And she said, "Peter, that's our club." That was Carol to a T. That summed her up perfectly. From the ashes, the phoenix. I just thought, Fucking hell, you're right.' The Factory Records building on the corner of Princess Street was bought for £350,000 in a quick deal. The licence appeal for the premises involved a touch of shadowy legalese, gifting Dalton and Ainscow another *Evening News* front page. 'In hindsight it was great publicity for us. We'd just opened and were on the front page of the paper.' Paradise Factory was born. Again, the stars kept coming. 'Lee Sharpe, Ryan Giggs, Pet Shop Boys, Take That, David Beckham, they all came through the door,' says Dalton. 'It was famously the place Michael Barrymore was spotted when he was being followed by the tabloids, outing him. He actually copped off with a friend of mine in there and, fair play to him, he never sold his story – never said a word, and was offered a lot of money to.'

Outside of Dalton and Ainscow's empire, gay Manchester itself was starting to sprout legs along Canal Street. First Metz, the bar-restaurant on the other side of Canal Street from Manto, opened, another independent venture with strong gay heritage, managed by Michael 'Polly' Pollard, the old New York New York manager, and part-owned by Manchester's drag queen in residence and city-centre fixture at Foo Foo's Palace, Frank 'Foo Foo' Lammar.

Breweries began sniffing around for venues in the newly christened 'gay village'. Bars opened up on Canal Street with breathtaking speed: Via Fossa, Prague V, Velvet up at the top end, towards Piccadilly train station. The Manto dollar became synonymous with the 'pink pound', a lucrative new revenue stream of gay men and women unencumbered by childcare and flush with disposable income. Gay Manchester never looked prouder.

The winds of change in nineties Manchester were starting to blow across the country. 'In that 1991 to 92 period,' says Payne, 'everything changed. It becomes an urban-regeneration and redevelopment story, an archetypal, blueprint one. It's canal-side, it's disused Victorian buildings, the huge investment that not only Peter and Carol put into Manchester, but also Via Fossa, Metz, Bar 38, Prague V. The street life was bustling. Then you get the gay doctor. The gay centre moves to a purpose-built venue. The two big cab firms, Village Cars and Street Cars, operate from out of the village. You've got the Village Hairdressers, the Funky Crop Shop and the Village Chippy.' Perfectly Manchester. 'I think what the huge investment in all of those bars did in a short amount of time was a vote of confidence in urban regeneration that couldn't have happened anywhere else.'

Toward the end of the nineties gay Manchester felt ready for its close-up. The area around Canal Street had blossomed into some unforeseen configuration of Peter Dalton's take on Le Marais and Tony Warren's Salford. How precipitously close-up that would get was percolating in the imagination of Russell T Davies.

Really Doing It

It was a ten-year period between Manchester's No Clause 28 rally and the city becoming camera-ready for commercial inspection on a Channel 4 drama series. Russell T Davies says he hadn't thought about writing a gay drama until he sat down to script the first episode of *Queer as Folk*. He had felt some movement in gay characterisation on TV with Warren in *This Life*, played by Jason Hughes in Amy Jenkins's London legal flat-share drama of the mid-nineties. He had noted the absence of any gay characters in *Cold Feet*, the pre-millennial twenty-something Manchester drama. He was excited by the possibilities of sex on TV opened up by Kay Mellor's *Band of Gold*, the sensational comedy drama about a frank-talking gang of Sheffield streetwalkers. 'Once you've seen a man who owns a chicken factory wanking himself off to a stripper then anything goes, really,' says Russell T Davies. 'On ITV at prime-time? Wow.'

Davies didn't connect directly to the worlds of Manto, Flesh and the Paradise Factory. Like Tony Warren before him, his writer's eye preferred the chatter and concerns of the little people. He began fleshing out dramatic potential from the obvious change in the city. And, again, like Tonys Warren and Holland, Davies had axes to grind on screen. 'I was massively railing against Tony and Simon on *EastEnders*, bless them,' he says. 'Whenever they went out on the gay scene they sat in chrome bars and wore shiny puffa jackets and all their friends were immaculate.' This was not a gay life he recognised. 'It looked revolting. Gay people looked shiny and all their conversations were about AIDS, and going to a gay place seemed slightly glamorous. I just thought, I want completely ordinary people because then those ordinary people could do extraordinary things.' He built edicts into his writing: 'Don't start with the drag queens. Don't start with the fireworks. I was never the youngest thing in the world, I was never the trendiest thing in the world and I was never the sexiest thing in the world, so I felt slightly out of place in those places. You didn't find me in the Haçienda. When this place was the coolest place in the world and everyone was talking about Madchester and getting off their head on drugs, I was sitting at home working. Weirdly, that acted in my favour. You ended up with a drama that was a lot more accessible to people.'

The central character of *Queer as Folk* is Nathan Maloney, the 16-year-old Manchester schoolboy who finds himself on Canal Street for the first time and goes on to enjoy a baptism of fire. Davies spotted an archetype of gay life in the time he'd spent in the less aspirational ends of Canal Street during its mesmerising transformation into the village. 'Two friends, one of whom is beautiful, one of whom isn't, and the less beautiful one is in love with the beautiful one. And the beautiful one knows it.' *Queer as Folk*'s twenty-something duo Stuart Jones and Vince Tyler sprung to life.

When filming *Queer as Folk* began in 1998, Canal Street was awash with rumours about the show. Yet from inside the production, Davies says there was no palpable sense of buzz building around it. The head of drama at Channel 4, Gub Neal, related a story to Davies about having been for dinner with Andy Harris, the head of drama at ITV, and Kevin Lygo, head of ITV, and telling them about the programme. Neal told him they had mercilessly taken the mickey out of him for commissioning the gay drama. 'Gub came back bristling, saying I can't wait for them to see what we've got. They imagined that soft, nice, liberal drama, with everyone saying, "I'm awfully worried about Roger, he's not taken his pills." When you used the words "gay drama" people imagined something trembling. Soft, middle-class people crying in the rain, which was exactly what they weren't going to get. We knew what we had.'

Queer as Folk began its screen life disastrously. Channel 4 rented a 250-capacity cinema in London and filled it with press. 'The launch was utterly hostile. There was a Scottish gay journalist sitting at the back, furious that we hadn't visibly got a condom into the sex scenes. Of course, Stuart and Vince would've known about safe sex. It was understandable he'd bring it up, but we had to sit

there and say, "That's not what it's about."' On the Saturday before
the first day of broadcast, Davies came down to talk about *Queer
as Folk* on the Radio 4 arts show *Loose Ends*. 'Ned Sherrin was so
coolly and coldly sarcastic to me throughout the entire interview.
We all had to go to lunch afterwards and he was talking about what
escorts he would hire, about dusty old Soho. It was the last roar of
the dinosaur in a way. He could not have been more unwelcoming.
For a long time gay men in broadcasting were this cool, waspish
London elite. Gin, opera and a Brazilian escort, nothing to do with
the real world at all. But it was actually dying out.'

When it was broadcast, the show grew an instant head of steam,
finding street-level fans in unusual places and opening a new, true
dialogue about gay men, Manchester and the wider world. 'Literally,
there was a hysteria to it,' Davies says. Charlie Hunnam, the young
actor from Newcastle charged with bringing Nathan Maloney to
life, became an instant pinup. Madonna invited him to tea when he
took a work trip to Los Angeles he never returned from. He is now
one of the three Hollywood actors handled by Brad Pitt's manager.
'I can remember once being with Charlie in some London hotel
and we bumped into Baby Spice,' says Davies, 'and she couldn't
get over meeting him. Oh my God, it's you from *Queer as Folk*!'
Davies's personal publicity cycle reached a surreal conclusion when
he was invited onto *Top Gear* to talk about Stuart's jeep, despite not
being able to drive.

Part of the homespun hysteria ignited by Davies was down to
his breaking a sex taboo in the opening episode. He took gay sex
to new realms on television when Stuart asked Nathan, 'Do you
like rimming?' before proceeding to instruct him on a new realm of
pleasure. 'I didn't just mention it, I showed it. That was absolutely
deliberate and I wasn't just being salacious. It had to be a mind-
fuck for Nathan. You'll only stay with a sex scene if there's some
drama in it. He had to encounter something more than the teenage

gay boy wanking to a pop star or their favourite boy at school. They might imagine kissing or even fucking, sucking, but I don't think they imagine rimming. Maybe they do now, but then it certainly wasn't part of a conversation or a fantasy. It was an area of sensation that Nathan wouldn't even have imagined.' It provided a satisfying dramatic tangent for Davies. 'You can't really show someone having the fuck of their life. You can't really dramatise that. You can't even really see that in porn. But there was one form of physical contact, a sexual act that would literally take him into a new world. So it was genuinely important because it's beyond his imagination. The normal version of that scene would be him getting to do the things he's been imagining doing for years – hooray! – but in this version he gets to do something that he's never even imagined for himself.'

In episode two, Davies gifts Nathan the catchphrase, 'I'm doing it. I'm really doing it.' A recurrent that would be passed around school yards, gay clubs and private conversations – a new rallying cry for Manchester itself. With power came responsibility. Davies was invited along to a gay teachers' conference and mostly applauded for the visibility and talking-point notoriety of *Queer as Folk*, until a teacher stood up to tell him that, buoyed with confidence from watching the show, the student had come out at school and promptly been beaten to a pulp, attacked so violently that his cheekbones had been crushed. 'There's a direct, absolutely ineradicable chain between what I wrote and him being beaten up. Presumably his face is still a mess to this day. I have to live with that.' The story made it to the pages of the *Gay Times*. The full story, Davies reasons, was that after the incident the school was so appalled by the behaviour dished out to its student that they initiated one of the first anti-homophobic bullying programmes in the country. 'That bit wasn't in the story so there was a sense of some fighting between your own kind. But that responsibility comes with it, of saying, "Did I do a bad thing? Should he have come out?"' *Queer as Folk*'s effect on Manchester's gay life was incalculable, just as it was on some of those involved in the programme. Davies went on to find incredible success reviving *Doctor Who* in the noughties, and Charlie Hunnam went to Hollywood. And one almighty argument broke out on Canal Street about what would happen in the next millennium.

Canal Street: The Hangover

The problem with being seen on television is that everyone can see it. The word on Canal Street was that the special area that had managed to incubate the secret world of gay life's growth while still keeping its cool had lost its edge. *Queer as Folk* was seen by some as the last nail in the coffin of the secret kingdom. The most familiar argument in Canal Street by the end of the twentieth century was not about the arrival of the big breweries that had initially turned down Peter Dalton's invitation to modernise gay Manchester. It was about the arrival of hen nights. 'Everybody famously says that *Queer as Folk* ruined Canal Street,' says Davies, 'because it got the hen parties in there. But actually, on screen in *Queer as Folk*, in episode three, they complained about the hen parties. So clearly I didn't invent that because I have Vince and Stuart talking about the hen parties in the first series. It was documenting what was going on at the time.'

Peter Dalton thinks the tipping point for Canal Street was not the airing of *Queer as Folk*, but the opening of Mash & Air, the fancy multi-storey restaurant and bar in a disused warehouse at the end of 1996. 'By the time it was on TV,' Dalton says of *Queer as Folk*, 'the mass market had turned up.' Mash & Air was the brainchild of Oliver Peyton, the Irish restaurateur who cornered the new market in rock-and-roll gastronomy with the opening of London's Atlantic Bar and Grill, just off Piccadilly Circus, in the mid-nineties. For a season, Mash & Air made Manto look like old news. 'There was one little point when it looked like the village could become Manchester's version of Shoreditch, a point when it could have gone down that route. Mash & Air was it.' Visiting celebrities had lost the impetus to stop off at Manto now there was a new kid on the block.

There was a period in 1997 when you couldn't go to a gay man's flat without stubbing a cigarette out in a stolen bespoke aquamarine ashtray with the Mash & Air logo on it. Visiting bands had their after-parties there. The high-end retail sector, buoyed by the arrival of Harvey Nichols and Selfridges after the IRA bomb redevelopment, had its new favourite social hangout. Vidal Sassoon hairdresser trainees were no longer interested in having a croissant at Manto. 'If the next three or four places to open had been of that ilk,' says Dalton, 'it could have been too cool for us. As it turned out, everything else was naff as hell, and Mash & Air was far too cool for where it ended up. It was completely in the wrong part of town. As soon as the mass market turned up, all the cool crowd had left.'

In 2003 Dalton and Ainscow decided to sell their business. By 2005 the places that had shaped gay Manchester's renaissance and made it a San Francisco of the north, had shut their doors and been sold on to new investors. The next wave of Manchester socialising congregated around the Northern Quarter, far enough away from the gay village to form its own identity, but close enough for gay folk interested in the next trend around the corner to stray from their natural home. The gay scene soldiered on regardless, some of it splintering off into the Northern Quarter, some moving from a night-time economy to something more community-minded. The park in Sackville Street became home to the first monument to those who had lived and died with the HIV virus in the country. Every year, over the August bank holiday, up to 100,000 visitors crowd the village for Mardi Gras, a highlight of the city's social calendar.

The parade is traditionally led by a visiting gay dignitary, followed by the first float featuring the rotating cast of *Coronation Street*. HomoElectric, the gay wing of the city's defining post-Haçienda night Electric Chair, opened with a mission statement setting itself deliberately at an obtuse angle to the commercialisation of Canal Street. There is still night-time mischief to be found among the old totems of the pre-Manto gay village, most of which proved surprisingly robust in their business plans. Velvet opened a fancy boutique hotel on Canal Street. The more fertile end of the club scene shifted from Canal to Bloom Street. The Eagle opened. The internet happened, cementing the twenty-first century's predominant social spaces as virtual, not physical. The most fertile social world in Manchester could now just as reasonably be adjudicated as being the Facebook group Mint, a breeding ground of Manchester's gay life past, present and future, as it could be Via Fossa or Churchills bars. The Company Bar kept the flag waving for a touch of the old Mineshaft sleaze that neither James Anderton nor the shifting sands of social inclusion and digital engagement could dampen.

Peter Dalton moved to the suburbs and took over the Horse and Jockey pub on Chorlton Green in leafy, bohemian south Manchester. 'These days I feel really proud of it,' he says of Manto. 'At the time we closed, everyone was moaning that the village was too straight. My attitude was, Well, when I was 20 I was going on marches for equality and acceptance.' Times had changed. 'We've got it now. We've got acceptance. We've got civil partnerships, we've got gays in the military, an equal age of consent. We've got equal rights and legal protection. We've got a massive amount of social acceptance. What is a gay village actually for anymore? We've demanded all this. We can't suddenly turn around and say, "Oh, you can't come here."'

He suggests that something similar may happen to Manchester's gay community that happened to the Indian and Pakistani communities in Rusholme. 'The curry mile was where the first Indian immigrants went to in the fifties and sixties. They settled there, and it wasn't until a while later that they'd taken over so many businesses – a takeaway here, a restaurant there, a shop here – that it became for everyone. The indigenous and second- and third-generation populations would all still go for big celebrations, for Eid, for events in their calendar, but the rest of the time they're getting on with their lives all over the place.'

He thinks this might be a way for Manchester to move forward, setting a new template for how gay life moves incrementally forward in the country. There are, after all, gay villages in Cardiff, Glasgow, Newcastle and Leeds now. 'I didn't realise at the time but we really should have been going out and opening bars and restaurants all over the place. That's what we fought for.'

4. IMPOSSIBLE PRINCESS

Enjoy Yourself

I was attending an induction day to work for a record store during the Christmas period in 1989. A dozen twenty-somethings sat around a boardroom table. I was 18. The manager-type conducted a boring talk about till-receipt rolls, smoking restrictions, fire escapes, dinner breaks and order forms, before attempting to liven up proceedings up with a question: What was the last record you bought and loved? The majority of folk around the table picked records I knew but wasn't especially interested in, mostly, I guessed, learned from recommendations in the staple student tastemakers of the times, the *NME* and *Melody Maker*. This being a boardroom looking onto the lonely, underfed, unkempt pigeons of Manchester's Piccadilly Gardens, a lot of local music figured. Someone mentioned the Chameleons, another the Railway Children: bands I learned later that you didn't hear much of elsewhere in the country. Here, they were gods.

Someone broke the tedium. A tall man with the most fantastic pout, voluminous blond quiff, fruity Yorkshire accent and scuffed biker jacket entered into a passionate soliloquy on the talents of

screeching gothic diva Diamanda Galás. I'd never heard anyone
talk about music with this idiosyncratic force before. Each sharp
sentence of effusive cheer swept towards the next, as if the forensic
dissection of Ms Galás's virtuosity had been rehearsed for a win at
the Grammys. The room was temporarily dazzled by his passionate
showmanship and liberal use of the local superlative 'fab'. With the
tacit recognition you learn swiftly on first accepting, then embracing
your sexuality, I turned and smiled to the fellow, silently hoping
he'd end up in my branch (he did).

Buoyed by the clear message of this man saying everything you
needed to know about him in a three-minute music monologue,
could I take up the baton? Certainly, I had the armour ready. My last
music purchase was the second Kylie Minogue record, *Enjoy Yourself*,
bought at the reduced price of £3.99 from a barely reconfigured
warehouse called Power Cuts at the back of Oxford Road. I couldn't
remember another. It was a brilliant year for music: De La Soul,
S'Express, Soul II Soul, Neneh Cherry, the first *Warehouse Raves*
compilation, an esoteric Michael Nyman soundtrack you'd hear in
the Cornerhouse bar. These, I knew, were the correct answers. But
in a quiet moment of personal exposition, I decided to tell the truth.

I'd developed an inexplicable and growing adoration for the
Australian soap actress. She was just that little bit older than me,
and perhaps the most notable, famous face of the Hit Factory
stable of record producers Stock Aitken Waterman (SAW). The
three made a joyful conveyor belt of Hi-NRG hits, each one an
undeniable mainstream appropriation of the gay disco subgenre.
Pete Waterman's music was crafted with callous precision, free of
any cerebral angle; his own plastic, neon and poppers version of the
Motown conveyor-belt model. The stars that fronted his records
were as oddly other as their songs were inclusive and everyman.
Pete Burns, Divine, Sinitta, even pint-sized lesbian superhero and
perennial Gay Pride fixture Hazell Dean.

There is something about a slightly demented character striking a populist chord that will forever warm the cockles of British gay men. It's perhaps our version of the biblical idea of the meek inheriting the earth. When someone weird stands centre stage, we don't look away. We are the first to dissect the signals hurtling them to popularity. It's a seventh sense you learn from being looked at for no apparent reason other than being yourself as a kid, then wondering and eventually understanding why.

A SAW song simplified the confusing gamut of grown-up emotions you would see played out on *Neighbours*, the TV show that threw Kylie Minogue into the British tabloid spotlight. With her hatless hat brim, wild curls and spectacles pin-badge, she was not one of the weird kids. On entry into the British pop milieu she was perhaps the least weird of them all. She represented a kind of suburban purity and homespun pluck that radiated goodness. She was on the front page of the papers all the time, in a real-life love drama with co-star and onscreen boyfriend Jason Donovan, a teen romance that felt almost chaste, beamed from a photo-love story in *My Guy* or *Jackie*. That music, that TV show and that relationship were just the easiest ways of working out what an adult life might feel like before the complicated business of living one.

So I made my own little tribute to the joy of Kylie Minogue, effectively coming out to a table of unexcitable Hüsker Dü fans from Stockport wearing frayed jumpers and roll-up ciggies behind one ear. In a first moment of personal triumph in reconciling the private and public me, an unexpected feeling of whistle-blowing liberation was counteracted by something peculiar and new: a feeling that, once the cork was out of the bottle, there was no chance of squeezing it back in; that subtle new ways of recalibrating the phrase 'I am gay' would have to be found in the perpetual motion of identification that accompanies coming out. Nobody tells you that you'll have to do it over and over again, boring yourself with answers to a carousel of the same questions asked over and over for the first five years, before you've worked out subtler ways of short-circuiting this ritualistic moment in which your sexual fancy becomes other people's property.

This wasn't punching the air on the dance-floor in the Number One club with like-minded inebriates. It was still months before the Manto story injected gay bar culture with sophistication and light. No, this was something quite different. It was identifying yourself during the daytime, at the workplace, on the verge of a first salaried position (£11,500 per annum, no benefits). Standing behind the counter, no longer would I have to be self-conscious of my vocal inflections, propensity for standing at a funny angle or stone-cold clichéd inability to throw a ball, in the unlikely event that should be necessary while positioned behind a cash register. This was just who I was: somebody who loved Kylie. Job done.

This was telling a bunch of strangers you weren't like them at 11am on a Monday in a corporate office suite and letting them make of it what they will, learning that no one cares, really, unless they've been brought up with a pernicious and specific reason to. Then starting the magnificent, mind-bending, evolutionary process of learning, yep, actually you were just like them – as good as you – with the added cultural baggage of a higher beats-per-minute count and a sincere affection for the work of a ditzy Antipodean pop princess in which you could countenance the tricky transition of turning boy to man.

Express Yourself

When Madonna arrived in Britain she was already layers-deep into the formation of her unassailable gay iconography. Her dance teacher at school in Michigan, Christopher Flynn, was referenced loud and often as her earliest inspiration, the first gay man embedded into her tale. The second, her gay brother, Christopher Ciccone, was her first backup dancer and choreographer, later her interior designer. He only needed to be her hairdresser and air-steward to complete the set, really. Madonna knew the latticework of the gay club culture of Downtown Manhattan before she'd recorded a note. She'd road tested white labels of her earliest records at Danceteria. She wore a Vivienne Westwood skirt with cartoon print by her friend Keith Haring, the peerless gay street artist, in early promotional shots and the brilliant video for 'Borderline'. She was steeped in Warholianism. Her eye for lending liberally from gay culture, whether it be tuning into the exact visual frequency of Robert Mapplethorpe or popularising entire countercultures like the Harlem vogue balls, was notable for its note-perfect execution and timing. In the popular (straight) consciousness, so much of gay culture was touched by Madonna for the very first time. She was its academic mistress, confessor, songbird, cheerleader, champion, thief and public mascot.

Madonna's tale chimed with several still-recurring key gay faultlines, not least the inner struggle she played so extrovertly, reconciling her own blatant, open sexuality against the restrictive tenets of an Italian-American Catholic education and upbringing. She had a doctorate in defying and disobeying repression. Madonna sat at the coalface of the cultural interchange with the AIDS pandemic, most publicly with the deaths of Haring and Flynn. She repaid her gay audience time and again for its loyalty, setting a pattern that is followed to this day in pop-marketing configurations, weaker imitations of her pioneering blueprint. If Madonna was the first pop artiste I understood to court explicitly the gay male audience, Kylie was the first to stumble upon that specific loyalty, admiration and dedication by accident. Trying to locate the beginnings of Kylie Minogue as gay icon, however, can demand just as much of a hopeful accident.

Lucky, Lucky, Lucky

On 5 April 1987 a letter was sent on headed Mushroom Records notepaper from label boss Michael Gudinski to his A&R staff. 'Gary and Amanda,' it began. 'I've just listened to this demo. It's a cover of the old "Locomotion". Sounds kinda cute. I think she's got something. Might be worth taking a punt on her. Get back to me.' A picture of Kylie Minogue was attached to the letter with the tart stylistic appendage: 'PS Can we do something about the hair?'

'To which my response now,' says Kylie Minogue, 'is *he* can talk.' Gudinski and Minogue are still close friends, fellow Australians who threw a stick in the spokes of the indigenous male rock machine, unsettling its course with a bubblegum-pop cover of a 20-odd-year-old Little Eva song. 'He's like family to me now. I had dinner with him ten days ago.' Over the meal, Gudinski told Kylie about her first coming to his attention as a possible pop singer. 'Interestingly, he said that he tested the idea of signing me with his kids.'

From the hair comment, one might assume Gudinski to be gay. '*Au contraire*,' she corrects. 'He said, "What would you think if Kylie released a record?"' His children drew a blank. 'They were like, "Nah, what, who?" It didn't make any sense to them. Then he said, "You know, Charlene from *Neighbours*?" and they went, "Oh, yeah!"'

Kylie Minogue grew up the eldest child of three in Melbourne suburbia. Her first brief interchange with fame came as a school kid, with a role in wartime soap opera *The Sullivans*. She didn't bother to get an agent; Dad could do the paperwork. Like all showbiz pre-teens, the existence of gay men in the industry was assumed, unlearned. 'It was just normal for me, starting work at 11. There wasn't anyone in particular at that age that I registered, but you can bet your bottom dollar that there was a gay man who would've been around at work. I wouldn't have known what that meant. I mean, that was around the time of the Village People, and I didn't even know what *that* meant.'

There were no forbidding ecclesiastical demons in the Minogue family closet. 'I'm not steeped in religion in any way,' Kylie says, 'so I didn't have that to deal with.' Her partner in familial crime when it came to showbiz ambitions was not her brother, but her younger sister, Danielle, who refashioned herself Dannii and signed on early as an all-singing, all-dancing child star on *Young Talent Time*, Australia's version of *The Mickey Mouse Club*. 'It was very shiny, there were a lot of sequins. So that was around my peripheral vision, too. It never felt like being gay was different or dangerous.'

Kylie's pop awakening was the soundtrack to the film *Grease*, featuring her first and only role model for what a female pop sensation could achieve outside of the macho Australian rock circuit on an international stage, Olivia Newton-John. 'I don't know how gay you can say *Grease* was. It was showy. Abba, obviously. I loved shiny pop.' Quite gay. Her first major crush was Adam Ant, who, though plastered in make-up, top to toe in Viv Westwood and responsible for the unlikely re-ignition of the career of the British Marilyn Monroe, Diana Dors, had turned out to be a local hero predominantly among curious straight schoolboys. 'I loved Gary Numan, who was not a manly man.' Another glorious British pop oddity with a penchant for heavy blush, occasionally in electric blue, who seemed to miss the strategic cult of gay admiration completely. 'But I thought that Adam Ant was the most beautiful man ever. I mean, he just was.'

The only poster she had on her wall as a teenager was of the artist with whom she spent most of the eighties obsessed: Prince. 'They all dressed to the nines and traded on their sexual ambiguity.' The first gig she attended was Culture Club's Melbourne date of the *Colour by Numbers* tour in 1984. 'I went with the ribbons in my hair. Can you imagine from the size of me now how little I was at 14? I got dressed up as Boy George.' Kylie is 5-foot, 1-inch tall.

It was only on her second TV engagement, signing up to play dungaree-clad tomboy mechanic Charlene Mitchell in *Neighbours*, that the word 'gay' made real-life sense to her. Charlene was introduced as part of a freshening-up of the show on Australia's Channel Ten after it had endured a sketchy start. The new cast members were not provided dressing rooms. Two weeks' worth of scripts would be delivered and memorised in a day. 'Learn it. Do it. Forget it. I think my brain still operates like that.' Much to Kylie's delight, the walk from the smoky green room where the cast would get into costume to the *Neighbours* set in the Channel Ten studios involved passing the gates which had earlier doubled as the scary entrance to Wentworth Prison, home of the camp, cult Australian TV classic *Prisoner: Cell Block H*, a favourite in the Minogue household. From the outset, *Prisoner* had a lesbian character in the form of Franky Doyle, a biker serving a life stretch for armed robbery. 'Franky was gay,' recalls Minogue, 'and it was considered totally scandalous. My God, these things do come back.' Franky met her untimely death in episode 20 in front of her girlfriend Doreen, shot by a police officer on a roadside in a tear-jerking farewell. A nation mourned for the first time a homicidal gay heroine. It was Franky who gave the fascistic prison boss Bennett her immortal nickname, but 'Vinegar Tits' had long since left the building by the time Kylie arrived on the same plot to shoot *Neighbours*.

Kylie's initial *Neighbours* contract was for a week. 'When I started there was definitely a makeup artist and possibly a hairdresser too that were both gay,' she recalls. 'You were in the chair every day and someone's doing this to you,' she imitates a blusher-brush application, 'so you notice. But I didn't have any gay friends. I guess that early *Neighbours* period, when Jason and I were dating, his father's an actor and I'm sure there were flamboyant characters around their place. So, yeah, I wish I could say, Oh, there was this defining point. But it was just osmosis in some way.'

Neighbours was a circumstantially anodyne affair, part of its broad-based international appeal. Because the sun permanently seemed to be shining on Australia, the cast were often semi-clad, another cause for its success on these shores. 'There was always the illusion of sunshine in *Neighbours*. Even if it wasn't always the reality. We didn't know what *EastEnders* and *Coronation Street* looked like. Now I know, of course, that if you're going to shoot in England and you're going to shoot it outside, then it is going to be grey most of the time. As we all started coming over here and got to understand some of the cultural differences, we got to appreciate more what the Brits saw in *Neighbours*.'

In a Britain barely recovered from the miners' strike, embroiled in the early horror narratives of AIDS, at the cusp of Clause 28 and preparing itself for the second wind of Thatcher's breakdown of society, school kids took their bronzed, toned, sun-bleached visions of nirvana where they could get them, in this case on the cul-de-sac of Ramsay Street. Yet the G-word was conspicuous only by its absence in the drama during its formidable first decade. 'I mean, there was obviously the wishful thinking of all you guys,' notes Minogue, 'for Scott and Mike in their speedos to get it on.'

Within six months of being on air, Kylie had made it to her first magazine cover, on the Australian car magazine *Royal Auto*. The headline read, 'The Female Mechanic: Fact or Fiction?' – a bluff indictment of the mid-market gender politics of the time. It featured Kylie as Charlene sitting on the bonnet of a pickup truck, wearing her dungarees and a baseball cap, holding a spanner triumphantly aloft, smiling. As with all the best soap-opera characters, we had become fine-tuned to the face of Kylie Minogue smiling and crying a lot in the late eighties. It, too, had by osmosis become part of our psyche. Within a year, she sang 'The Locomotion' on the pitch before an Australian football game.

Kylie's *Neighbours* years chimed especially with a smitten audience of straight male admirers. 'There's an age range of guys who were lusting after us *Neighbours* girls, whether it was Plain Jane Superbrain or me or whoever. Now when I meet them they'll go to a place I've learned to recognise, which is "remembering Charlene".' In a passage he wrote for a well-engineered coffee-table book on Kylie in 1999, the era-defining Scottish author Irvine Welsh surmised the rite of *Neighbours* passage for straight men succinctly. 'I can proudly claim,' he wrote, 'to be one of the original Kylie fans. With my friends Willy, Stuart and Sandy, I would waste away a large part of the eighties on the dole, smoking hashish and tuning into the Aussie soaps. If there had been digital television back then, you would never have heard of *Trainspotting*.'

The Locomotion demo found its way to Michael Gudinski and Mushroom Records. 'Michael was used to signing rock bands,' says Kylie. This was Australia's macho music culture. 'There was very little pop music on the radio. It was dominated by the Eagles and people who sounded like them. I had to ask him recently, "Honestly, did you sign me as a joke?"' She meant it sincerely. 'OK. I get it. It's business, whatever. And he said no. I don't think he would have foreseen the story, as it unfolded. But then I don't think anyone, least of all me, would have foreseen it back then.'

Like most of the commercial upswings in the early years of Kylie's professional life that took her to global recognition, her first interaction with the PWL Records Hit Factory of Stock Aitken Waterman was by chance. When Gudinski green-lit the recording of 'The Locomotion' for commercial release, Kylie was dispensed to Sing Sing Studios in Melbourne to record her vocal with a proper studio engineer. 'Mike Duffy, who was an engineer from PWL, was in Australia doing some production and remixing work for Mushroom, so they gave it to him. That led to meeting Pete Waterman. So if Mike Duffy hadn't been in Australia at the time, Stock Aitken Waterman may never have happened. It probably would never have happened, anyway, considering that when I arrived, they didn't even know I was there.'

Minogue's first trip to London to record at the Hit Factory was hampered from touchdown at Heathrow. Left hanging with her newly acquired manager Terry Blamey – brought in from the local rock-band bookers circuit, only because her dad couldn't work out the wording of Mushroom Records' one-single label contract – she arrived on a Sunday for a week's work. She was sent away to see the sights of London while the three producers finished work on mounting deadlines for other projects. The Hit Factory was then wallpapered with gold discs. By Friday, she'd done the lot: 'Double-decker bus tour, Harrods, Madame Tussauds. You name it, we were there. Terry and I were kept waiting for days and days.' Blamey put in a stiff call to Pete Waterman's CEO, David Howells, on the morning of their final day in the UK, and Howells dispensed a cab to collect Minogue and Blamey from their hotel to wait in reception until studio time was free.

Kylie had little prior knowledge of the work of Pete Waterman. 'I'd have known Bananarama,' she says. 'But Rick Astley was around the same time as me so that hadn't happened yet. I don't think the others had really happened in Australia.' It was customary practice for Waterman to take stars like Pete Burns, Hazell Dean and Sinitta to the local, the Gladstone, then a gay pub positioned round the back of his studios on Borough High Street, SE1, for a celebratory pint after finishing a particularly pleasing song he felt might be a hit. Because Kylie and later Jason Donovan were so famous, he had to curtail this courtesy for his newest stars for fear of causing an unnecessary incident in the pub. Kylie says she had no knowledge of her straight producer working in the evocatively gay musical tradition of Hi-NRG. 'No, not at the start. I was only 19, remember.' On her second visit, she brought along her mum as chaperone.

When Howells told Matt Aitken that he had an Australian soap star waiting in reception and that the trio had to come up with a song before she left the next day, he turned to his boss and said, 'She should be so lucky.' Within the hour, Kylie Minogue was in the vocal booth, singing a song written line by line in the few hours she had left in the country. She took a plane back to Australia on the Saturday and went straight on set at *Neighbours*, having neither sung nor heard her debut single in completion. 'That was all I did in the early days – work, work, work.' Her friends back home would ask how the first single proper from Kylie Minogue sounded and she would answer, 'I have no idea.'

The Great, Dark Man

In 1968, Quentin Crisp's *The Naked Civil Servant* was published, a book about the crisis and quandary of life as a gay man that would later be televised with a moving performance from John Hurt as the captivating, curious ideologue and man of letters. Homosexuality had only been legalised for a year and here was its agent provocateur: 'I, an effeminate homosexual.' In the book, the brilliant polemicist – Gay Britain's Ghost of Everything Past – posits the idea of the great dark man, the imaginary individual that all gay men are certain to have their hearts broken by. The great dark man is the wonderful zenith of masculinity, the one whom we all desire. Yet the circularity in Crisp's version of events, the great plight and tragedy of homosexuality and the chink in its armour, is that if you love the great dark man and he loves you back, then he is no longer the apogee of that thing you once desired. In the act of loving another man, he has become less great, less dark, less man.

'There is no great dark man,' he wrote. 'Even under an exterior as rugged as a mountain range, there lurks the same wounded, wincing psyche that cripples the rest of us. Where we are led to think we will find strength, we will discover force; where we hope for ruthlessness, we shall unearth spite; and when we think we are clinging desperately to a rock, it is falling upon us. Even with a man whose neck is thicker than his head, if we are not careful, we shall be involved in an argument about who most loves whom. The trouble is that, if you find that by mistake you have bitten into a soft centre, you can't very well put it back in the box.' The glass in Crisp's house was rarely anything other than half-empty, however wittily and intelligently he speculated refill.

The German group Gina X Performance was the first to knowingly fashion a pop song from Quentin Crisp's theory, on the brilliantly subversive new wave classic 'No GDM', an unsurprising smash across gay European dance-floors in 1981. The male idyll is a concept woven through Hi-NRG like Classical mythology. Songs on the great dark man theme piled up, ready for airing on the dance-floor at Heaven and its equivalents elsewhere: 'He's a Saint, He's a Sinner', 'Searchin' (I Gotta Find a Man)', 'So Many Men, So Little Time', 'The Boys Come to Town', 'Primitive Desire'. By some coincidence and a little design, the lyrics Stock Aitken Waterman fashioned for Kylie Minogue's first recorded output in Britain read close enough to Quentin Crisp's thesis to warrant note. The verses are dream sequences, in which our heroine imagines being loved by the fantasy man she wills to life. So unimaginable is love to the young singer, she can only fantasise about the idea of it. The nursery rhyme meter is offset by a feeling that is both hopeless and hopeful.

With 'I Should Be So Lucky' Kylie Minogue achieved an insane new level of fame. Yet the swift empathy levels she received from some gay male listeners was equalled in antipathy from some corners of the straight world. 'Oh God, there was all sorts,' she says. 'I think when the music started – and a lot of it I understand now, with emotion aside and the benefit of hindsight – it was because I had not earned my stripes. Especially in Australia, where it had been a rock-band culture. You were INXS or you were Midnight Oil or Men at Work. You wrote your own music and played pub gigs and travelled around, and that's what they knew.' Like reality TV contestants now from *The X Factor* or *The Voice* bypassing the traditional route to the top without touring little venues and establishing a name for yourself, soap stardom was seen as a shortcut to hotwiring musical fame that broke one too many trad-rock rules.

'I must have upset a lot of people within the industry,' she says. 'Do you remember the time that a radio station in England put up billboards saying, "We've done something to improve Kylie's records. We've banned them."' The Virgin Radio campaign stung hard but, after intervention from her lawyers, it was quickly taken down so that she no longer had to see her name as a byword for trash, staring at her from lay-bys. 'I just thought, Wow, that is really ironic. You're still using my name to advertise your radio station, but I am very hurt. There were lots of things like that at the start.'

Negativity followed Kylie shadow-like throughout her early career. 'You had all the scandal stories and people either being for you or against you, which can be quite frustrating because how do you respond? I'm loath to ever get into it. Who was it who came up with the expression "never complain, never explain"?' She took the message and ran with it. 'Back then you just had to kind of swallow it, really. There wasn't much you could do.' Yet from the start of her musical career, Kylie Minogue was delivering a sentiment that found the ear of a gay audience. She arrived in London with a head filled with the possibility of professional and personal fulfilment. She was 19, not yet herself. Her road to discovery was uncertain, each step followed incrementally by a judgemental viewing public.

'We all wish that we could find that person and have the dream. "I Should Be So Lucky" worked for everybody.' She smiles. 'I'm sorry to inform you, I'm not a gay man.'

The Culture Club

One of the first customers to ask Peter Dalton for a job at Manto didn't waste any time in doing so. 'We had our opening night party on the Thursday,' he says, 'and William came in on the Friday after school, still in his Manchester Grammar School uniform.' William Baker was 16 years old, bolshy, cheeky, cute, clever. Dalton immediately took to him, though he recognised he was clearly underage, for both bar work and gayness, which was then still stuck at a rigidly unequal 21-year-old legal age of consent. 'He started working in the kitchen, helping out with the prep and the washing up, and then he moved onto the floor as a pot collector. He eventually made it to the bar.'

As a child growing up in Wilmslow, in the heart of Cheshire's footballer belt just south of Manchester, William Baker ticked all of the boxes growing up gay and suburban presented to a child of the eighties. Like Kylie Minogue on the other side of the world, his first great pop love was Culture Club. He remembers exactly when he first saw them: 'It was the night George was singing "Do You Really Want to Hurt Me?" on *Top of the Pops*, 1982. I would have been eight or nine. I just felt really attracted to it and didn't know why.' At that age, a feeling for a pop song is at its most intuitive and unconsidered. 'I was never that interested in music on its own anyway. It always involved the look, the personality. There was Boy George, then Madonna later on. I came back from Cub Scouts in Wilmslow in a hall near the rugby club – horrific, awful, hell – and Culture Club was on *Top of the Pops*. I actually stopped going to Cubs because it was on the same night as *Fame*.

He was not afraid of what he saw. 'No. I've never really had any fear about sexuality or anything to do with that. You hear really sad stories of people who are terrified of their own gayness and I've never really understood that.' Nonetheless, at an age not yet in double figures, he knew better than to keep his love of this alien new creature at least temporarily quiet.

It was the Culture Club song 'Victims' that really hooked the young Baker: 'I guess it was just the poetic nature of the lyrics and how sweeping and grand it was. There's a real romance and loss to it. It's something that really stayed with me. I still associate love with something that is painful, which he articulates so well on that song.' He picked up the book *Boy George: In His Own Words* and learned of George's own great dark man heartbreak, his love affair with Culture Club's straight drummer Jon Moss. The words 'loving would be easy if your colours were like my dreams' in the ritualistically derided 'Karma Chameleon' took on a stinging new tone. 'It was a really big part of my attraction to George's music, the heartbroken sadness to him. I think it was a Chrissy Iley interview I read with him where she said that no one can do emotion quite like him. It was always the things he would say about love or sexuality that were really brilliant, almost quite traditional in a way, a very romantic idea of love. Because, as we came to know later, of his affair with Jon Moss.'

George was the great suburban eye-opener to the great dark man story. 'I really loved him towards the tail end of his massiveness,' says Baker. 'He was on the front pages of the tabloids every day. He was a massive star. I really started liking him when it all started falling apart, when the press really turned on him, when he just became really over the top and indulgent.' William may be the only George devotee who can mount a persuasive defence of 'The War Song'. 'Oh, I loved him between *Colour by Numbers* and *Waking Up with the House on Fire*, when he went really quite drag.'

George's notoriety from his first *Top of the Pops* appearance had been cemented with the 'is it a boy or a girl?' irritation of grumbling eighties dads, when George confronted fears of male effeminacy head-on, with sensational bravery and a side of unapologetic metropolitan fashion savvy. Later, when the story of his affair with Jon Moss broke, the terror that sits at the heart of some homophobia – that we are only here to steal your brothers, husbands, cousins, sons – slid into view. Through it all, through the sheer force of his personal charisma, George was loved. For a brief period of their international omnipotence, Culture Club looked like a magnificent avant-garde re-appropriation of the Beatles in which their gay manager Brian Epstein was the frontman.

For young gay viewers, the space in between binary genders that George seemed to visually occupy – a place beyond drag, high fashion and clubwear, one bountifully borrowed by Madonna in her first fame assault – was a useful identity loophole to start negotiating our own relationship with masculinity. 'Towards the end of Culture Club it was completely plastered on,' says Baker. 'I remember on *The Tube*, they did a big special on Culture Club in Japan. They were having a whole spat backstage about him wanting to wear a wedding dress on stage. He was like, "I want to wear a fucking wedding dress, I want to wear one." I just really loved him for it.'

As the wheels started to come off his career, George provided a shortcut to a second taboo starting to tickle a further scare valve of the British suburbs: narcotic dependency. A heroin habit made him the very definition of a fallen idol. He tied neatly into the end of the 'Just Say No' campaign that had kicked off so many schoolyard drug conversations, provoking as much young curiosity as it did fear. 'When the whole heroin stuff came out, that's when I really, really liked him,' says William. 'The look became more real, somehow. When he was on heroin he was more like a boy; he wasn't so much the painted dame. He was a guy, who was sexual. He was a boy in make-up.'

Initially, Baker had no one to talk to about his burgeoning fascination with Boy George. Baker was the only out gay boy at Manchester Grammar School during his eighties education. It was a position he enjoyed so much that when another lad tried to come out of the closet in sixth form, he essentially sent him straight back into it, for fear of his notoriety being usurped. 'Everyone in Manchester was part of a tribe back then. All my friends were into the Smiths. They were all in their cardigans with gladioli and floppy hair. Then I had friends who were Goths and into the Sisters of Mercy. Manchester is a city of tribes. The Smiths fans later became Stone Roses fans. Even then, they all had quite a distinct look and a distinct message. It was visual, but it was also lyrical. At that time it had gone really tits up for George.'

At school and at home, William belonged to a tribe of one. 'Manchester is, for a start, a city of Mancunians. There's a hardness to it. Everyone drinks and everyone drinks a lot. Friday night and Saturday night, everyone just gets pissed. There's no stop button. You get pissed and end up throwing up outside. It's a double-edged thing. There's this great personal and tribal freedom where you could do anything and look like anything, but there was always this undercurrent that you'd get beaten up by some skinhead outside a club for it.'

William developed his own look based on George's. He wore flat caps with button badges pinned all over, wide ties, a fedora, something old, something new. He discovered the work of Vivienne Westwood and Jean Paul Gaultier. 'I never felt that I was a victim of homophobia when I got abuse for it. There is such a weird feeling of everyone loving each other in Manchester, too, which I think really got going when everyone started taking ecstasy. So it never felt like a personal diss. It was just people being pissed. Everyone there is really gobby.'

William first saw George perform at a tiny club in Stoke-on-Trent. 'There were about 20 people in the audience. It was 1987 or 88. I jumped onstage. He remembered when I met him a few years later and he still brings it up. I used to get my mum and stepdad to drive me around to all these dodgy gay clubs. He played at the Number One once and this dodgy place in Leeds. Clubs in shopping centres.' The further into his teenage years he went, the more devoted to George he became. He'd travel down to London and camp outside the star's Hampstead house, making new friends of the fans alongside him sleeping by the driveway gate. 'Then I had people I could talk to about it. The sexuality thing was just taken for granted. If you were a fan then you were just gay, I guess.'

He made his first gay friends at 14, sitting in the café at the Oldham Street alternative shopping arcade Affleck's Palace. 'I had loads of badges and a cap and was plastered in make-up, and I met two boys who were a similar age in the café, by the poster bit. One was called Dominic and he was a skinny Goth. The other was called Jonathan; he was more of a denim queen. My mum went mental at that point.' For eighties mothers assuming that living a fulfilled life as a gay man might equal early death, this was a forgivable prerogative. 'I used to have to put my make-up on on the Wilmslow train to Manchester. I was really bad at it. Really bad. I wore it to school. No one gave a shit.'

William would meet up with Dominic and Jonathan on Saturday afternoons. 'One day they said, "Have you been down the centre?" and I hadn't a clue what they were talking about.' The Manchester gay centre was positioned on Bloom Street, adjacent to Canal Street, a short walk from the New York New York pub. 'We went down and I was completely shocked.' The Centre was far removed from the glitzy triumph and tragedy of his gay pop hero. It was all about workshops, talking through your feelings, grabbing the odd fumbling episode of human contact, reading leaflets and drinking from 10p coffee machines of the sort you'd find in municipal swimming baths. 'It was very social worker and pretty much all about abuse, really, halfway between a battered wives centre and, in true gay tradition, a knocking shop. Everyone in there had slept with each other. There was an actual pink triangle on the door. It was literally underground. It was a dump. Youth group was on Saturday evenings between five and seven and everyone would go to the New York afterwards. Everybody fancied this lad called Andy. It was funny.'

Beneath the tatty exterior, the centre provided a vital function. 'The AIDS adverts on TV just unified all gay kids. I remember asking a lot of questions at that time, about why people were getting sick. It was hard and really scary. There was a definite fear about physical contact, even just about touching someone's dick. That fear of AIDS was kind of what that centre was there to deal with, really. There were phone lines you could call. I remember calling one once, convinced I'd got AIDS after touching someone's hand or something. I remember thinking that you could get AIDS just by being gay, and when I started wanking, loads, thinking that I would be HIV-positive. I was that distressed, even enough to phone an anonymous line and ask them what to do.'

The 'AIDS: Don't Die of Ignorance' leaflets were posted through the door of every home in the country at health secretary Norman Fowler's insistence, despite Margaret Thatcher's warning to him that he would become known as the minister for AIDS. 'It suburbanised the issue of being gay,' says Baker, 'and for most families these were the first conversations they'd ever had about it. Of course there was Steven Carrington from *Dynasty*, but that was a whole other story. That affected me a lot. I remember being quite repulsed by Colin and Barry on *EastEnders*. But Steven Carrington, I totally got. And his mother being Joan Collins. Also, it was so dramatic. I was obsessed, totally. Other people at school weren't obsessed with Alexis Colby. They liked *Dallas*. They wanted to grow up to be J.R. Ewing.'

His love for Joan Collins's *Dynasty* character was shared among fledgling gay youth at the time. 'Like with Boy George, I could always identify with the wronged woman. I never had gender confusion but there was no one else that was so present. There was a huge thing about Rock Hudson kissing Linda Evans in *Dynasty*, so suddenly AIDS was everywhere.' Hudson, the archetypal Hollywood pinup during the 1950s and 60s, had lived his professional life in the closet. His death from AIDS-related illnesses was a galvanising moment for America. 'People had to explain what that was, what it was about, how you got it. Anal sex was on the *Six O'Clock News*. That was the start of this move towards equality. It unified a whole section of society, in suburbia. It started reaching to the outskirts.'

Some high culture found itself into the youth group at the Manchester gay centre: '*A Boy's Own Story* by Edmund White. That was entry level. You had to read that, then move on to *The Beautiful Room Is Empty*.' Baker became obsessed with the art of Robert Mapplethorpe and Andres Serrano. Prior to his death, Mapplethorpe had been embroiled in a scandal surrounding his exhibition of explicit homoerotic photographs in the US. The story was a useful cross-continental forebear for what would arrive in Britain with Clause 28. 'I remember going into Central Library to find out about them both, pretending to be over 18, looking at Mapplethorpe's work and being completely gobsmacked by it. The Mapplethorpe vision I could understand straight away. It was basically Madonna's *Vogue* video with cocks.'

When Manto opened, William Baker was keen to move up a social grade. 'My experiences of gay men up to that point had been these slaggy kids down the gay centre and older men into drag queens in the New York.' He remembers meeting Peter Dalton and asking him for a job the day after opening. 'Peter and [then boyfriend]

Steve were in their twenties, they were cool. The crowd that Manto attracted was very youthful but it was sophisticated. There were straight people there, too. There was an atmosphere of normality that I think to people of our generation felt genuinely new. It wasn't something we knew existed.' He says his inquiry about the job was delivered in the best way he knew how. 'I flirted with Peter.'

As a Manto pot collector, William Baker touched local stardom for the first time. Besides Boy George, his great pop fascination was Madonna. His imaginative habit of following his idols' unique dress sense began to develop a secondary, part-time drag wing. 'It's such a cliché now, but I was obsessed with Madonna and would regularly dress up as her. I just used to identify with these incredibly strong women. What I loved particularly about her was all the art references and the intelligence behind the pop star. She still is, but definitely was a pop artist in the Warholian sense of the word.' The year before walking into Manto, Baker had enjoyed his second Damascene pop moment after Boy George on *Top of the Pops*: 'I went to Blond Ambition with some of the girls from Manchester Girls School. There were four of us. It was a religious experience for me. It changed my life, totally. I've never seen such an incredible synthesis of fashion, art, pop and personality, before or since.'

Madonna's Blond Ambition tour was the first time British gays and girls got to claim ownership of the thrilling communion and euphoria of a stadium show, delivered at optimum star power by a generational hero. Every aspect of Madonna's theatrical enterprise, from its Jean Paul Gaultier costumes, tales of onstage masturbation and sacrilege, legion of physically dextrous dancers, Herb Ritts's programme photography, and the subsequent documentary film *In Bed with Madonna*, all set to her immaculate collection of platinum-plated hits, set a new standard for pop performance. Madonna wrestled the stadium show from old blokes with guitars and gave it to young female performers, a tradition that lived on through Kylie

Minogue before filtering through to the Spice Girls, Britney Spears, Rihanna, Miley Cyrus, Taylor Swift and its most prominent and successful current exponent Beyoncé. Somewhere between the Folies Bergère, Pier Paolo Pasolini, Mapplethorpe, *The Last Temptation of Christ*, Jean Genet, Hot Gossip and Studio 54, Blond Ambition was our Live Aid, with taste. Its function was just as charitable to the voiceless masses taken into its warm, ferocious embrace.

'It was an emotional journey,' says Baker. 'It was a piece of art. It was incredible to watch the religious thing being so beautifully subverted.' This wasn't the crystalline evangelism of Bono singing 'I Still Haven't Found What I'm Looking For' in a battered Stetson to lager-soaked dolts. It was a modern icon, named after the mother of Jesus, converging religious ecstasy with the female orgasm and the power of the pop song. 'The male body was so exposed in it, beautifully. It was really, really gay. It came out of a place of genuine struggle. If you look at the difference between girls then and now, she had insurmountable levels of influence. A door swung open and sex was suddenly a subject that could be talked about.' Young female Madonna fans and gay male fans came together as one at her altar.

William Baker was there and made the most of the moment. 'My friend Atol entered me into a *Manchester Evening News* search for a Madonna lookalike competition. The prize was getting to be on some stand at a music conference in Manchester.' In a moment of minor local scandal, the trailblazing 16-year-old schoolboy in drag won. It, too, made the six o'clock news in the Granada region. 'I won it, but they couldn't have me on the stand because I was a bloke.' His winning costume was a perfect replica of Madonna's Gaultier conical bra and corset getup, complete with ice-white topknot ponytail, red lips and black fishnets. It was made by Jackie Haynes, a fashion student William would visit during his lunchtimes at the Toast Rack polytechnic building, tucked behind the playing fields at Manchester Grammar School, where she was studying for a fashion degree. 'I always had school friends and then older friends that went to the Number One who were at fashion college in Salford. I became aware of this new thing called a "stylist". There was Ray Petri and there was Judy Blame. I knew about Judy and Leigh Bowery because of Boy George, and I read all the magazines, *Blitz*, *The Face* and *i-D*. One of Jackie's friends, called Trish, had a cousin that worked at *i-D* and she fixed it up for me to go and meet up with Judy. I was still at school.'

Kylie, the Metamorphosis

Judy Blame is the great alchemist of modern British fashion. His great skill is to make something out of nothing, to see beauty in the trash others might step over. He is a stylist, jewellery- and image-maker. For Judy, the distinction between the gutter and the stars in aesthetics is invisible. For young fashion scholars, both in and out of academies, his name and that of his old, late friend Ray Petri's are the first they hear associated with the word 'stylist'. His creative relationship with Petri began not long after he'd finished promoting the club night Cha-Cha's at Heaven in the early eighties, where he'd first worked on the cloakroom. Ray would ask for jewellery pieces to be made for his pivotal work with Buffalo, the luminescent new London taste barometer and a line in the sand still drawn for British fashion.

Judy's most familiar muse, Neneh Cherry, worked with Ray Petri during the recording of her debut album, *Raw Like Sushi*, but when it came to scheduling her first single, the song that would take Buffalo from the underground to the world via MTV, Petri was too ill to see the project through and Blame stepped in. Ray Petri died in 1989, at the height of the British AIDS pandemic. 'We were losing quite a lot of people at the time,' Judy says. 'It was difficult. It was quite confusing, that whole era.' In his last months, Ray was suffering with Kaposi's sarcoma, the rare and easily identifiable skin cancer most commonly associated with AIDS. 'I shall never forget as long as I live,' he says, 'Jasper Conran wanted Ray to go to his fashion show and Ray had a stick and a few Kaposi on his face.' These were vicious times, even in a fashion industry peopled to the hilt with gay men and their supposed friends and allies. 'We took a car up there, went in, took our seats and people just moved away. This is front-row fashion people we're talking about. All of a sudden there was a gap either side. I shall never forget Sally Brampton, the *Elle* editor, got up off her chair and walked over and parked her arse next to us. Then Debbie Mason, the stylist, walked over and parked her arse on the other side of us. Gradually, people that knew us were coming over and filling up the seats.'

Boy George's twisted pearly king years were Judy's inventive handiwork. 'Before I was doing work with Boy George, Ray was doing a lot of George's styling. He'd go, "I've got to shoot George, would you make me this and that."' The two connected further through the indomitable figure of Leigh Bowery, the resident alien force of London nightclub and fashion nature, who also died later of AIDS and is often attributed as the subject matter of Boy George's wonderful ballad to a gay man's death, 'Il Adore'. It was Judy's work with Boy George that William Baker was most interested in. He says of meeting Judy: 'He was drunk. The whole time. He was utterly amazing. He was like a legend, such a force of nature and personality.' His was a world Baker was primed in, self-schooled and ready to step into.

By 1990, now onto the promotion of her third Stock Aitken Waterman record, *Rhythm of Love*, Kylie Minogue was prepped to make the same leap. She approached Judy Blame about helping her out with imagery. 'I must have had a reputation of being good with the women,' says Judy. 'I met up with Kylie at her hotel and we got on well. I thought she was quite a laugh.' Judy green-lit Kylie's ascendency to style-magazine cover-star status. He shot her for *i-D* wearing a latex corset, a quantum leap from her stretch on *Royal Auto* in dungarees. 'I kept it quite loose to start with. I said, "What's a couple of things you'd like to do?" and she said she'd always wanted to be on the cover of *i-D*. I went, "OK, let's give it a go then, shall we?" I went in to see *i-D*'s founder Terry Jones and said I've been asked to do Kylie Minogue. It was as easy as saying, "What do you think about doing her on the cover?" He was into it, and that was that. Sometimes it works best when you don't overthink these things.'

Blame was instantly impressed by Kylie's fashion instinct. The early naïvety of her presentation only heightened the astonishing visual progress she was making. Her chrysalis to butterfly transition was played out in full public view. 'That's what I liked about her,' he says. 'She was really knowledgeable. She wasn't a bimbo. We used to go out to dinner together. This girl knew what she wanted and knew what her capabilities are. She was great – good fun and knew how to wear Alaïa.'

Kylie's musical success was such that she'd decamped to London and was living in Chelsea. Her adventures around the capital were succinct and intuitive. She shopped at Kensington Market, Hyper Hyper and the Garage on the King's Road and took full advantage of the city's burgeoning post-acid house club scene, a street glamour she wore sensationally well. Her great style hero was Lady Miss Kier of ultimate New York club kids' outfit Deee-Lite. 'You could see a shift,' says Kylie. 'By that time I had my little shorts and crop top that I would've got at the Garage. I was meeting English fashion people and liked them, a lot. It was later that I'd meet Azzedine Alaïa and Gaultier. I played Deee-Lite non-stop, watched the videos all the time and then worked with Towa Tei much later.'

Judy Blame introduced her to the pivotal fashion photographer Juergen Teller to shoot the sleeve of her fourth and farewell Stock Aitken Waterman record, *Let's Get to It*. Blame also introduced her to the exceptional hair and make-up team Sam McKnight and Mary

Greenwell. 'She couldn't believe that Mary and Sam had to go and do Lady Di in the morning and then come on to our shoot. Kylie was gobsmacked. "Jude, Sam's just come from Princess Diana?" So sweet.'

William Baker wasn't a particular fan of early Kylie: 'I kind of liked Jason more. I really fancied him. He's very me.' Jason Donovan bore enough of a similarity to Stephen Carrington in the first flushes of his success, the good-as-gold blond pinup. 'That, too. I hated "I Should Be So Lucky" and "The Locomotion", but "Better the Devil You Know" changed everything. You already had that sense of intimacy with her because of *Neighbours*. For men our age, we'd grown up with her being on TV twice a day, every day. We learned about relationships through those characters. They became part of your life, like *Keeping Up with the Kardashians* now. You know about these people even if you're not interested in them. Reality TV now was soap opera back then. When she started playing with fashion and started attracting the attention of the fashion press, I sat up and listened.'

The first song Kylie herself was consulted on by Pete Waterman was 'Better the Devil You Know', the tune and video which slipped her out of the interchangeable Hit Factory model, beginning an iconoclastic, sensational run of disco hits which, song by song, subliminally alerted grown-up audiences to take a second look at the singing soap star. 'Pete asked me, "All right, kid, what song do you like?"' she recalls. 'And I said D-Mob and Cathy Dennis's "Come On and Get My Love".' Dennis would later co-write the definitive Kylie hit, 'Can't Get You Out of My Head'. 'You know that the D-Mob song had the woah-woah-woah bit at the start? "Better the Devil" is woah-woah-woah-woah-woah, so they put two extra notes in. I was happy.'

Prior to her first London fashion awakenings, William had thought of Kylie as little more than the prettier, more successful Hazell Dean: 'At that point, I think she was. A big thing, post-AIDS, post miner's strike, was that England was really in tatters, and Australia, which was being beamed into the family home every day, represented a kind of suburban paradise. Interestingly, I think that's why people in London weren't that impressed by Kylie, because a lot of her appeal was suburban.'

Judy Blame's time styling Kylie was pivotal but short. It rubber-stamped an astonishing turnaround in her from populist puppet towards genuine iconography. Suddenly, magically, nightclubs were full of women who dressed exactly like the new Kylie Minogue. 'I put her in things like John Galliano,' says Judy. 'It was just a way of playing, really. I didn't last that long with her. Then one of my assistants, David Thomas, took over and did the Ellen von Unwerth/Azzedine Alaïa thing with her.'

Overnight, Kylie changed from club kid to Bardot-esque sex bomb. Her ascendancy was complete. It felt close enough to a young gay man's trajectory of finding his feet, the confidence to be his true self, to carry that growing subset of her audience adoringly along with her. Her catalogue shifted from songs of innocence to experience. She sauntered away from the Hit Factory conveyor belt and signed a worldwide deal with the non-more-vogue British dance imprint Deconstruction Records. Fashion flocked to her. Fans simpered. Straight men remembered just what it was they loved about Kylie in her earliest incarnation, the promise of what she would become. Women copied every inch of her styling. She became our Impossible Princess elect. 'And then, of course,' says Judy Blame, 'William met her.'

Kylie Minogue and the Great Dark Man

The first time Kylie Minogue really noticed her gay audience was when walking down Oxford Street in the heart of Sydney's gay district one evening with her straight manager, Terry Blamey. 'Somebody told me there was a Kylie night at the Albury,' she says.

'The Albury was *the* gay pub on Oxford Street. I really wanted to go but Terry said, "No, you're not, that's going to be way too difficult."' He was fully aware of the riot that would have ensued. Kylie had not long since filmed an Australian commercial for Coca-Cola. 'Apparently, someone had put Coke cans in their hair. There really would've been limited references to dress as me back then. I think I'd started to go into SexKylie mode, not that it was called that at the time. So that was the first penny-drop moment, where I thought, What? My God, impersonators? I didn't know anyone was doing that.' She was in a good place. 'I was dating Michael by then. You know?'

She had a similar Albury experience four years later and was this time ready to enjoy the occasion. 'It was maybe 1994 or so, when I was in Melbourne. I'd been to see the Lemonheads – totally not me – and someone said afterwards, "Oh, there's a Kylie night on at this place. Shall we go?" And I said, "OK, let's do it." There are pictures of me from that night and it was pretty weird to feel the least Kylie-like person in a club. I was wearing my hair wild, no make-up on, a little suede and crochet top on, not "What Do I Have to Do" get-up, and I think that was the first time I'd been up close to real drag queens doing me. I felt like an imposter: What the hell am I doing here?' On occasions like this since, she has learned to adapt. Kylie is happy to hand over the Kyliest veneer of herself to the drag community. 'Of course. Go for it.'

In 1989, Kylie's fashion awakenings coincided with the start of her relationship with Australian rock goliath Michael Hutchence, singer in INXS, a visual union not only sizzling enough to be made in paparazzi heaven, but one that symbolically linked their home country's old rock tradition with the figurehead of a new pop sensibility. Conclusions about the physical leap Minogue had made from Jason Donavan to Hutchence were not difficult to draw for her gay and female audience.

On meeting Michael Hutchence, gay men's interest in the Kylie story skyrocketed. It was the start of a new decade – the nineties! – and hope loomed large. After five years of blind panic spent renegotiating sex habits, libidos were running explosively high. And there on stage was a new, improved, significantly less innocent Kylie Minogue, singing songs that had started prodding the pop consciousness sideways. Kylie tells a great story of one particular detail of Hutchence's courtship. One night in Hong Kong, when they had arranged to meet on a stopover, crossing paths from London to Sydney, both travelling the opposite direction across the globe, he invited her to dinner. After eating, they retired to his apartment, where he plucked a book from his library shelf and read aloud to her a passage from a Milan Kundera novel. Their relationship at this stage was strictly under wraps, though hot rumours had started circulating. 'The question it asks,' she says of the passage, 'is, Would you rather sleep with someone – spend the night with someone – and you couldn't tell anyone. Or not spend the night with them and have everyone think you did.' The line of interrogation, read aloud by the rock star of his moment to the pop princess of hers, could not have been any hotter in the retelling. 'You've really got to stop and think, haven't you?' Have you really? One of the great unspoken truths of Kylie Minogue's gay iconography is the simple fact that she clearly just really, really likes men. 'Yes,' she nods, laughing, as if one of her great life mysteries has at last been solved. 'Yes.' The physical difference from Jason to Michael marked the shift from boys to men. 'Yeah, and even since. Mostly, and there's a couple we'll just skip over for sure, but more often than not they are *men*.'

Kylie is not abreast of the great dark man theory, but likes it when she hears it. 'Even Michael himself,' she says, 'I cannot imagine gay men not loving. He was gorgeous. He was Byronesque. He was everything you could wish for.' He was the great dark man. 'His was a universal sexuality. You either have it or you don't.' Within a universal sexuality there is something both amenable and totemic. You have to imagine getting a little drunk with it before the fireworks. 'Just add alcohol.' She laughs. 'He was so sexual. He oozed it. Even if you see him interviewed you can spot it. I don't know any of his stories with any dalliances but it wouldn't surprise me if he was the kind of guy who had had a moment with another man.' Perhaps he espoused every riveting detail of the great dark man theory. There is something, after all, in the possession of a universal sexuality that implies curiosity and the confidence to carry it through. 'Yes, for everything in life. That was the first man that I was like that with.'

When a favourite pop star becomes transfixed with an undeniable pinup, there is the sense of a portion of her audience willing her on, shouting, 'Go on, girl!' from the cheap seats. Madonna arrived in the pop landscape fully formed, but we travelled Kylie's journey together. Madonna didn't need to grow into her sexuality. Kylie couldn't have delivered 'Like a Virgin' on her second album. It would have felt icky, awkward. With Madonna, a lyric like that is allowed to drip slowly from the melody. With early Kylie, it would've clung to it. After Michael, those stabilisers were off. 'Kylie didn't come with the political agenda of Madonna,' notes William Baker. 'It can be weighty baggage. There was no agenda.' Just real-time movement toward happiness, fulfilment and a complete sexual identity. 'I think there was a sort of natural hunger for her to be in some way corrupted. It appealed to that corruption that you want for yourself. I think she was quite unique. Madonna frightened a lot of people sexually. Madonna can make sexuality look a bit like being put through your paces, a bit of an endurance test.'

Kylie is aware of the limitations of selling sex and the parameters around this transaction with her audience. 'It's a two-dimensional offer. More often than not I've got it where I'm happy with it. Sometimes I've gone further than I should have. This connects to that universal sexuality, about being accessible or available to everyone, but actually you're not at all.'

Once she had a gay audience, Kylie Minogue began to metamorphose into a broader, rangier artist. During her time at Deconstruction you could even call her experimental. She was courted artistically and socially by the defining musicians of their era: Primal Scream, Saint Etienne, Pet Shop Boys, Boy's Own producers Terry Farley and Pete Heller, and Manic Street Preachers. Encouraged by her fellow countryman and fan Nick Cave, she reconfigured 'I Should Be So Lucky' as a tone poem and read it deadpan at the Royal Albert Hall. Later, she recorded a homicidal duet with him, 'Where the Wild Roses Grow', posing as his Ophelia in the lake on the cover art and in the video, and gifting Cave his first chart hit.

The nineties were Kylie's difficult gay twenties, a time of personal exposition and revelation. 'It's not just going out and partying and pretending everything's all right. It's more introspective and thoughtful. There's something very close about a song like "Confide in Me". It's not exuberant.' Implicitly, an exchange was occurring, a mutual nod, an understanding that you may have been seen as one thing on the outside, but underneath you are something quite different, then daring to vent that angle. Madonna bowed to the temple of gayness. She celebrated it, elevated it, cut it free of shackles and oppression and rejoiced in its raw, decadent power. On another corner of the planet, Kylie Minogue was sort of living it. After her relationship with walking sex machine Michael Hutchence ended, Kylie developed a new close personal male, a fresh emblem of the shifting social sands of the times.

The Gay Husband

William Baker met Kylie while he was a theology undergraduate at University College London with a Saturday job at the Vivienne

Westwood store on Davies Street, W1. 'Without being spiritual about it, I think it must have always been something that drew us together,' he says. Not long after moving to London, he saw her at a party Judy Blame had taken him to, 'in some weird Notting Hill cinema. She was all Galliano'd up. The Kamen brothers were there, Curiosity Killed the Cat. It was quite fabulous.' He didn't speak to her.

At 19, Baker was dating Westwood's right-hand man, Murray Blewett, a man who significantly broadened his fashion horizons. He attended Paris couture shows with him and was schooled in the practices of the atelier thanks to him. He met significant figures emerging in the London fashion demimonde, recasting its horizons for the international stage in a new decade after all the business disasters of the eighties. Building a sideline portfolio as a stylist, Baker commissioned some sketches of Kylie wearing Westwood, to send speculatively to the pop star. Murray showed William a video of *Ciao! Manhattan* and Baker became temporarily fixated with the figure of Edie Sedgwick, spotting in the new Kylie something of Warhol's muse. He read George Plimpton's edit of Sedgwick's autobiography. Not long after, Kylie was shopping in Westwood. Baker stepped forward to introduce himself as the man behind the sketches. A friendship struck up.

The two did multiple test shoots for Deconstruction, often with their mutual friend, the photographer Katerina Jebb. 'I started working with Kylie properly,' he says, 'when she did the Nick Cave thing. That's when we became kind of inseparable. I can remember her going, "Who's Nick Cave?" I didn't have a clue who he was either.' Their work was honed with the help of another Minogue boyfriend, the French photographer Stéphane Sednaoui. 'She really wanted to, or he wanted her to be really challenged. It was a big growth point for her.'

Immediately, Baker saw her connection to the gay audience and the potential for her to really start enjoying herself with it. He'd seen it first-hand in Manchester and watched it grow the more time he spent with her on public engagements. 'She's always had it. I think it's gays that are properly into her. It's the gays that get it. It's really funny seeing her work with so many people over the years and, really, with very few exceptions, straight men just do not get her. Whereas gay men just completely get it.'

What is it to get? 'She's a star, isn't she? She's like an old Hollywood star. It's the same as why gay men like Judy Garland or Joan Collins. It's why people like Liza Minnelli. Maybe at times it's more like Julie Andrews with Kylie. But it is stardom, in the old sense of the word. There's a character in the Jake Arnott book *The Long Firm*, Harry Starks, the gay gangster who's obsessed with Judy Garland. Gay guys really are like that.' The harder we are, the softer we look to. Gay iconography is not chosen arbitrarily. To earn it there must be the fulfilment of a unique function. 'British gays have a very personal relationship with her. Madonna is remote. For a start, she's American. There's not a warmth or intimacy. Whereas with Kylie everyone thinks they know her.'

As their work and friendship grew to capitalise on Kylie's natural, imperial hold on gay culture, Baker and Minogue would socialise together, but rarely at gay clubs. Yet still they became indelibly linked in her audience's mind as pop star and her image-maker, perhaps as the more accessible version of Grace Jones and Jean-Paul Goude or Neneh Cherry and Judy Blame. Over the first years of their creative partnership, an epoch that took her from the introspection of 'Confide in Me' to her biggest selling single, 'Can't Get You Out of My Head', Kylie and William worked on a succession of touring extravaganzas that took the original Blond Ambition blueprint and built it into something bespoke for her work, something cosier and closer.

Her gay audience grew. 'It is like every gay guy at school,' says Baker, 'who has the girl who understands him on his arm. She is that person for a whole country. I don't mean she's a fag hag. She's not. But most gays at school have a female best friend. Kylie is that person when you grow up. The survivor thing is generational, growing up together and going through different life experiences together.' Their relationship has sometimes been fraught. 'I remember a time when my mum seemed more interested in her than she was in me.' Again, she's Kylie Minogue: mum's prerogative. 'You almost stop existing. I'm not her. And she's not me. We don't exactly help ourselves and I think that has been very difficult for her, too, at times. Because she's not a gay man.'

Like all the best marriages, Kylie and William endure through love. 'I just think that she's really underrated. I think she's genuinely very talented. I think we genuinely brought the best out of each other. I probably gave her confidence and likewise she gave me confidence in what we both do. When I say they don't get it, I guess what I mean is that I do always think of her as kind of an icon, because that's how she always was to me. That's how Terry always managed her, as a superstar. He made her quite untouchable, almost.' William remembers one particular blazing row they had, over the 'God mic' – the microphone used by the stage manager for announcements – at a rehearsal for an arena tour he was creative director of. 'I look back and cringe. The band, the dancers, everyone can hear us going for it. She said, "There's only room for one diva in this show, and if it's going to be anyone, it's going to be me."' The argument was over a pair of shoes.

Yet when they coalesce, the convergence of Kylie's enticing exterior and her gay husband's creative interior has become one of pop's most enduring partnerships. It touches a gay demographic with particular, special joy. 'These are men of our age,' says Baker, 'they are people who weathered growing up in the shadow of AIDS. I remember Pete Waterman saying that Kylie is like a razor blade dipped in whipped cream. That is perfect. She is gay culture. It's this frothy, pink, glittery thing, and underneath there is a sword.'

All The Lovers

'I was thinking about the videos that I've done with Kylie and how they've been these milestones in my life,' says director Dawn Shadforth. Dawn first met Kylie when pitching a clip for 'Spinning Around', the song that popped Kylie's introspective nineties bubble and returned her to pop supremacy in the new millennium. It was the video in which William Baker styled the star in a pair of gold hotpants, found at a Parisian flea market, which would become a publicity fixture of their own, ending up in the Victoria and Albert Museum as a prized fashion exhibit. Dawn is an exceptional visual artist, particularly known for her work with a succession of brilliant female artists. She's found new visual languages and directed career-changing work not just for Kylie, but for Alison Goldfrapp, Peaches, Shirley Manson and Florence Welch. 'What all these women have in common is that they're not completely mainstream. Kylie knows her thing, the character, what the product is, yet we know the person less so. They're all writers, they all have very strong stylistic identities that belong to them as well as the product they put out, and I really love them all.'

Like Kylie Minogue, like the last 30 years of British gay culture, Dawn Shadforth knows that to make an imprint on the popular consciousness you might have to present something that is not mainstream in a mainstream way. For 'Spinning Around', she shot Kylie's body with a sensuousness and loving eye that a straight male director could never hope to match. The angle of the camera with a pair of hot pants like those is essential to anticipating and altering and the viewer's eyeline. It is the Kyliest Kylie video ever, even more so than their next work together, the zenith of commercial Kylie, 'Can't Get You Out of My Head'. 'I think it's to do with how she is a character, not an object,' says Dawn of 'Spinning Around'. 'Kylie is Studio 54 in that video. She's carefree, not attached to anyone.

She takes the boy to the dance-floor. She just wants to dance. She knows when she's given you the performance. She will turn around on set and say, "We've got that now, haven't we?"'

The ability to present the best – or most commercially viable – version of herself is a special skill of Kylie's. To keep back the more curious elements from public display, just close enough to warrant interest, without approbation. 'Part of that in a public sense,' she notes, 'as a celebrity, is that I'm not offering you everything. We've all got our private lives, and we're all complex creatures and we do right and we do wrong. I guess we do that in our lives as well as on a public level.' She has a further skill, for hotwiring an elegant approximation of pure, unapologetic camp. She understands the relationship Britain has with it.

When camp faces opposition, Kylie and her creative director are there to don armour. She can turn into a miniature Joan of Arc figure in order to fight the good fight. 'The music industry,' says William Baker, 'is fundamentally run by straight men, and that can be a problem.' After 'Spinning Around', Kylie faced her first proper gay dilemma. The obvious next single from the record was a song penned for her by the new British Hit Factory, the songwriting duo of Robbie Williams, the most famous man in the country at the time, and Guy Chambers. 'Your Disco Needs You' had been fashioned precisely with her gay audience in mind. 'And written by Robbie and Guy,' she notes. 'Who are open to that. Half of Robbie's show is his flirtation with that, from Take That's start in the gay clubs to his continued ambiguity and his playing up to it.' From the fan's perspective this was all adding up to commercial gold dust, the single that could turn out to be Kylie's 'Dancing Queen', her 'YMCA' – that one undeniable gay classic that becomes the wedding-disco fixture. 'I mean, it is,' she says.

The label considered it too gay. 'I've had so many battles with record labels about being too gay,' says William Baker. 'What the fuck does that mean? That is still a slur? Really?' The follow-up was changed to 'On a Night Like This', a sleek number delivered in the manner of her then closest international rival, Jennifer Lopez. It delivered another number one for the artist. Was the label right? 'The record company were afraid of that one,' says Kylie. 'Not others, but that one. We got in trouble. I still often think, Who knows that song? It wasn't a single; it wasn't a hit. But when we do it in concert it brings the house down. It's so amazing. Even if it didn't have the proper hit package treatment. Or maybe people love it because it's their little secret and it wouldn't have happened in the same way if it wasn't. Maybe that's why people love it.' She noticed that the song was used by Russell T Davies in his unofficial follow-up to *Queer as Folk*, *Cucumber*, the 2015 tale of middle-aged gay men negotiating sex, life, love and the universe in post-equality, post-Canal Street Manchester. Kylie understands that it had to be that song, for that audience, for that story. Everything finds its fitful home in the end.

Sometimes winning the war is about losing the battle. Kylie has found subtler ways of incorporating gay motifs into her shows, her music and her entire creative world. 'I don't think any of my songs have been aimed specifically at a gay audience, which is good, because that goes along with my way of thinking. Now we have the moments in the show where you know, of course, the gay audience is going to love that. We can customise things. But it's still really in my world. I believe in equality. That's part of who I am.'

In 2010, 22 years after the release of 'I Should Be So Lucky', Kylie bookended her unwitting thesis on the great dark man with another diamond-plated, cut-glass, quintessentially Kylie pop classic that might hold special significance for gay men. 'I love that song,' she says of 'All the Lovers'. 'And I love that it has taken on that significance.' The chorus looks back at a life full of love, of great dark men that came and went, never quite working out, until *the one* finally arrives. The hook-line is simple: 'All the lovers that have gone before, they don't compare to you'. It is not just the plurality implied that strikes a chord ('I mean, no one wants to sound like a strumpet') but the ambiguity of 'that have gone before'. 'I always thought that could be interpreted as being people lost to AIDS,' says Baker. The song is Kylie incarnate, hopeful, a little sad, smitten, joyful, resigned and knowing. It seems to encapsulate in a clever moment the very thing that Kylie has always brought to a gay audience: pure, unadulterated escape. 'I have to say, it's the video that did it,' she says. In the video for the song a panoply of underdressed couples of all gender varieties engage physically with one another, forming an outsized human mountain of polyamorous interaction. At the top of it all sits the Impossible Princess herself, singing the final chorus.

'You had guy on guy, girl on girl, guy on girl,' says Kylie. 'It's all there, everything in the world. It's just what you choose to see. It looks like a blur of bodies, our world, our society. Who you zoom in on, who you relate to, who and what you are attracted to in that is left up to you. The eye eventually finds what it needs to find.'

5. HOSPITAL WING

The First Mortality

I had – still have, actually – a wonderful friend called Alison. Hers is one of those deep friendships that you only really forge on dance-floors. It was the early nineties and Alison was the person who, when a rush was rushing or pill was peaking or the opening bars of a particular song started nudging up the mix, you would actively seek out, running the whole length of a club to find. A moment was better with her around. She's just that sort.

Once, at the Haçienda's gay night, Flesh, Alison was out with another girlfriend. The two of them met a guy. Good-looking, worked out, young, fresh, nice clothes, good hair, into her. At first, in the heat of the moment at 1am in the sensory splendour of smoke machines, strobe lights, mirrorballs and elevating sound, he looked like a convincing catch. Encouraging elbows shifted them together to dance. You always wanted your straight friends to cop off at gay nights because, firstly, it seemed so unfair that you got all that end of the fun, and secondly, it would make socialising easier later, for them to have a girlfriend or boyfriend who implicitly got the detailed minutiae of how a great gay club differs from a great straight one – the hustle and escape at their core. Clearly, this dream theory of how friendship pans out is not foolproof and is open to some misunderstanding. It was that night, anyway.

Alison spent the next three hours until the lights came up with this fellow my lad. Her friend came over intermittently to give her the protective northern eye that says, 'Are you sure about this one?' Yep, she was. This was definitely on. As they stepped out of the club hand in hand into daybreak, her perspective skewed a little. The more the high wore off, the more reality seeped in, and, Alison could see, the gayer the young man looked.

So obviously – because what is the adventure of the night-time but an excuse to make mistake after mistake and retell those tales afterwards in the broad light of day? – she invited him back to a friend's house in Rusholme, where everyone was carrying on the party. In the taxi she turned to him and said, 'I don't even know your name or what you do.' Spangle-eyed and sweat-soaked, he said, 'My name is Simon and I'm a steward for Monarch Airlines.' At this point, the 'Are you sure?' eyes turned to a 'Really?' stroke of the chin.

Back at the house, before Simon could take Alison off to another room to make his move, he needed to iron out a couple of social niceties first. He didn't know her name or what she did either. So he asked.

'My name's Alison and I work at the London Lighthouse.'

'What's that?'

She patiently explained that the Lighthouse was an AIDS care unit, a centre for excellence in the treatment of the disease in Notting Hill. He might very well have heard of it because Princess Diana had been there once or twice, anointing it with her saintly, beatific gaze, one not a million miles from Kylie's in pop culture or Alison's on the dance-floor. Some women just have that thing.

With each word the look of terror on his face increased, until by the end his jaw had dropped in full horror. 'I hope you wear rubber gloves,' he responded. She introduced him to her boss. 'What, you work at the same place too?' And he said, 'Well, I don't fuck my clients without a condom and I don't share a needle with them. So I think we're all right.' And that was the end of that. As friends had predicted earlier in the night, nothing happened with Alison and her mystery man, then or ever again. No one, I suppose, could have predicted the specifics of why.

I wish I could say I'd never been as dumb about the long shadow HIV cast over coming out back then, when the promise of sexuality was pockmarked with the fear of death. But a repressed memory came back to me when talking to Alison about that night, of the first person I ever met with AIDS. You don't forget.

Vincent was the flatmate of the first gay couple I ever knew, Dan and Paul. Dan was – still is – a kind man. He saw a kid a little lost in the Number One club, where he worked the bar. The next time I went to buy a can of Breaker lager from him he batted back the money and gave it to me for free. It became a ritual. We'd talk in the club. He fell into the role that some are charged with, of accidental mentor. Gay men in gay clubs can tell you the secrets your family cannot, of how this new culture and world to which you are drawn might work out for you.

Our friendship turned from night-time to day. He'd make me mixtapes of amazing music I'd never heard before and talk about books and films I knew nothing of. I'd go round to Dan and Paul's flat in Longsight and anthropologically observe for the first time what looked very much like a functioning gay couple, only five years older than me, in a home that was their own. You can see this stuff on telly or read about it in books and magazines as much as you like, but nothing quite allows life's smallest, most infinite possibilities to compute like encountering the meat and bones of the real thing.

Dan worked as a chef in a briefly fashionable restaurant on Piccadilly Plaza, a cooperative called Basta Pasta. He was the first person I ever heard say the word 'cappuccino'. We went to matinees at the cinema together. He listened to what I had to say, treated me like I was cleverer than I was, the kindest of all social niceties. His was another face that lit up the night, but it was the daytime stuff that mattered. We tend to think of our first boyfriends as defining figures, but your first gay friend is the man you want to remember, not the one you want to forget. There's none of the trial and error and inevitable disaster of first love. Your first gay friend is how you imagine your first gay love to be before reality bites: funny, tender, trusting, unhurried. You are on one another's side.

For the first year of my friendship with Dan, Vincent was dying upstairs. He was beautiful and fragile by the time I knew him, but spoke with a waspish vocabulary and wit that is almost a unique other language to gay Scousers. I heard about his years as the darling of Liverpool nightclubs. He went out once in the time I knew him; a farewell to disco. We didn't speak a lot, and never about his health. I could never quite find the words to ask anything useful or the capacity for comfort that conversation required. Dan would tell me mundane domestic details about Vincent's condition. One time we went to see *Honey, I Shrunk the Kids* at the Odeon on Oxford Road, a 2.30 screening on a sunny afternoon. I took a bag of sweets upstairs to Vincent for while we were out.

The details Dan shared would get less mundane, more visceral. Then one day we met up and Dan told me that Vincent had gone back to Liverpool to a hospice for respite care. I had to look up when *Honey, I Shrunk the Kids* came out in the UK to date all this. There is such a confusing and elemental angle to being at two steps' remove from death happening in front of you, such a selfishness and drama to meeting the first person you know with AIDS, a memory to be deposited away for when you need to lean on it later. You feel helpless, even a little cruel about it because you are making someone else's death your problem. It was 23 June 1989. I was 17. Vincent died at 34. 'One of his things,' says Dan, 'was he'd look in the mirror and say he looked gorgeous for whatever age he was.'

A Passage to Terry

Rupert Whitaker's childhood was not a happy one. 'I was deeply depressed for a lot of my teen years,' he says. 'I'd had rather a tough childhood. I tried to kill myself first when I was seven years old, and it didn't get much better from then.' As a child Rupert attempted to hack at his wrists but found it too painful. 'I didn't tell anybody about it at the time.' The incident was connected to trauma in his home, where his parents were separating in acrimonious circumstances. 'My mother was an alcoholic and a drug addict and my father was a failure of a father but trying his best. I think that's the kindest way to put it.' There were other related issues that he couldn't quite reconcile at the time. 'I knew I was different, but I didn't know what that meant.'

His mother died as he entered his teenage years. He helped clear her house with his father in the aftermath and found deposited around the property black-bin-bags' worth of empty Valium bottles. 'They must have given them out like sweets,' he says of her doctors and pharmacists. 'That was my first introduction to medical malpractice.' There was more to come.

In an act of uncommon bravery for a 15-year-old boy from a rural background boarding at Lord Wandsworth College, Hampshire, Rupert came out in 1977. The reaction, he recalls being surprisingly muted. 'I was sufficiently ... I wouldn't say popular at school, but I fitted in enough. When I wanted to be, I was good at rugby.' He says that the decision to come out came from a place of moral compunction. Rupert is a charming, passionate, serious man.

'I had to have a sense of integrity. Nobody's perfect in terms of their integrity, by any means, but I had to be true.' He had an older brother at the sixth form, 'so if there was going to be any problem I always had him to fall back on.' Rupert's coming out did, however, come with one unfortunate downside. 'Well, it was the first of a number of strategic failures on my part,' he says dryly. 'It meant that, as the only out gay kid at school, I never had sex with any of the other boys, who were all screwing each other like mad. Because they weren't gay, you see.'

Rupert was aware of his sexuality from a young age. A bright scholar, he was lifted two school years ahead of his age. 'I had a crush on somebody at school. He was a couple of years older than me but we both entered junior house together. He was already shaving at 11. I just couldn't get that. He had a very wicked, funny sense of humour.' As one might with a first crush, Rupert followed his adult progress as best he could. 'He eventually became a senior homicide detective and is now ugly as sin. So there you go.'

For most of the teachers, Rupert's declaration of sexual identity at 15 was greeted, 'not well. The chaplain was just fine. He was a great bloke. He was the person that took me to my first clap clinic, which was an education in itself. The first time you have sex you think, Oh my God, I've done something dreadful. And you assume that you've caught some disease.' Another master proved to be educational in a more significant and academic regard. Rupert's touchstones for gay life were not the pop-culture heroes of the seventies – Bowie on *Top of the Pops* or *The Naked Civil Servant* – but divined from the classics. 'I was the only kid at school studying Greek, and I was fascinated by the stories of guys in literature having relationships. My teacher was superb. He did not hold back on the descriptions or details. He really knew how to engage kids in learning.' Forty years later, Rupert can still recall the Latin verbs for buggery and fellatio. 'There's a poem by Catullus – "16". I think "I'll shove it up your arse and shove it down your throat" is "*Pedicabo ego vos et irrumabo*". The fact that God knows how many decades later I'm still remembering fragments of poetry, typically Catullus, that are ecstatically lyrical is just astonishing.'

Perhaps not. Upon completion of his A Levels, with a place waiting at Durham University, Rupert made the executive decision to discover a gay culture closer to his own time and place: 'I took a year off between school and university in order to come out properly.' Paternal connections found him a job in Hamburg. 'My father was in publishing so he organised work with a colleague of his who ran a publishing distribution company. When I got there I didn't speak any German and I was met off the train by this extremely frightening woman in a full leather trench coat. She was like something straight out of a spoof, and of course turned out to be lesbian.'

He started to get the inclination that there was unusual interest from a senior colleague in the company. 'He was ugly and I was lonely. But he was very kind to me and we developed a relationship. He was 36 and I was 17 at the time.' The age difference made the couple illegal, but Rupert saw it as part of his new informal education on what a gay life might look like. 'I knew he was a bit younger than my father, but he was a completely different person with a completely different mentality. At that age they know things that you don't know, and they understand life in a way that you don't but that you want to; you feel a need to, in order to be able to swim in those waters. That is part of acculturating as a young gay man.' Or at least it was in the 1970s, when information at school, church, in the political establishment, on TV and in the family unit was scarce. 'I moved in with him, not knowing it was not the done thing to do. And he introduced me to the gay scene.'

The gay men's culture of Hamburg then revolved around Tom's Bar, a cruisy leather joint. 'We walked in and I was just saucer-eyed at what I saw there.' The furniture was very much to Rupert's taste. The Tom of the bar's name was Tom of Finland, the gay illustrator and caricaturist Touko Laaksonen, whose specialist black-and-white drawings of men with rippled musculature and outsized genitalia sporting artistic facial hair and a strict uniform of gay classics, usually in a state of fetishistic sexual unrestraint, has followed gay culture since the artist's first contributions to the magazine *Physique Pictorial* in the 1950s. Only at the start of the twenty-first century did Touko gain revisionist appreciation from the world of high art, as a figure light years ahead of his time, in touch with the realisation of some of the most redolent and very real edges of male taste. The Tom of Finland estate now produces a range of bedding.

Touko's invigorating art of male sexuality in its rawest form came as quite the revelation for the young scholar of the classics. The men at Tom's Bar were the stuff of Rupert Whitaker's unrealised fantasy made flesh. 'At six in the morning, both very drunk, having not slept all night, we went to work. So that was an introduction.' His partner was not happy with the chosen venue. 'He hated anything to do with leather. He associated it with Nazism, which is an understandable mistake, but a mistake nonetheless. It's more of a biker thing. His antipathy towards it stemmed from the volunteer work he did for the Simon Wiesenthal Centre, hunting Nazis.'

Rupert is not sure whether he was in love with his partner of that time. He was 17, after all, and who knows the distinction between desire, the yearning for bodily contact, the gratitude for any attention, the relief of consummation and the complicated business of learning a brand new emotional repertoire at that age? 'I was very fond but I was also very afraid of everything. I grew up afraid of my own shadow.'

Despite having outed himself at 15 and entering a world of German leather bars and trench-coated lesbians at 17, Rupert thinks of himself as a late learner. 'You have absolutely no idea about the rules. What do you do? Even what do you do in sex? I remember trying to shag a schoolmate and thinking, How do you get that in? How does that happen? So with my first partner I learned a lot, let's put it that way. I also got HIV from him.'

With no public knowledge of the virus, Rupert's is a life story he has had to piece together jigsaw-like in the aftermath of its defining moments. 'I got ill with what is now known as a classic conversion syndrome.' He began suffering from severe fatigue and night sweats. 'Mine looked a lot like it was an Epstein-Barr virus, which is a typical thing teenagers get when they get an infection. I never felt quite right after that.' This was 1980, and the Human Immunodeficiency Virus was still years from being identified and named. The international volcano had not yet erupted. Nobody knew anything of Acquired Immune Deficiency Syndrome at Tom's Bar. There was a curious innocence to the times, despite its rigorous dress and amplified testosterone.

When his tenure was up at the publishers, Rupert ended his relationship and moved back to England. On return, his father had moved to London and taken lodgings in Bloomsbury, close enough to the emerging, loose connection of gay venues at the Charing Cross Road end of Tottenham Court Road and Oxford Street for his son to find out whether a local equivalent of Tom's Bar existed in the capital. 'I trawled down Tottenham Court Road, empowered by what had happened in Germany, and went to Bangs down in the basement. I can still visualise it because I went there several times. I first saw Terry there.'

Terry was Rupert's second boyfriend. 'It's bizarre how well I can remember that night.' Given his age, shyly adventurous nature and the succession of events to follow, it would be more bizarre if he couldn't. In the following decades, Terrence Higgins has become the name most synonymous with the start of the British national health panic around AIDS. It was Terry's name that was honoured by the enduring charity.

'I can still visualise the way he used to dance,' says Rupert, 'which was this kind of slinky, weird way of dancing. I've never seen anyone else dance like that. It wasn't a particularly hot way of dancing, but I was entranced by it. I was also, more importantly, entranced by him.' Terry was a familiar type. 'He was the classic clone: big, black moustache, short hair, checked shirt. I was really attracted to that.' Rupert liked his demeanour, too. 'He was very cool and there was no keenness on his part. But he was warm and open and friendly, and that was all it took to talk to this person. I'd spent years being tongue-tied and very, very shy, lacking in confidence. We went back that night and just kept on doing the same.'

Terrence Higgins was of working-class stock, from Glamorganshire, south Wales. Like Rupert's boyfriend in Hamburg, Terry was 36 when they met. 'He'd been in the navy, tried to get out of it on the gay card and when they wouldn't let him he went over the side of a ship and painted hammers and sickles on it. So they kicked him out. That was very him. He had also apparently been a journalist and a Hansard reporter. He was not stupid, but he was also not taking life seriously.'

Terry shared a flat in West Kensington, close enough to the gay venues of Earl's Court – or 'Girl's Court', as it was affectionately known among its gay denizens – on the third floor of a mansion block towards Barons Court tube. 'I could even point out the place to you,' says Rupert. 'It was a walk-up with a kitchen down the hall, shared, then a bedroom and a main living room, which people would crash in.'

Dipping into Terry's world was not a private and solitary encounter, as life with Rupert's publishing boyfriend had been. 'He had a few interesting friends who were also new types to me. When I met Terry I met loads of guys from completely different classes; it was an eye-opener to me. I didn't know how to relate, but it was really interesting and I had to learn a lot, working out who you can trust, who is going to take advantage and who isn't. Interestingly, there were a lot of older men with whom I had friendships and learnt a lot, but never had sex. They helped me understand what it meant to be gay. I'm very grateful to them.'

The social whirl of Girl's Court at the Coleherne, the Catacombs and Bromptons was new terrain for Rupert, but Terry knew the codes of the day and the lay of the land well. Rupert liked his friends. 'They all seemed to have lots of confidence and I didn't. Also, they all seemed to have lots of drugs and I didn't.' They smoked pot, took MDA, dropped acid and PCP, sniffed poppers. 'I remember New Year's Eve, when I'd taken God knows how much and I was fried. I was sitting in a seat for hours.' He enjoyed these socially disinhibiting rites of passage. 'That's part of learning about gay life.' He liked the existence of a shared, secret vocabulary too. 'Terry had that aspect of gay humour. I learned about Polari from Terry and his friends. He had a very dry, sardonic sense of humour.' Rupert says Terry was not particularly politically motivated. 'Like everyone, he hated Maggie Thatcher, but that was it really.'

The pulsating Hi-NRG music of the time became a new soundtrack to Rupert's life. 'The music that you heard in all those places, mainly disco music he introduced me to, was so wonderful. It was Lime, Patrick Cowley. For years afterwards, whenever I heard that music, it would just trigger this intense grief. I listen to it occasionally now, and it's funny, it can evoke intense feelings much more easily than even talking about it. That music just echoed life.' Patrick Cowley's residency at the EndUp in San Francisco was the social storage cupboard of America's post-Stonewall gay revolution prior to his own premature death from AIDS. 'Because I'd studied music,' says Rupert, 'I could analyse it, and I didn't think there was much in it.' It didn't matter. 'Some things are just bloody great.'

Rupert liked dancing. 'On both sides of the family there have been professional dancers and that did come down in my genes, no pun intended.' He was delighted to meet among Terry's friends Mark Tyme, the Hot Gossip dancer. 'Every time I would walk into Heaven with Terry, Mark would meet me by doing the splits or wrapping his legs around my neck and saying, "Hello, darling." He was just sex in motion, and a beautiful dancer, just beautiful.'

When Rupert moved away to Durham University, he and Terry would talk for hours from phone boxes at opposite ends of the country. Back in London, when Rupert was on holidays, Terry would even come over to Rupert's dad's place and sit on the wall opposite the flat while Rupert readied himself for a night out. 'Terry used to come and visit me. He'd tell me a particular time, I'd look out of the window and see him on the other side, and I remember this particular one time when he had this light pink sweater with no sleeves on it. He just didn't give a shit. I really loved that about him, too. I'd go out and meet him on the street and we'd go out from there.'

Unlike his first boyfriend, Rupert Whitaker is sure that this relationship was built on love. 'I did fall for Terry,' he says. 'And he fell for me, although I didn't really know it. I had to check later. It did happen. As he was dying, apparently I was the one thing he was asking for.' Their relationship didn't last long. 'He died within a year.'

For the Love of Freddie

Broadcaster, writer, intellect and Britain's unofficial professor of pop, Paul Gambaccini first met Queen's gregarious frontman Freddie Mercury while running the Boston, Massachusetts, radio station WBZ, 'one of America's ten biggest radio stations at the time.' It was 1976. Gambaccini was in the thick of a sensationally promising media career after graduating from Oxford University and briefly returned home to his native America to take the position. Queen were in town on tour and introduced to the aspiring young broadcaster at the then unknown *Cheers* bar, the Bull & Finch. Queen, Gambaccini and *Cheers* would all eventually take their place in the upper tier of the pop culture canon.

'We were chatting,' he explains, 'because they knew that I'd been in England. Freddie impressed me so much because he gave as much time to my assistant, who was a black woman, as to any person of greater power. She adored him, obviously.' There were few that didn't. 'I thought, Here's a real man, a real gent. When I shortly thereafter returned to Britain, I saw more of him in social situations.'

He visited Freddie at his house in Earl's Court. 'His home was quite near, within walking distance of the Coleherne pub. I only went in there once.' Paul's broadcasting buddy, the fantastically unhinged comic Kenny Everett, would often tease his more temperate friend about his social conservatism. 'Kenny had this habit,' says Gambaccini, 'of saying to me, "Oh, there's this great new place that you've got to go to. I'll meet you there. See you there." I would show up at these places – at the London Apprentice, the Subway and the Coleherne – and Kenny would never turn up. He enjoyed the concept of having me going into an environment where I would feel intimidated.'

Unlike many other BBC professionals of his illustrious vintage, Gambaccini never hid his homosexuality. 'In my normal personal life, I was not intimidated.' Nor were his tastes of the same sort as Rupert Whitaker's. 'I walk into the Coleherne and I'm thinking, This looks like the New York Police Department, and I've moved away from that; I don't want to be here.'

For many men of Gambaccini's age, who have weathered the storms of AIDS, watching first-hand as friends disappeared one by one, congregating in hospital wards and seeing whole communities decimated, there is a reflective, there-but-for-the-grace-of-God sense of having cheated death by only a whisker. In retrospect, he thinks Everett may have saved his life, by introducing him to people and places that were not to his exact taste at vibrant venues like the Coleherne. 'It was,' he says, 'the supposed origin of AIDS in Britain.' The late Dr Charles Farthing, a brave, talented AIDS specialist, schooled the DJ in the disease's local origins. 'He told me that they'd traced it back to two locations, one was the Coleherne, where a gay American had called, and the other was an American drug-using sailor up in Edinburgh. That's how it spread among the intravenous drug-using population of Scotland, its second original site.'

Of all the British pop intellects, it is to Paul Gambaccini that the establishment turns, time and again, as for true, scholarly punditry. He understands the sociological significance of mainstream pop culture, its context, pretext and subtext, perhaps better than any other pop zealot. He is a man who lends the shallowest cultures their depth, treating each passing trend with the significance of a historical epoch. He knows precisely how to translate a gay ear for the consumption of a wider audience. His broadcast voice is one twinned with intimacy and gravitas.

'The role of popular music in the sixties was so much stronger than it is even now,' he says. 'It was our social media. I know it's difficult for anyone under 30 to imagine a world without the internet, but how did you share messages? There was no Facebook. And you shared feelings through, in my case, pop music and the silver age of comics.'

Paul Gambaccini was born in the Bronx, New York, 1949. He was ten years old when his comic-book love ignited. 'Beginning in 1959, DC Comics started reviving in earnest its World War II superheroes and in 1961 Marvel began. I took that wonderful ride of about five years, when all of the characters that now dominate popular culture originated.' Paul has two siblings. 'Our comic books were all signed by the three brothers for ownership. My brother Peter did the Batmans, my little brother Phil could only afford Justice League of America, which was later valuable. The rest were mine. We would have gone ape if one of us had tried to sell one of the others' comics.'

Then there was pop music. 'It was an explosion,' he says of hitting 17 in 1966. 'The so-called British invasion of the Beatles, Motown, protest music and rhythm and blues, all at the same time. Now, the important thing is in the early sixties there was no gay liberation.' He mentions The Mattachine Society, an early incarnation of gay liberation whose heroic work is so underplayed in a history that sees global gay pop culture beginning with the Stonewall riots of 1969 that their name is barely remembered. 'So whenever there was a song relating to injustice against any people, we could relate to it. I think gay people were attuned to the suffering of black people during the Civil Rights Movement, because that was the group at the time that was fighting and receiving public attention. So there was this deep appreciation among gay people for soul music – for rhythm and blues, Motown, music made by American black men and women. We got deeply into that emotion.'

For gay men and women on both sides of the Atlantic, a fragile and exceptionally talented new British figurehead emerged in the immaculate form and sound of Dusty Springfield. 'Gay people didn't need much of a signal to know that Dusty was lesbian,' he says 'and they clutched her to their bosoms. Here was, first of all, a world-class talent accepted by everyone. But someone they knew was going through what they were. It's not transference. It's empathy. And hence, people who were alive in the sixties have a deeper relationship with the music of their day. This is not to insult the music of today or the people of the day, it's just saying that our energy went into that area. You also have to remember the words of Marshall McLuhan: "The medium is the message." In the late fifties, merely to make a rock-and-roll record was a statement of rebellion and otherness.'

In a modern age where pop music is everywhere, blurred by appreciation across age, race and gender lines, it feels almost anachronistic to think of it as once being so bound up in tribal generational identity, in defining characteristics that would move political change forward. 'It was the sense of oppression that we related to. People were searching for empathy in a world without much understanding.'

The seventies, he says, was a transitional period. 'Then the out pop acts of the early eighties in this country finally put that to rest. OK, Boy George is the turning point.' Paul Gambaccini and Freddie Mercury made a pact with one another that George unknowingly interrupted. 'Freddie once said to me, "One day we're going to do an interview that will shock the world." I knew what that meant.' He was going to tell the world about something hiding in plain sight, that Freddie was gay. 'But it turns out that events overcame that. Boy George happened.'

Freddie told Paul a story. 'They were on the same aeroplane once, not travelling together, and Freddie sent a note to George saying: "loved 'Church of the Poison Mind'".' Underneath the compliment lay pathos. 'George was what Freddie had been unable to be a decade previous, which was actually no more outrageous than Freddie but, if we're allowed to say this, he showed more of his feminine side, whereas Freddie was showing more of his butch side. Suddenly, this was 1982, and for anyone who can read, the church doors are open.'

'MTV comes along,' he continues. 'It's ironic that it's because of "Bohemian Rhapsody".' Queen's defining hit single was the first promotional video to be heavily rotated on *Top of the Pops*. 'The record industry thought, Woah, this is a real sales tool. So Britain gets a lead on making pop videos, MTV opens in America and most of the supply is from Britain. These groups who had mastered the video, such as Duran Duran and Eurythmics, immediately had this entry into America that any act in any other period of time could only have dreamt of. Suddenly, you make a video and you're guaranteed a national television show? Incredible. So all of these acts break America in a major wave, and it's called the second British invasion.'

The reach of the pop video and MTV was not just a record-label marketing tool; it sent out a broader signal. The most arresting examples of this new format played with visual identities, often connected to sexuality and gender. 'So you get the outpouring of either people coming out directly or implying it very strongly or playing with gender confusion, as Annie Lennox did.' In the wake of this sexuality shake-up, *Newsweek* printed its infamous 'Britain Rocks America – Again' cover with Boy George and Annie Lennox on it. 'Pop stars hardly ever made the covers of the news magazines. That's how big it was.'

For Gambaccini, this shift was scintillating to watch. 'By this time I was over 30, so I did not need this for my own development. But I was thrilled.' For Freddie Mercury, a new challenge was at hand. 'Freddie was overtaken by both the overt, such as Holly Johnson, and the covert, such as Pet Shop Boys. I can quite imagine him thinking, Oh, my contribution here is not needed. As a matter of fact, it might be considered passé.' His major response to the shift was the video for 'I Want to Break Free', in which all four members of Queen dressed in drag, with varying degrees of evident facial hair, just like characters from *The Kenny Everett Television Show*. 'What a marvellous bunch of young men those four were. They understood that in unity there is strength.' Nonetheless, it was Mercury who was unashamedly their star. 'I mean, Freddie was Shirley Bassey. When I saw that "I Want to Break Free" video, I said to him, "I love the way you double-time the movement from one room to another so that you minimise the time that you're out of vision."' Mercury smiled at Gambaccini. 'He said, "I'm glad you noticed it. That's my favourite part."' The video killed Queen's career in America.

Paul Gambaccini has borne witness to all shades of the sexuality spectrum on the British pop rainbow. One of his first professional assignments was interviewing Elton John for a coruscating profile in *Rolling Stone* magazine in 1973, in which Elton's gayness is spelt out in all but name. 'This was a profound episode in my life,' he says, 'because it was the first time that a public figure had been comfortably and openly gay in my presence. Obviously, there had been gay public figures throughout my life, but here was a beloved figure, just being himself. Two of the great musical figures of the sixties, whom I clearly cannot name, said to me some years ago, "I hope you'll pardon me for not coming out, but if I did it would be like admitting I was a liar during the 1960s." Of course, it was completely understandable why they didn't come out in the sixties, because it was illegal. So society repressed them and made it impossible for them to be honest subsequently.'

He thrilled at times changing. 'There was the definite transformation from the seventies into the eighties as homosexuality exploded into public view.' He attended the opening night of Heaven. 'Who was my guest? Paula Yates. I used to accompany Paula when Bob Geldof was away on tour. We became great friends. Of course, Paula loved it.' London's night-time celebrity circuit all turned up. 'The stars of *Cats*, most of whom were not remotely gay. Wayne Sleep said to Paul Nicholas and Elaine Paige to come down to this amazing nightclub, and they came down and nobody said, "What are you doing here?" The fact was that what had been inconceivable when I came to London, a mass public celebration of gayness, was now possible. We had this amazing, short period pre-HIV when we were chic.'

For anyone wishing to emulate the career of Paul Gambaccini, he has one golden rule. 'I have always believed,' he says, 'that if you are to live a full life, you must engage with what there is in your time, even if it is unpleasant. So then there was 1983, the year that changes everything.' When the next significant shift in pop culture happened, he did not – he could not – avert his eye.

'I went to the Gardens, Sunday night, gay night, and was dancing to the 12-inch of "Flashdance … What a Feeling". It was a great record, actually. The next day I went to New York, where I was staying at my parents' place, which was 2nd Avenue and 57th Street, near Bloomingdale's. To walk to Bloomingdale's I had to go past the newsagent's, which was fine by me because that's where I bought *Variety* and *Billboard*, the two show-business bibles. As I was buying them, I noticed on the cover of the gay newspaper *New York Native* the headline "Swine flu at last?"'

It was a reference to President Gerald Ford's attempts to have all Americans vaccinated against swine flu in the mid-seventies. 'It didn't happen. Swine flu never had an epidemic. But now there were gay men who were developing symptoms of animal diseases, as told in Randy Shilts's book *And the Band Played On*. The *New York Native* headline showed you the extent to which we desperately sought an explanation. That was my introduction to the world of horror.'

It was the first Paul Gambaccini had heard of AIDS. 'It was like losing your virginity; one day you are a virgin, the next day you will never be a virgin. One day, I'm dancing to "Flashdance" and there is no disease. The next day, I'm dancing to "Flashdance" and, oh boy, there is a disease.' That very same day, on that very same trip to Bloomingdale's, the disease took on its first personal significance for Gambaccini. You never forget.

'I quickly learned how serious this was,' he says, 'because as I walked down 8th Avenue with my best friend from university, David James Carroll, who was then a stage actor in New York, a bunch of his friends come up, chat, chat, chat, and one of them says, "We'll see you on Wednesday." He goes, "Wednesday?" And the friend says, "Joe's funeral, didn't you hear? The new disease." After they left, David said to me, "Excuse me for a second," and he retired to a side street to sit on a porch and weep. He then said to me, "Joe was the man I loved most in the seventies." At the time I thought he was weeping for Joe, but as I soon came to realise he was weeping for himself. He had been told, without the others knowing it, that he would die. And he did, in one of those sagas of horror and heroism that typified the era that was to come. He and his partner were so heroic. As with so many other couples, I saw examples of dedication and courage the like of which I've never subsequently seen.'

Pop culture was to take on a deeper new dimension for Paul Gambaccini, to lead him down the unexpected road of philanthropy and activism. 'Now, it was great to be engaging with the Beatles and pop music, the sixties,' he says. 'I made my career out of it. But there was also HIV in my lifetime, and I felt I must engage with it. I thought it was a moral obligation. How can people not?'

The First Public Mortality

'Terry was the one who became ill first,' says Rupert Whitaker. 'When I called him from university he would complain about headaches. I'd always known him as more or less a slender guy, but he was known as "Fat Terry". He had obviously lost a lot of weight.' Terry had been to see doctors, but none gave him any inclination of what might be wrong. 'No, nobody. Nobody knew a thing.' Rupert says Terry had some loose skin, 'which never bothered me. He had a furry matt for a chest which I just adored. At 17, 18, you don't really know what's what, anyway. He would cook for me, but he wouldn't really eat. He didn't have much of an appetite. I would be concerned by that but would think, Well, he knows what he's doing; he's a lot older than me. I thought it was part of his cool demeanour.'

Rupert Whitaker had been offered a music scholarship at Cambridge, which he turned down in favour of Durham. His instrument was, and remains, his voice. He went on a short tour of France, singing in duet at concerts with a friend who played the lute. 'When I got back from that I heard that Terry had collapsed and been taken into isolation in hospital.'

Rupert's father's flat was positioned fortuitously around the corner from London's notorious first gay book shop, Gay's the Word, which the young student would brave his way over the threshold into, schooling himself in news stories from the more detailed American gay press, in which some early medical flares had been sent up. 'Nobody knew what it was. There was no mention of anything, even though I had suggested to the physicians that it could be this American disease, which obviously it was.' AIDS was then medically referred to as GRID, Gay Related Immune Deficiency. 'I'd read a little bit about it, I don't know how. It must have been in an American gay magazine. It was a shit experience from then on.'

There were moments of mordant humour to prick the overwhelming sadness of Terry's impending death. On his nineteenth birthday, Rupert received a card from Terry, telling him in all seriousness that he had arranged a surprise to be delivered by Elizabeth Taylor. 'He was delirious,' he recalls. 'But it must have been what Terry wanted for me.' He still has the card. Rupert took what he intended to be a year off from Durham University and visited Terry at St Thomas' Hospital. 'I remember looking through a glass panel and seeing him unconscious in bed, talking with Martyn Butler and other friends there, and not knowing what was going on.'

Terry Higgins died. 'It was very quick. He had something called PML, or Progressive Multifocal Leukoencephalopathy, which is an infection of the brain. It was very traumatising.' The cause of Terry's death was pneumonia.

For first-year university student Rupert Whitaker, there were pressing concerns. 'I was already starting to feel ill myself, and I was losing my energy,' says Rupert. 'I moved from Durham to London to be near a specialist because I was getting ill.' His father's Bloomsbury flat was on the third floor and Rupert was weak, having to stop at each level to sit down in order to collect his breath and get his energy back. 'This was me at the age of 19. I was sick as a dog.' He was sweating so much in his sleep that he had to put towels underneath his sheets and change them several times a night. 'I was losing a lot of weight myself. I didn't have a lot of weight to lose. You could count every one of my ribs. So I was expected to die in that year.'

'They were fine with him,' Rupert says of Terry's doctors, 'and the nurses were nice with me. I didn't know anyone else in the situation. The undertakers were nice too, interestingly. My experience was good. We cremated Terry at Golders Green. I still remember going in to see him … the viewing of the body.'

To The Lighthouse

On the subject of the part she played during her decade working at the frontline of the British AIDS pandemic, Alison Randall is pretty categorical. 'I don't think you need anything from me because I was nothing in it,' she insists. 'Absolutely nothing.'

For her third year's training in occupational therapy at a northern technical college, Alison took the decision to specialise in HIV and AIDS. She wrote a lengthy dissertation on new working practices in the field, still in their infancy. 'It was so fucking shit,' she says, recoiling in horror when asked if the paper still exists. The thesis was written 30 years ago, in her early twenties. The mind can play tricks on you. What Alison can recall is why she was the only person in her class who decided to work in the field of AIDS. 'Because I went dancing with everyone, you know?' She was a favourite fixture on northern gay dance-floors. 'It touched my life in so many ways that I thought, Oh God, there has got to be answers and there have got to be ways of helping people.'

While a student, Alison took a part-time job at an art-house cinema, collecting ticket stubs. 'Remember there was a little old man that used to hang around outside there? Staff used to get two comps every night and I'd give him mine.' So he could keep warm, rather than to see the latest works of Wim Wenders. 'They constantly reprimanded me for getting him in.'

After college, Alison travelled out to work in HIV and AIDS treatment at the Bindura General Hospital in Zimbabwe. She stayed for five months. 'I went to the front line. It was mad. There were 20 people on the women's ward there and 13 of them were HIV-positive. It was the maddest, maddest time. I learned about the decline. It was so harsh. Within days people would just die.' She says the atmosphere on the ward was not the hysteria often relayed from African hospitals on British TV in the eighties. 'It wasn't all screaming and shouting. But it was a rapid thing from them testing the blood, which took so long because it wasn't a developed country. Patients came in with babies and the babies were all positive, too. It was just horrendous.' She worked closely with the kids. 'A lot of them lived in huts and would fall onto fires in the middle of them. So I did a lot of splinting hands and fingers, all burned, but being really careful because everyone was HIV-positive, including a lot of the nursing staff. A lot of them knew that they had finite time as well.' Death changed shape in Alison's mind in Zimbabwe from something far away to a fact of daily life.

On returning she volunteered at the northern outpost of the Terrence Higgins Trust in Ardwick, Manchester, before getting her first proper salaried post, a job at Chiswick social services in west

London. 'Because it became such a crisis, social services allocated teams. If you were diagnosed you might have a social worker, an occupational therapist and hands-on nursing care, like a community nurse. My role as a care manager/occupational therapist was to provide equipment to people so that they could remain at home, and so that families felt confident about treating someone who was so ill. It was really practical care.'

Her first client lived with his mum. 'She was looking after him and she knew absolutely everything about him. His boyfriend was around.' He was still a teenager. 'He was in the living room and I went in and showed them how to lift him and move him and tuck him in, and took him a commode. We talked the mum through money things with a social worker. We got him comfortable. That was what the job was about, making people comfortable. They were working class, honest and really, really lovely. They were open about his sexuality, which was not the case with everyone.'

Her work was physical. 'Clients were so thin that the skin was breaking and there were pressure sores, the things that you get with really old people when they've been ill for a long time. It would all happen so rapidly.' It was palliative, too. 'I was occupational therapist to a vicar. His boyfriend was an American guy and for some reason he really wanted a *Blue Peter* badge. I knew the PR for *Blue Peter* at the time so I organised to get one for him as his boyfriend's care manager. The vicar was great. He spoke out very openly about being gay and HIV-positive and what we had to fight against. So many people didn't.' Sometimes the sweet token gestures she could bring to clients to alleviate something of their personal and medical trauma veered toward farce. One couple of intravenous drug users she helped wanted to marry, a ceremony complicated by the groom's testicles being so outlandishly engorged by his condition he couldn't walk. 'So I measured him up and made him a sling so that he could walk down the aisle.'

Her work was sometimes open, often covert. 'I had two clients who lived next door to one another. I'd spend my time parking my car about a million miles away, walking down and making sure that nobody could see me going in. I'd arrange different times, when the neighbour was out, because I wasn't sure that either one knew about the other.' This secrecy was understood to be a part of the job. 'One day I went to see one of them and the other one was there too, having a fucking barbecue. I didn't know that they knew one another because they'd never told me, and obviously I couldn't ask. They were both gay men but you can't assume anything. I'd been to these ridiculous extremes to make sure neither knew I was visiting the other for a year and a half.'

A position came up for an occupational therapist at the London Lighthouse, the Notting Hill centre for excellence in the field of HIV and AIDS that was considered among the world's pioneers for treatment and care. Alison applied. 'I was so excited to even get an interview because, to me, it was like the best job you could ever imagine.' She can recall getting so stressed about what she'd wear on the morning of the interview that she didn't realise she was wearing odd socks until halfway out of the door. 'I was so shaky and out of my depth I said it out loud.' She got the job. 'It was one of the most thrilling things, to be given the opportunity to work there.'

The Lighthouse building, she says, reminded her of the chic industrial clubs and bars she'd known in the north. 'It was really like the Haçienda or Manto. It was that industrial eighties blue and metal. It felt really open and modern. To the left there was a really wide counter that had lovely receptionists who would really welcome you and ask you how you were. You could just go in and have a coffee. There was a beautiful garden to the right and a lovely café.' One of her favourite staff members when she began working at Lighthouse was a kitchen boy. 'He was looking after the menus. One day it had shepherd's pie on it, and all the lesbians had changed it to "shepherdess" pie, which he loved.

'Some went there to die, but it wasn't only that. As funny as it sounds, it was quite a positive place. It had a day centre, just for general support and coffees. All the staff that ran the kitchen prided themselves on making really healthy, amazing food.' By a stroke of good fortune, the prize-winning gardens at the Lighthouse were tended by the first gay friend Alison ever made, growing up in a small Midlands hamlet. Paul was the son of her mum's best friend. By the time he'd moved to London, he was reinvented as Polly and working the door at Brixton nightclub the Fridge, in full drag. 'It was the most beautiful garden that he worked on. All herbs and scents and loveliness. I really think it did help cushion all the heartbreaking news that went on there. There was a little chapel downstairs. You spent time there even if you didn't mean to. You had to.'

On her first day, she was told by her new boss that the occupational therapy equipment was kept in the onsite morgue, one of several baptisms of fire. One incorrectly opened drawer and you never knew what you might find. 'It's amazing what you just deal with,' she notes. She would work two days a week at Chiswick, three at the Lighthouse. Often cases overlapped as a client's health swiftly declined. 'I had this one guy who was a chubby-chaser. He was a big guy himself, really massive. I was his care manager.' He was diagnosed with PML, the same brain disease that began the steep decline of Terry Higgins. 'I went round to his house and he'd had this diagnosis and was saying, "What the fuck am I going to do?" I said, "I've got you a place at London Lighthouse." If you'd got a bad diagnosis and there was space, you could go there, but there wasn't always space.

He said, "You've got to help me, you've got to help." He could barely speak and he could barely move. He was into big, larger men and he was going, "You've got to help me clear under the bed."'

He pointed to a stash of sex paraphernalia and apparatus under the mattress frame. This was not a new activity for Alison or any of the health workers dealing with gay men and AIDS. 'I've seen loads of things and I've helped a lot of men hide a lot of things,' she says. 'But this one, I was like, Bloody hell ... did you used to ... what?' It only made her love him more. 'He was such a brilliant guy. So I helped him hide all these things because he didn't want his family finding any of it. There was all that side of it. I couldn't care less what he got up to. But that was the heartbreaking thing, in a way. He went in and he was really scared of everything and saw me as the point of contact. It was so hard because I couldn't be with him the whole time. He had family coming in and out, but suddenly you become aware that you are the one that knows everything about him.' Alison was present at this man's death. 'He held on so tight that I had marks on my hand when he let go. It was absolutely heartbreaking when I had to leave the room.'

Working in HIV and AIDS before combination therapies was not the kind of job you switched off from when you went home at night. 'I would just worry about clients all the time.' Alison was living with two friends in Belsize Park. 'We all drank too much red wine.' Nor was it the sort of work you could talk to friends about. 'You were so sworn to secrecy over things. I mean, quite rightly. It was like panic, people were floundering.' In the framework of this sombre and frantic vocational calling, you begin to reappraise mortality. *Carpe diem* takes on a radical new slant. 'That definitely happened to me. I went out a lot, barely slept.'

While the country was exploding in an ecstatic haze of post-acid-house euphoria, some people needed the outlet and temporary nirvana of nightclubs more than others. 'I'd be out clubbing at the Fridge, and people would know me in there. Some would come up and say hello and chat. Some of them were actually in respite at the Lighthouse. Then you'd bump into them at Trade. That happened. I was so young. But I lived and breathed it. I was so connected to it, in my outside life as well.' By the magical powers of youth, her night-time activities didn't so much hamper her work as help it. 'I felt like I was really good at it, too. I knew it. I could do it.'

And then there were, inevitably, the funerals. 'I went to so many. In Chiswick there was this amazing funeral director. She took on most of the deaths from HIV when a lot of funeral directors were really against it.' Acts of professional cruelty of this magnitude are almost unthinkable now. 'It's insane. They wouldn't deal with corpses. She was the one that they all went to because she was so good with them and so good afterwards at making them look their best. You'd get so, not hardened to it, just that you couldn't allow it to make you go goose-pimply and cry because otherwise you really would just be a fucking wreck the whole time and no help to anyone. You have to just go, Right, this is what it is, this is what we're doing, we have to find a way to help.'

One day, after a late and impromptu midweek bender, Alison went into the Lighthouse – when she was supposed to be at Chiswick. She stood in the staff kitchen making a cup of tea. 'And my boss said, "Alison, you're dancing to the toaster."' She'd subconsciously mistaken the Dualit toaster's distinctive ticking sound for a drum pattern. 'It was such a fancy kitchen. It was a really fancy place, the Lighthouse. Of course it was. It was gay men. There was a standard to keep up. It felt almost five-star. The food was gorgeous, the toaster was Dualit, the furniture was lovely.' But under all that surface prettiness? 'You do think, Life is so short. If you can live and breathe and dance another day, then you just have to do it.'

Alison ploughed head on with work. 'I was hedonistic, but I was right on it, in a way, too. I knew everything I had to and read everything I had to and more. I knew about every treatment. You had to know it. You had to be on it. People were absolutely brilliant there.' A lot of parents that came to the Lighthouse to visit sons wouldn't know it was an HIV centre. No signs were put up on the walls alluding to the disease, so that discretion could be upheld when it was needed. Alison says it was not always religious families who chose not to believe their relatives were dying of AIDS, and that it was an idea that could take root in the minds of all families.

From her experience, it was clients who had caught the virus by blood transfusions who wanted to remain quietest about their condition in public. 'That's another story, another subsection who felt totally fucked over. I had a whole family, a man and his wife and his two children and they were all diagnosed. That's nothing to do with gay culture, but it was so absolutely mental.' She pauses. 'Fucking hell, don't ask me any more questions because I will go. I had this one client,' she says hesitantly. 'He was a Compton's queen. Biker, moustache, did a bit of modelling. He was absolutely gorgeous. He was so aware of his looks and how he presented himself that he was completely secret about everything to his family.' For this one client, the signs on the wall made no difference. He refused to see anyone but his carers. 'As a result, he died in such a lonely, terrible, terrible way. I was his one thing. He was on the phone to me absolutely constantly. And he asked me to kill him.' It was not the first time she'd heard the request. 'No, it happened quite a lot. They'd go, "Please, just help me to do it. I can't bring myself to do it. You have to. Just help me, just help, do the morphine." That happened loads. Oh my God. And do you know what? I've never,

ever talked about it.' Once ingrained in the secrecy of a job, it can be hard to open up. 'It was such a massive part of it. But I didn't even register it because it was all so mental. I'd just be like, Oh, fucking, shitting hell I've got to go and see someone else now, then someone else. You barely had time to consider what happened in a day before the next day was here.'

Her beautiful client got under Alison's skin, to a recess of her brain she could never have imagined when she was a student. She started to dream about him. 'Because nothing was ever good enough. Nothing was ever right for him. He had Kaposi's sarcoma, and he had it all over his face and he didn't want to see anybody because of it. He lost all of his support network because he thought that it was all about him being this body beautiful and most gorgeous thing, and he didn't want to accept anybody coming in. He didn't want to be seen as anything other than the thing people would remember him as.'

In the decision to cut off communication with life around him, he turned on his carer. 'I was his punchbag, in a way. That's why it was so heartbreaking to me, his death. Every night I thought, Shit, is he going to die now? I was so filled with fear. He was so reliant on me. I know he didn't want to carry on: even another day is really hard; another hour is horrible when you can't breathe properly, you can't eat, you can't walk. It's horrible. I felt really close to him and I could understand it as well.' Alison was schooled enough in gay men's thinking to understand the depth of a shallow concern like physical appearance. 'Why did it happen to you? Why the disfigurement to somebody who is so beautiful. It felt like that for a lot of people. He was so angry and critical to me and, oh God, he was angry at me. He couldn't physically do things so I had to say, in the end, "I'm not going to put more morphine in."'

Who knows in these circumstances what the right thing is to do? In the end, it can only be the legal thing to do. 'I tortured myself because he was in agony.' Years later, the man appeared in another dream. 'I had a weird dream about him where I felt like he apologised to me. It was a dream, but it wasn't a dream; it was an awakening thing. He said, "I'm grateful for what you did for me."' Sometimes the interdependent relationship between carer and client became this consuming.

Often, Alison would try to explain to her mum what her job entailed, without giving too little or too much away. 'She was petrified for me. My mum prayed so much for everybody in there. She's an absolute church fanatic. But she wore a little red HIV badge before anyone else did, because I gave it to her from the Lighthouse. She explained to people what it was in her church in a village, where there were apparently no gay people. People were really horrible to her about it. If that's the one thing I did in the world, then I'll take that.'

Terry's Trust

The Terrence Higgins Trust was founded as a matter of charitable urgency after Terry's death. 'When we were setting it up,' says Rupert Whitaker, 'I wrote to the physician in charge and I asked him what Terry had died from. He said, "Are you a registered charity? Because without that I'm not letting you know." I had told him I was Terry's partner, Terry's boyfriend. Despite the fact that I was the only one who was in any way the only relation or next of kin named by Terry; despite the fact that I had collected the body and paid for the funeral out of my student grant, this arrogant shit of a professor wouldn't deign to tell me what he'd died from. I spoke to one of his juniors. He said, "We're writing it up and you can read the autopsy in the *British Medical Journal*." So that's what I had to do. They wouldn't tell me.'

It was just the kind of inhuman act Rupert Whitaker needed to inspire him to help affect change. 'That was a major trigger and has remained a trigger because, actually, very little has changed in attitudes.' Though an excellent and rational speaker, full of controlled, righteous fury, Rupert Whitaker says that activism did not come easily to him. 'I was never comfortable with standing up and speaking, which is a bit weird given that I'm supposed to be an activist. It meant I had to take my courage in my hands, in many ways. Right at the beginning, after Terry died, I didn't ever intend to be an activist. It was simply that you do what's put in front of you. It's always been circumstances. I am bloody-minded and I do speak up when I see something's wrong. But I am very much a reluctant activist and I always have been. I hate the contention that is engendered by it. This whole experience of activism has been a trial by fire, if you will, of learning how to articulate and express myself.'

The charity was the idea of Terry's great friend Martyn Butler. 'He had the idea for the charity, and the original intention was to raise money for research. Martyn was involved in the club scene, in events, promotions, laser-shows, that kind of area. He had a flat in Limehouse, which seemed like the other end of the earth.' They began raising money in pubs with a group of friendly and concerned volunteers, 'which was badly organised and didn't go well. Then London Lesbian and Gay Switchboard was organising an event and they wanted us to speak. So Martyn and I spoke.'

The meeting was at Red Lion Square, Holborn. 'We said we needed people to help organise, and people offered, one of whom was Tony Whitehead, who was a firebrand in those days. He scared the hell out of me. He was just another volunteer who'd got this committee meeting together. I can remember some of the people on the committee who really put their back into it. We then got it registered as a charity.'

Between the Red Lion Square meeting and it being registered as a charity, the Terrence Higgins Trust switched its aims so that it would offer direct services. They set up buddying services, education materials, mental-health services, counselling initiatives. 'I put my shoulder to the wheel with all of those and helped out. The thing that I was most involved in was safe sex.' Rupert Whitaker was determined that these materials would not pull their punches. 'Trying to get those first campaigns, the "On Me, Not In Me" campaign, there were all sorts of discussions to be had. You've got a safe-sex campaign but you're not allowed to show a penis. You can't actually use the word penis. Oh, for fuck's sake. You can't use the word "fuck". I think we were pretty radical because we said you have to use the word "fuck". You have to speak in the language of the people that you're talking to. We were ahead of the curve there.'

Rupert had to diagnose himself as HIV-positive. 'Because the test wasn't out yet when I became ill.' For a while, his hospital thought it was cancer and removed one of his lymph nodes. 'I told them that Terry had died.' There was no provable medical connection to be made yet. 'I went abroad to start studying psychology in Canada. In 1985 I moved to Boston where I also started studying immunology. The lab I was in was very interested in HIV, because one of the researchers was a gay guy. He took my blood, we ran a western blot and, sure enough, all the proteins were there.'

From his first admission to Middlesex Hospital, the now-demolished Victorian Gothic building behind Goodge Street tube station, Rupert feared death. 'Oh yes. I always assumed that I would be dead within a year, for years. Living with that, year after year after year, and when, on top of that, everybody else is dying but for some reason I'm not? I looked at the statistics and the chance of me being alive is something like 1 in 200. So 199 other people in my situation are dead? OK.'

He had friends to talk to at the time. 'I did, but I tend not to now. I've worked through a lot, and I don't find talking to other people in my situation who haven't processed a lot is helpful. There are a lot of damaged people in my situation, through absolutely no fault of their own. At the time, I don't think there was any way to avoid the damage, and I have to admit that I am damaged myself. But I have worked very hard on repairing that, which is why I'm in psychology now. It is the only way through this. You don't happen to bounce back. You do not bounce back from this. It is not possible. It is a long, hard journey.'

The quasi-religious language that surrounds disease of any sort in Britain doesn't help. 'It's framed as a fight against an object, whereas in fact it is a fight to determine what your life is going to be. It is a fight with life. To say, "No, it's going to be this way," which means I'm going to survive. It's not a fight with a lump that's called a cancer or this microscopic virus. It's a fight with life.'

The British celebrity deaths in the late-eighties and nineties – Freddie Mercury, Kenny Everett and chat-show doyenne Russell Harty – brought AIDS back into the family living room after its initial death toll. 'Definitely, they changed perception,' Rupert says. 'By then I'd left the UK, but I stayed in touch very much because Tony Whitehead was still in charge at the Terrence Higgins Trust. I was hearing a lot about what was going on. It made a huge difference. Also, Princess Diana visiting the London Lighthouse made a massive difference.'

Diana Takes a Trip

At the end of 1984, the Terrence Higgins Trust, headed by the impressive figure of Tony Whitehead, gave a gala screening at the Everyman Cinema in Hampstead of *The Times of Harvey Milk*, a documentary about the San Francisco mayor whose pioneering local work changed perceptions of LGBT people the world over. Paul Gambaccini was on the invite list. 'I was an admirer of Tony Whitehead from afar,' he says, 'because he was writing a column at the time, maybe in the *Pink Paper*, maybe *Capital Gay*, and in it he was discussing on a weekly basis the progress of his HIV infection. Well, this was unique, that someone was so far out they were even discussing their journey into the unknown. Going along with him on this trip was his partner. I just thought, Clearly, Tony Whitehead is as brave a person as has walked the face of the earth.' Tony was an activist by choice, not circumstance. He stood proud at the battle lines of the Gay Liberation Front during the seventies. Whitehead asked Gambaccini to become a patron for the charity. 'I saw Tony and thought, Anything this guy asks, I'm in there. You either answer the call or you hide.'

As part of his duties, Paul would visit the London Lighthouse, 'because there were so few HIV charities at the beginning that you checked out every one of them. You have to fight.' Gambaccini did not just bring a bevy of celebrity connections to the Terrence Higgins Trust, but a loose link to royalty, too. 'One of my visits to the Lighthouse was because Princess Diana was taking Prince Charles. On that mutual tour of the Lighthouse, Prince Charles turned and said to me that he was enthusiastic about it because it was investigating alternative therapies, and that alternative therapies were a topic for him. So I think it's quite possible that Diana said to him, "Well, you know they work with some alternative therapies?" And he'd said, "Oh, I'll go along."' Not that this was a vanity move on behalf of the heir to the throne. 'He was fully committed to that visit. Anthony Sher was there, which helped, because he is close to Anthony. He had a rigorous conversation with service users and employees. That was probably the peak of the Lighthouse.'

Diana's spiritual kinship with the plight of gay men throughout the eighties and right up to her death in 1997 is impossible to underestimate. What does Gambaccini think was that special connection? 'You, being British, are talking about her role in Britain. I, being a man of the world, having come from another country, am well aware of her significance outside of Britain. She was a world star, as big as there has been in my life. She's up there with Elvis.'

The alignment of events necessary to anoint somebody to this level of stardom cannot be planned for: 'You have to have right place, right time. It's always a big factor with charismatic individuals. But they always have an inner sense of how to steer the career. Because a true groundbreaking world star has to be rooted in the now but with a sense of where we're going to next – and being one of the first to get there. People like Bowie and Madonna, as you know, if only because they gave credit, took inspiration from avant-garde artists and adapted their work into their own, and thus seemed to be, to the general public, the pioneers.'

Diana, he thinks, did the same not with artistry, but with the fundaments of human empathy. 'Diana didn't originate any of the attitudes to tolerance that we felt, but she was listening to that frequency. She tuned in and got there first among the leading world figures. She was so clever, in a way that I'm sure irritated people who didn't want her to be so clever. She was clever beyond the expectations of role.' Like Kylie Minogue, Princess Diana first appeared in a blizzard of news and television coverage, seeming to be one thing before transforming into quite another in full public glare.

Gambaccini first met Diana at her brother Charles Spencer's twenty-first birthday. 'I had known Charlie already. I'd done an interview with him for the Eton newspaper and he'd asked me to do a talk for the students, which I had done.' Gambaccini was delighted to note that the entertainment for Earl Spencer's twenty-first was provided by the American singer Phyllis Nelson, beamed in via satellite from a rooftop in downtown Los Angeles. Nelson's earlier career coincided with what Gambaccini calls his brief 'disco-bunny' period, following the opening of Heaven. 'How many times did I dance to "Don't Stop the Train"?' he quizzes. 'There was that period of three years when I was out several nights a week, and there were a handful of records that the minute you heard the opening bars you had to get up and dance. There was that and the Disconet remix of Abba's "Lay All Your Love on Me", the 12-inch of "Don't You Want Me"; there was "Hit 'N Run Lover" by Carol Jiani and "Your Love" by Lime. Oh my God, I still play that. I would say they were the top five.'

Just prior to his twenty-first, Charles Spencer was grumbling about his stepmother. 'This is on historical record because Charlie said that she was selling off the family silver in anticipation of the death of his father, after which she would become less welcome in the house.' At the party, Gambaccini was introduced for the first time to the Princess of Wales. 'So I said to Diana, "Oh, Charlie's been telling me about your stepmother." Well, that set her off. Strangely enough, that got Diana and I off on a friendly acquaintanceship. This was obviously something that was bugging her.'

They remained on appreciatively nodding terms until her death. 'I don't claim to have had the relationship with her that somebody like Elton would have had. But Diana, I have to tell you, she was real.' He stresses the further importance of her embrace of gay lives, not just at the London Lighthouse, but as rabidly counterintuitive to the establishment thinking of the time, then most persuasively collated in the print media owned by Rupert Murdoch. 'I will go to my grave, which will hopefully not be until he goes to his grave, believing that he is the man in the western world who did more harm than anyone else in my lifetime. What a villain Rupert Murdoch is. This man was the great hate-monger against gay people in the 1980s. His publications persecuted people who had HIV and AIDS. You'll immediately start thinking of the *Sun* and the *News of the World*, and of course they were the most despicable publications, but *The Times*?' He is now fuming with rage. 'Let me tell you ...'

On the morning of an early nineties Terrence Higgins Trust benefit at Quaglino's – for which Gambaccini had organised the entertainment, in the shape of Elton John, Rory Bremner and Kiki Dee – the professor of pop was stopped in his tracks by a *Sunday Times* headline. 'Rupert Murdoch could have done a lot of good in his lifetime,' he says. 'And he chose to be a villain. So, Quaglino's, on that day, the *Sunday Times* has on the front page how AIDS is not caused by HIV; it's caused by gay men taking drugs, particularly poppers. This was the newspaper of record when it was published by the Thompsons. So that night, from the stage, Elton says, "Fuck the *Sunday Times*," and gets an ovation. You will find that when you speak the truth about Rupert Murdoch, people will respond. People will go mad with applause when you tell the truth.'

Gambaccini finds it hard to forgive the then *Sunday Times* editor. 'Andrew Neil, to his eternal shame, just says, "Oh, we got that one wrong." Excuse me? That is not sufficient. And to attack the Terrence Higgins Trust as part of the AIDS industry? This was the *Sunday Times* campaign that there was an AIDS industry and let's stop it. Nick Partridge, when he was chair of the Terrence Higgins Trust, told me that in South Africa the leading anti-AIDS campaigner, former president Thabo Mbeki, said to him that he had read the theories quoted in the *Sunday Times*. The *Sunday Times* gave a megaphone to this so-called scientist and Mbeki bought the act. It was later speculated that over 200,000 people died as a result of the theory being taken seriously. So Andrew Neil can't just say, "Oh, we got that one wrong." I'm not saying that he personally or that Rupert Murdoch personally has the blood of 200,000 people on their hands, but they were on the wrong side of history. And it should be noted that they were on the wrong side of it and have not atoned.'

After Diana's death, Paul Gambaccini was invited to St James's Palace by the executors of Diana's Estate to value the contents of her record collection. One of the simplest reasons Diana connected with gay men was her natural populist touch. No other member of the royal family at the time was an avowed Duran Duran fan. Her tastes felt novel and modern. 'It immediately became apparent to me that there wasn't much of value outside of provenance,' he says of the record collection, one he found curious given what he – and we – knew of Diana's taste. 'There was what was surely the greatest collection of Welsh male voice choirs, because they would all send a copy of their records to her. And there was a unique collection of performers from Commonwealth countries. Then there were some classic rock records like the Moody Blues, a few classical records like Tchaikovsky ballets and Beethoven symphonies. The only thing of value was a set of BBC transcription discs of *The Goon Show* programmes, with a letter from Peter Sellers to Prince Charles. So I said, "OK, this is valuable, but it's Prince Charles's. Where's the Diana stuff?"'

It started a train of thought. 'Is it a fraud that she was into pop music? The only vinyl record I can remember that had her name signed on it was 'A Single Man' by Elton John, scratched to uselessness, obviously listened to a lot. There was a copy of Dire Straits' *Brothers in Arms.* But where's all the Duran Duran? I thought, Well, that's a puzzle.'

At the turn of the millennium, the mystery as to the validity of Diana's pop taste was resolved. 'When the Paul Burrell trial came up I was asked by Scotland Yard if I would go to a secret destination in south London to view materials seized from him.' Diana's former butler had been accused by the Crown of stealing multiple artefacts from his previous employer. 'And there it was, the CD collection, each of them signed by Diana. Here were all these CDs that were part of the Diana image, all the artists that she liked.'

The deaths of both Freddie Mercury (24 November 1991) and Kenny Everett (4 April 1995) hit Gambaccini hard. 'I was more affected personally by the death of Kenny because I was not in Freddie's inner circle, and in his final months he drew the wagons close.' Freddie had chosen a path to his end that was familiar to Alison Randall and the staff at the Lighthouse. 'Freddie was one of those people, and I pause because I'm immediately caused to think of some of our other dear ones who chose not to be seen as they physically diminished, like Marlene Dietrich in the film by Maximilian Schell where you hear her but she refuses to be seen. And some of our dear ones did not wish to be seen when they were diminished. Although, professionally, of course, he did make his last videos.'

Freddie's farewell to his fans was a simple, direct message to camera in the song 'These Are the Days of Our Lives'. 'When he looks to camera and says, "I still love you," you have to be hard of heart not to break into tears. That's Freddie's goodbye.'

Kenny Everett had talked to Gambaccini about his illness. It was not a secret. The consummate comic, he used humour as his primary defence. 'He came to my birthday party and said, "Well, it's a good job Capital Gold is in mono because I've gone deaf in one ear." To the very end he was telling jokes against himself. We were once arranging lunch and I said, "Can you do Wednesday?" He said, "Well, I'm having brain surgery at three so maybe we could have lunch at one?"'

The timing of Everett's death, less than a year before combination therapies changed the life expectancy of HIV-positive people, stung hard. 'With Kenny, the great frustration is, if only he could have hung on for a few more months. There's a group of a few dear lost ones, including my PA, Terry; if only they could have held on for a few more months there would have been hope. They can torment you the most. And you know there are still some moments when you're stopped in your tracks because you now have cause and opportunity to grieve for particular individuals whom at the time you just wanted to give a decent funeral. So many were dying and you were attending to everybody, and almost nobody got their due amount of attention. We just had to stay afloat as a community. Now we have time, when somebody's name is mentioned, to think, Oh my God. What happened? What would've happened had Freddie lived? Would we have got to Sir Freddie? I think, inevitably, we would have. What a wonderful subject to speculate on. He was a figurehead. He would have come out. We would have had that interview.'

Diana's death, he says, is rivalled only by John F. Kennedy's as the defining moment of his lifetime. 'Diana will never grow old. She will always be a heroine.' In the immediate aftermath, Gambaccini found himself passing by Buckingham Palace on his way to work. 'There was this Woodstock of grief. Which got bigger, not smaller every day, and people were singing songs of comfort: "Yesterday", "Candle in the Wind". This was before anyone asked Elton to do it, but it was the perfect, appropriate song.'

HIV, The Change

Combination therapies may have changed the life of Rupert Whitaker, but they did not shift his brilliantly agitated temperament. 'After that,' he says, 'the main biomedical discourse became, "Oh, you've got pills now, what are you complaining about? Get on with your life. You're lucky. You survived." It's all about pills. Do what your doctor says and you'll be fine. It doesn't matter that you've lost 50 people, you can't get out of bed because you're depressed, your adherence to the medication that's being dished out is affected because of the people you've lost, and that your life has been ruined by this. You're told, "Here's your pills, get on with it."' To which his response is? 'Well, fuck you, frankly.'

Rupert Whitaker has not lived the astonishing, unique life he's lived to pipe down now, in his fifties. He has received doctoral qualifications in Psychiatry, immunology and neurology. He is chairman of The Tuke Institute, an independent research organisation that works in the health service, and he has worked and been published across the world. His great heroes are the US AIDS activist Larry Kramer and our own one-man human-rights militia Peter Tatchell ('one of the awkward people who will not shut up, and thank God'). 'There's a lot of people who are my age or older that have found the re-entry into "normality" very hard.' His own academic work in psychology has helped him find an understanding of the mental side effects of long-term survival. 'I've been working with complex post-traumatic stress disorder, which is considered to be a sub-type of post-traumatic stress disorder. It happens particularly with multiple loss or interpersonal traumas that are chronic. It fucks you up in a brand new way. It really does.'

He recognises familiar psychological patterns in people in his situation. 'I've seen this with a lot of long-term survivors. You get this inability to relate. You cannot risk relating deeply again. I have had some trouble with this. Either you hermetically seal yourself in with someone in a relationship or you just keep avoiding. You're like Teflon with relationships; even if you think you want one, you just cannot risk engaging. It's a subconscious thing. It damages your sense of identity. It damages your ability to relate to people. It damages your sense of the future and your ability to plan for the future and to enjoy life. Your ability even to have pleasure is severely blunted. It also overlaps a lot with depression, and you find a lot of self-destructive behaviours associated.' Amazingly, since his first experiments in Terry's Barons Court flat in the early eighties, Rupert has never taken recreational drugs.

Sometimes the medical profession's attitude to living a long life with HIV reminds him of finding the bin bags full of empty Valium bottles in his mother's house when he cleared it out at the age of 13. 'Physicians think that a lot more has changed than it has. They are so out of touch. They always have been out of touch. They're typically overpaid and under-competent. I've put a lot of my life into changing that and they don't want to know. They're not interested in getting better. They're interested in being in charge.'

Rupert's life has been significantly shaped by his early diagnosis. 'Because I was right at the start of sex education and the safe-sex campaigns, my sex behaviour changed. It didn't change fast enough because I had unprotected sex when I was highly infectious, as I know now but didn't know then, and I am sure that some of those guys got HIV from me. But I didn't know better.'

In 1981 nobody knew. There was no information. 'Exactly. But after that, yes, I've always used condoms. I've not had unprotected sex in decades. With one early boyfriend, who was a policeman, he wouldn't have sex with me because I had HIV. But he would go and get fucked on the towpath without protection. So that ended. You think, Well, that's so totally dumb. And, of course, that's irrational behaviour, but sex is not a rational activity.'

Such have been the advancements in medical technology that Rupert is now not infectious, even without a condom. 'And I have had some people wanting me to fuck them without a condom, and that's not comfortable for me. First of all, how do they know that I'm not infectious? All they've got is my word for it. It radically changed my sexual behaviour. Shifting back to a more "regular" or "usual" form of sexual behaviour, I wouldn't feel comfortable with. But I've always been rather inventive with sex anyway.' He laughs.

In the mid-nineties, Rupert's medical condition was complicated by a stroke, from which he is now completely recovered. 'I was severely affected by that for years, though it doesn't show now. I also have epilepsy from brain surgery for the stroke, so there's been more than one thing to deal with.'

He cannot imagine a life different from the one he has lived. 'The reality is that if I hadn't had the stroke, say, I would probably have a good professorship at a major university and an international career in that way. That would have been what I wanted. But because I had the stroke and I got knocked off that, I've continued trying to forge my way ahead. I had to learn to walk and talk again, to use my memory properly and control my seizures, but having got to a certain space I've got back up on my feet.

'And what would life have been like if I didn't have HIV? I think I would probably have been an opera singer. A linguist, perhaps. I probably would not have ended up in science or medicine. I would not be the person I am today. I would not be half as worked out as I am. I would probably still be struggling with deep depression and not have faced that or its causes. And I would have lived a very different but still fairly miserable life.'

He laughs his deep, atonal laugh. 'This life has, at least, been full of meaning, full of passion, full of the chance to make a change. And I think that is a life worth living.'

How much of that is due to Terry?

'All of it.'

6. DEPARTMENT OF CULTURE, MEDIA AND SPORT

Things Can Only Get Better

I suppose we should have known something was afoot for gay folk by the decision to use D:Ream's 'Things Can Only Get Better' as the signature song for New Labour's winning election campaign of 1997. It was a strange choice, if only because culture was swimming chin-deep in Britpop. What had once been considered the musical alternative and confined to the margins was now the mainstream. In the Gallagher brothers, Liam and Noel, British music had unearthed new nonpareil working-class heroes, the sons of an abusive father and doting Irish Catholic mother. Their band's name Oasis, a high-street variant on the woozier American Nirvana, represented its own tenacious allusion to a new kind of paradise.

Perhaps Oasis's tale from Burnage bedroom to the world was too redolent of old Labour to soundtrack the administration's christening party (perhaps the band's extraordinary story of untrammelled personal ambition was too unwittingly Thatcherite?). Perhaps, with the obvious musical references to a Britain past and long gone, in the shameless appropriation of the Sex Pistols, the Beatles and every simian stage gesture Ian Brown had threatened to cauterise the establishment with, and the unwavering, open lyrical triumphalism, Oasis was just too unsubtle a gestural klaxon to sound even for Tony Blair's communications tzar, Alastair Campbell. Perhaps a song like 'Rock 'n' Roll Star' would confuse Tony Blair in the public imagination with his early musical ambitions. Perhaps 'Live Forever' was too grandiloquent a claim for his haunting, ageless gay sidekick Peter Mandelson. Or perhaps there was just somebody at New Labour HQ who really, really liked the omnipresent nineties disco subgenre handbag house, put their hand up in a meeting and had a handy copy of *Hed Kandi Classics* to gauge whether 'Things Can Only Get Better' was up to the job. With New Labour 1997, it seemed as if almost anything was possible.

It's tempting to look back at the choice of 'Things Can Only Get Better' as Tony Blair's coronation anthem through a rosy lens. Was this as clever a configuration of what was to come during his tenure as it seemed, or just happy accident? We'd had a spookily prescient American campaign anthem immediately before Blair's 1997 landslide. The intra-marital strife and industrial levels of narcotic ingestion involved in the production of Fleetwood Mac's 'Don't Stop' – the song Bill Clinton chose for his first campaign – would all be echoed in the 'did he or didn't he?' secret toke conjecture of Clinton's early presidency and sewn through the stains of Monica Lewinsky's most famous dress. But Blair skipping to the conference podium to the strains of handbag house was something truly new.

Handbag house was a genre incubated and plastered all over the gay clubs of the north in the late eighties and early nineties. As well as the big divas fronting its most prominent tunes, it made temporary stars of straight men: the Beloved's Jon Marsh, M People's Mike Pickering, D:Ream's Peter Cunnah and the fantastically utilitarian remix squads Brothers in Rhythm and K-Klass. The classier forebear of these house-lite pop acts was the unlikely switchover from rock to house of Britpop messiah Paul Weller who, for a spell in the eighties, had recorded a dance-floor suite with his post-Jam band the Style Council, including a cover of Joe Smooth's equality anthem 'Promised Land'.

The name handbag house was a derisory invention, a reference to the 'Sharon and Tracy' crowd that would territorially plonk a handbag in the middle of a Yates's Wine Lodge dance-floor and proceed to get ripped to the gills before taking home a handsome ne'er-do-well in a nice button-down shirt. The obvious appeal of this demographic to gay men – of dancers who took the chin-stroking, essayist seriousness out of the physical impulse to move to music and replaced it with a cheeky mating ritual – was not tough to identify.

There was something different about Peter Cunnah to those other men, though, something that would for a season elevate him towards his pinup potential across gay Britain. He seemed to know by instinct the correct way to groom a Vidal Sassoon French crop. Irish men have always held a particular appeal, with an assumed alcohol intake (fun), bodywork inherited from navvies (hot) and unhindered storytelling agility (interesting). Cunnah's best songs were gender ambivalent. While touched with some of the hippie-ish thinking of the first acid-house wave, they had a significant connection to the tangential swell of hopelessness and faith that marked northern soul and Hi-NRG. 'Things Can Only Get Better' triumphed as a UK number one single in 1994, but before that came 'UR The Best Thing', a naturally ecstatic song re-engineered by club-hero DJ and producer Sasha into something almost symphonic.

Cunnah's gay credentials stretched further than physical admiration. He was an early cover star for the new gay magazine *Attitude*, which debuted in 1994. Famously, *Attitude* launched in the same month as *Loaded*, the British lads' magazine that injected a fresh new honesty into the mid-level men's publishing shelf, hoovering up the groundswell of national pride fostered by Britpop and reconfiguring young British masculinity into a flash, funny fantasy of itself, a geared-up, togged-up, intellectually idealistic yob.

The *Loaded* lad was sexier, funnier and better dressed than his aspirational, middle-class counterparts. He was the man in a bucket hat and 6876 windcheater emitting happiness on the Heavenly Social stairwell when the DJ dropped 'Life's What You Make It' after something by Carl Craig. *Attitude* was clearly publishing's response to handbag house, just as *Loaded* was to Britpop. The *Attitude* boy was the one beaming for joy in a Stussy T-shirt and Adidas Gazelles when the opening chords of 'U Sure Do' ripped through a sound system. *Loaded* lad and *Attitude* boy were just heads and tails of the same shiny coin, with a shared fondness for a gurning skinny girl in a crop-top and bunches holding a sparkler above her head on a nightclub podium, contrary to any or all in-house fire restrictions.

I bought the first copy of *Attitude* from a newsagent's on Byres Road, Glasgow, where I was sitting finals for an English degree. From the day I registered at Glasgow University, the building looked like something out of *Brideshead Revisited* to me. It still gives me a shiver up my spine every time I see it, even now. My favourite character out of all the books I'd waded through over four years in the splendid circular University Avenue reading room was Pechorin, the brooding protagonist of Lermontov's *A Hero of Our Time*. One afternoon, a professor took a tutorial out on the lawn of the spectacular university building, overlooking the splendour of Kelvingrove Park, the night-time cruisers of Kelvin Way and the sun-dappled art gallery at the bottom of the hill. The professor was a wise man with a silver beard. He spoke distractedly about *Lolita* and the moral line Nabokov so frequently swung either side of. He said, 'Show me a person who has never been abused and I'll show you someone who has not lived or is a liar.' I read narcotic literature: Irvine Welsh's *Trainspotting*, treated as a literary classic only a year after publishing, and my very favourite, Katherine Dunn's *Geek Love*. I read a new arch campness in Choderlos De Laclos's *Les Liaisons Dangereuses* and a doomy morality in Nathaniel Hawthorne's *The Scarlet Letter*. I reread Tennessee Williams's *A Streetcar Named Desire*, over and over, for the tenth, fifteenth, twentieth times. I sat open-mouthed at the climax of *The Tempest*, when the characters' moral worth is adjudged, divided and split down the middle not by their behaviour, but on account of their ability to awe at the wonder of the world. I could barely work out whether I'd fallen in love with the work of Christopher Isherwood and Walt Whitman or the men themselves, such was the generosity of time given to thinking about life and literature.

Peter Cunnah's cover interview in *Attitude* involved a story in which, blitzed on ecstasy, he'd gone to an after-party, and found himself being fellated by a man. It felt exactly like the legitimisation of stories you'd hear in bars and clubs and at parties, of the breakdown of male sexuality from something rigidly compartmentalised into something messy and nearly equal, in the correct sense of the word, the same but different. Good as you. It felt warm, naughty, real and proper, navigating a new British heartland of maleness that was built on empathy rather than antipathy. It was the terraces and transvestites, lager and Lucozade.

With a broadly supportive government in place, one whose ears were open to the changing social patterns of their times, and a brand new millennium soon to come, D:Ream sounded oddly perfect soundtracking the *Ten O'Clock News*. Things could surely only get better.

A First Political Hero

Chris Smith – now Baron Smith of Finsbury – was the first sitting politician in British parliament to come out as gay in 1984, a year after the young Labour backbencher had intended to. The same year as Frankie Goes to Hollywood's 'Relax' and Bronski Beat's 'Smalltown Boy', though any coincidence there is surely academic, as it was also the year of the identification of the HIV virus as the cause of AIDS. Chris Smith's astonishing upending of the assumed preference for privacy when it comes to homosexuality in public life can get glossed over in the revisionist reading of the amazing equality legislation quickly introduced under Tony Blair's first term as Prime Minister. But Chris Smith is no less an emblematic hero of his times than Pechorin was to turn-of-the-twentieth-century Russia. During a 21-year Commons career, Chris Smith lent gayness itself a patina of quietly unruffled, kindly establishment decency.

The day after Blair's 1997 election victory, Smith, who had been Shadow Secretary of State for Health, was summoned to see the Prime Minister. 'I walked into the cabinet room and he said, "I want you to do the Heritage job," as it was then called. It was a surprise.' He had the presence of mind to ask two questions, there and then. 'The first of which was, "Can I change the title of the job to Culture, Media and Sport?" and the second was, "Do we have to go ahead with the Dome?"'

He got the answer he wanted to the first question (yes, of course he could) and was saddled with the ongoing dead weight and cash drainage system of turning a retrospective exhibition of Britain located by the Thames in Greenwich into a tourist trap. Nonetheless, he says now, the Culture, Media and Sport role was a dream cabinet post. 'Oh, I loved it. It's the best job in government by miles. Partly because you're dealing with a lot of enjoyable stuff, but also because you're dealing with stuff that means a lot to people's lives.' He lists some of his work, painting a noble picture of government thinking marked by egalitarianism and optimism. 'There were always lottery fund allocations that were causing joy and media froth, restoring free admission to museums and galleries, setting up the UK Film Council, increasing funding for sport, setting up the National Foundation for Youth Music, establishing NESTA (National Endowment for Science, Technology and the Arts), rescuing regional theatres, starting the process off for digital television. There was a whole range of stuff.' Not much of his work had anything other than incidental connections to Smith's sexuality. 'Some of it had spin-off impacts on the LGBT community, but not much that was specifically labelled as such.'

Chris Smith turned 16 in 1967, the year of the legalisation of homosexuality in England and Wales. 'I was 15 when it passed and didn't really know that I was gay by then, so it didn't really impinge at all.' It did, however, excite his young political mind. 'It registered as part of the whole liberalising agenda that was going on under the Labour government. There was abortion and homosexuality reform, and there were various other things like the abolition of the death penalty. I remember being very conscious that this was a great liberalising, progressive moment. But it was a progressive moment, rather than an LGBT moment, for me at that time.'

Smith's coming-out story was a slow-burner. 'I took quite a long time to come to terms with my sexuality,' he says. 'It was probably just after college, rather than at college, that I really thought, Yup, you know, I'm different, I'm special.' With Chris Smith, the 'special' detail is significant. Before accepting his sexuality, he says, 'I concentrated on my studies and my politics.' Reading E.M. Forster and Walt Whitman, 'was of only academic interest to me at the time.' He studied at Pembroke College, Cambridge. 'The thing, of course, in those days was that being gay was definitely something that was unusual, and this wasn't what was expected of a young man growing up. So it wasn't that I was fearful, it was just that it wasn't the predicted path of one's life.' If he had done such a thing as plan for life ahead as a teenager, he supposes that, yes, a wife and children probably would have been expected. 'I didn't have any relationships with women, but I hadn't thought at the time that anything else might happen.'

The realisation of his sexuality came gradually to him. 'There was no one particular thing, just some fumbling experiments and then the sudden sense that, actually, there's a rather wonderful, vibrant community of people out there and we go to pubs and clubs and have fun, and I want to throw myself into this.' Living in pre-Granita Islington, he would visit the Edward IV pub sandwiched between the Angel ends of Upper Street and Liverpool Road, and the Fallen Angel, off City Road. 'There was a wonderful dance club up in Wood Green, called Bolts. And remarkably there were Monday nights at the Hippodrome that were big and blousy and spectacular.' He can't pick one particularly important individual in this thrilling stage of his personal development. 'I didn't have a role model. It was friends, people I met, one or two people I ended up having affairs with.' Though brought up religious, as a member of the Church of Scotland, he felt no conflict between his burgeoning sexuality and faith: 'It was all about an inclusive God rather than a condemnatory God.'

Smith had been a supporter of the Labour Party since his early teens and became a paid-up member on his first week at Cambridge. When he was selected as the candidate for Islington South and Finsbury in the 1983 election, the subject of how to deal with his sexuality was first tabled. Smith was openly gay in the party, 'but I'd never made any public statement about it. I had a conversation with my agent about what would happen if, at a public meeting during the election campaign, someone shouted out something from the floor.' She offered a solution. 'She was all for having a burly, working-class member of the party standing at the side in the room saying, "We don't want to hear about that, we want to hear about unemployment."' Smith had another idea. 'I said to her, "No, no, no. If this arises there is only one way to deal with it, and that is for me to say in answer to the question, "Yes I am, so what?" And onto the next question.' In the event, he didn't need to. 'No one brought the issue up.'

Before the 1983 general election, London witnessed one of its ugliest public displays of establishment gay prejudice in a by-election daubed clearly with the rotten, regressive hand of homophobia, in Bermondsey. 'Oh, that was seriously worrying because it was a very homophobic campaign,' Smith recalls. 'Ironically, all three major party candidates were either gay or partly gay in that election.' Robert Hughes was the Tory candidate. Peter Tatchell was standing on an openly gay ticket for Labour, a stance he was butchered for from both within the party and his opposition. Simon Hughes, a later admission to the openly gay Members of Parliament over a decade later but one firmly in the closet at the time, was the eventual Liberal party victor.

'I think Simon was more opportunistic than reprehensible in that campaign,' offers Smith, kindly. 'Although the Liberals rode the tide, the beast was unleashed by renegade members of the Labour Party, who were the old, white, working class of Bermondsey, and they were pretty vicious in their campaigning. I went and knocked on doors and delivered leaflets for Peter Tatchell, and it was very obvious that the election was slipping away from us.'

Four months later, Smith won the Islington South and Finsbury seat by a narrow margin, of 363 votes. 'The issue didn't arise at all. I remember for the next year or so after that election I kept on thinking to myself, At some point I need to say something about this.' Smith didn't have a partner at the time, though he was acutely aware of a British print media scavenging like hounds for clues as to any public figure's homosexuality, ready to routinely brand them with shame. 'There was a very good friend of mine, who was an MP and gay but never publicly came out. Everybody knew that he was gay, and he was being hounded by the press. He had reporters sitting in cars outside his flat all night. He had his dustbins ransacked. He had several break-ins in which nothing of value was taken, but papers were looked through. I just thought the only way of making sure that didn't happen was to remove the story. And you remove the story by being upfront and open about it.' His coming out would have to be chosen with pertinent timing. 'I'd sort of made up my mind that I needed to say something, sometime, but I didn't know when was the right moment. No one had ever done this before.' It was important for Smith to avoid pre-emptive strikes by the press. 'I don't think I was nearly important enough at that point to warrant it. I was a newly appointed Labour backbencher. Also, they hadn't really twigged.'

Eventually, the moment presented itself, at a town hall meeting in Rugby, Warwickshire, in November 1984 that has come to signify one of the most crucial moves forward in British gay equality. 'The incoming council in Rugby had decided they were going to remove sexual orientation from the list of things they would not discriminate against in their employment policies, and there was a big rally and demonstration. Because I'd said positive things about what we used to call lesbian and gay rights at the time, I'd been invited to go up and speak at the rally.' He took up the offer.

'I remember writing this very boring speech,' he says, 'and then I walked into the back of this rally, and the meeting had already started. I walked up through the audience to take my place on the platform, about ten minutes before I was due to speak, and I suddenly thought, Now is the moment. Because this is all about the right of anyone, no matter what their sexuality is, to be capable of doing a decent job as a council employee. Exactly the same principle applies to MPs. In that ten minutes I was completely terrified. Having decided I was going to do it, in front of this audience of a thousand people, my knees were almost literally knocking together. I stood up and began my speech by saying, "My name is Chris Smith, I'm the Labour MP for Islington South and Finsbury and

I am gay."' Parliament had suddenly, without fanfare, found its good-as-you moment. 'The entire place got to its feet and gave me a standing ovation.' He raises an eyebrow. 'I will add that it's the only time I've had a standing ovation one minute into a speech.'

The incentive for his action had an unlikely precedent. Earlier that month, Smith attended the Pretty Policeman's Ball, a London Lesbian and Gay Switchboard charity fundraiser against police entrapment, the risible practice of engaging handsome young officers in plain clothes from the Met to patrol public lavatories and pubs in the Earl's Court area. He'd marvelled at the candour of the lesbian actress Miriam Margolyes's opening gambit. 'She came on and she just stood in the middle of the stage and said, "I am ..."' and the place went wild. I thought, Same principle here.'

There were two events after the Rugby moment that stick in his mind. One is touched with comedy. 'The television cameras around the room had all been switched off because they'd obviously thought, There's just this unknown backbench Labour MP about to speak. When I did my "I'm gay" you could see them all struggling to get the cameras rolling. So the actual moment of me saying it is not recorded on camera anywhere.' The second was less amusing for the young politician, then barely into his thirties. 'The other thing was, having done this and knowing that it was going to be reported in the newspapers the following day, I suddenly realised I had never told my parents.'

He made the necessary call on returning home. 'I said, "Mum, there's something I've been wanting to talk to you about for quite a while. And, by the way, you're going to be reading about it in the *Observer* tomorrow morning."' Her initial reaction was sympathetic. 'She was fine at that moment. Then, a few days later, I had letters from my father and mother which were much less positive. Within a year or so they had completely come round to it, but it was difficult for a while.'

Smith remembers Neil Kinnock, the first leader of the Labour Party he served under, being vocally supportive after he came out in Rugby, and encouragement came from both sides of the House. His favourite moment was an approach by Edwina Currie while queuing for a cup of tea in the Members' tearoom. 'She came marching up to me and said in a very loud voice – everyone could hear – "Chris! I hear you've come out. Well done!" And she turned on her heel and marched out.'

For the next decade, Chris Smith remained the only openly gay Member of Parliament, the one authentic voice opposing a Tory government entrenched in anti-gay legislation, dealing with the biggest medical crisis of modern times, one which disproportionately affected the lives of gay men, their families, friends and communities. 'The Tory Party really intensively blew the anti-gay dog-whistle. There was a huge controversy in the 1987 election about a book called *Jenny Lives with Eric and Martin*.'

Jenny Lives with Eric and Martin is a children's picture book, written by Susanne Bösche and first published with photos by Andreas Hansen in Copenhagen in 1981. In 1983 it was translated into English by Louis Mackay for the publishers Gay Men's Press. It was reprinted in 1987, an election year. *Jenny Lives with Eric and Martin* opens with a double-page spread. On the right-hand page there is a picture of a smiling child in a pinafore. On the left, the text reads: 'This is Jenny. She is five years old.' On the next spread, a picture of a man in a plaid shirt staring contemplatively to the bottom left-hand corner of the page with the words: 'This is Jenny's dad. He is called Martin.' The third spread, another man with hair parted and plaid shirt. 'This is Eric. He lives with Jenny's dad.' On the following page there is a picture of the three of them, a happy family, licking ice lollies on the doorstep of their small Danish home. We learn of Jenny's mum, Karen, who wears a lace blouse, lives nearby and 'visits them often'. Jenny's infant life looks frankly lovely. It would become in the public imagination, with considerable help from the homophobia of the national press, the apogee of malign offensiveness.

Jenny Lives with Eric and Martin was the start of Clause 28, the bill to outlaw 'the promotion' of homosexuality in the classroom. 'It was a lovely, sweet book,' says Smith. 'Yet there was this huge controversy around it because one copy had been discovered in a teaching centre. In Islington, of course. And so I remember at that 1987 general election there was a big Tory billboard which had a picture alluding to the book and the words "Is this Labour's Idea of a Comprehensive Education?"' There was more. 'It was the same election that they had a photograph of a soldier with his hands up in the air, and against that were the words "Labour's Policy on Arms". It was pretty crude, brutal advertising. The gay issue was something they really wanted to push.'

Smith says that while the Tory Party were running another intensely homophobic campaign – one he suspects did not come from Thatcher directly but a cabal of close allies – the Tory Party locally, 'could not have been better.' They never mentioned his sexuality. It was considered off limits. 'They never talked about it, never used the issue at all, anywhere.' Antipathy to his sexuality came from Smith's other rivals instead. 'Meanwhile, the SDP, who were the main challengers to Labour in the constituency, didn't put anything down in writing, but they were using the issue on doorsteps. We had a whole succession of reports about canvassers for the SDP on doorsteps talking about it, and basically saying, "You don't want to vote for him, he's queer."'

Chris Smith's team devised a strategy. 'We were training our own canvassers as to how to respond to this sort of thing if it ever came up on the doorstep. We gave them three lines to use. The first one was, "Isn't it good to have an MP who is honest for once?" The second line was, "But you know that Chris Smith works for everyone, no matter who or what they are?" And the third line, if neither of those two worked, was, "You're not meaning to tell me you're prejudiced, are you?" No one, at any stage in the campaign, had to get to line three. And my majority went up. It was still in three figures rather than five, but it went up.'

The Currant Bun

In 1998, barely a year into Blair's first term, David Yelland took over as editor of Britain's most popular newspaper, the *Sun*. He had been hired as the tabloid's business editor in 1992 before relocating to take up the position of deputy editor at the *New York Post* in 1995. David and his wife Tania took full advantage of the city, and they had many gay friends. He arrived back on British shores with a more progressive agenda than might have been expected from a new editor of the *Sun*.

Prior to the astonishing stranglehold on the national temperament seized by the *Mail* in the new millennium, the *Sun* had always dealt in a kind of tell-it-like-it-is populism and catch-all humour that seemed to divine an essence of the working character of the country. From the triumphalist roar of 'Gotcha' during the Falklands war to the deeply weird tale of Freddie Star and his mate's hamster, the newspaper's front covers dominated bus-stop and barroom chatter. An MP caught with his pants down, a footballer with a 20-quid note stuck up his nose, a newsreader's casual trip to the local sex dungeon, the Currant Bun was there to capture it all in its cheekiest details. The style of writing often felt like being told the news by the funniest bloke in the pub, the one who could turn every cadence of a sentence into a quip or pun. You knew where you were with the *Sun*, man and woman. They spoke as they found.

Part of the national character, it was assumed through the collation of stories, pictures, horoscopes, crossword puzzles and attention-grabbing headlines was to define yourself not by what you loved and accepted, but those things you despised and ridiculed. Women had never faired well out of it, mostly reduced to their anatomy on page 3. People of colour were routinely treated with suspicion, if not outright derision. The character of the entire city of Liverpool was picked out for a specially targeted, senseless hate campaign under Yelland's predecessor Kelvin MacKenzie over the disaster at Hillsborough football stadium, and Liverpudlians still refuse to buy the paper.

Somewhere beneath all of this, there was an all-encompassing hatred, fear and derision – an almost molecular disgust – of gay men. You didn't have to do anything; you just had to be gay. The characterisation of gay men in the national tabloid – and, to be fair, the *Mirror*, the *Star*, the *People* and most broadsheets weren't much better back then – had stalled somewhere between the five figurines of the Village People and the noose around Justin Fashanu's neck. To offer sympathy or empathy to such an easily derided portion of the population was somehow to intimate a personal effeminacy or weakness, as if offering the hand of friendship was a declaration of your own faggotry. The result of all this, in the home, through families, into school playgrounds and then tracing you, the target, into the workplace, was a codified, viral culture of rejection and victimhood. The *Sun* said gay = shame. The simplest maths stuck.

As it was on the page, so it was in the offices over at Wapping, too. David Yelland says that British tabloid culture when he began work was steeped in homophobia, a prejudice that could shift on a sixpence between the newsroom, the front page, office gossip and editorial cartoons. 'I came to the *Sun* when Kelvin MacKenzie was editing, just as the eighties turned into the nineties, and it was deeply homophobic, often in a – dare I say it – amusing, English, Benny Hill-type way.' This didn't bother him so much. We'd all grown up laughing at *Carry On* films, at Julian and Sandy, even now at Julian Clary and Lily Savage. Surely this was all part of the same thing? 'But also not,' he corrects. 'Put it this way, anyone in public office or in the church, or a headmaster or choirmaster, anyone who was in that position and was gay was considered fair game. There didn't have to be a hint of any illegal behaviour of any kind.' It was not a culture he was comfortable with. 'If you could put a team of reporters on a vicar and find that he was gay, that he'd been seen in the loos or a club in Vauxhall, if you could basically back up the fact that he was a gay man then off you went and wrote it.' The practice was known in the industry at the time as fronting someone up.

Like the Houses of Parliament prior to Chris Smith's coming out, Fleet Street was not in the habit of encouraging openness among its staff. There was nobody Yelland knew of at the newspaper to present an alternative scenario to these accepted practices of hounding innocent people, based squarely on rabid and endemic institutional prejudices. 'If there were any gay staff on the tabloids,' he notes, 'they certainly were in the closet.' Britain's most outspoken campaigner on gay rights, Peter Tatchell, he says, 'had been vilified in the *Sun* for 25 years.' When he took the editor's chair, Yelland would receive calls from Tatchell without telling his staff on the editorial floor, for fear of the repercussions from siding with an assumed enemy. 'It would have almost been a firing offence.'

Yet by 1998, Yelland sensed softening in the public mood. He'd noticed conspicuous figures in public life wearing their sexuality openly and without friction. Mark Bolland was then deputy private secretary to the Prince of Wales and was thought to have played a major role in rehabilitating the Prince's image through the storms his affair with Camilla Parker-Bowles becoming public knowledge presented. Guy Black, once a Tory MP and the former head of the Press Complaints Commission, was and still is Bolland's partner. They formed a formidable power couple, and they were friends with Yelland and his wife. Elton John's partner David Furnish had stepped into the spotlight as his boyfriend without causing any unnecessary fuss or concern among Elton's fanbase. Only three years previously, when Nigel Hawthorne had been nominated for a Best Actor Oscar for his astonishing turn in *The Madness of King George*, his partner of 27 years, Trevor Bentham, was instructed by a ceremonial flunky to walk five paces behind Hawthorne on the red carpet as straight stars strutted hand in hand.

David Yelland's appointment by Rupert Murdoch was understood to be a modernising manoeuvre. 'I felt very strongly that the readers had changed,' he says. 'British people, although they can be quite fascistic in some respects, are basically much more tolerant than people give them credit for. Just the fact that Boy George was every mum's favourite says it all.' He liked the London he returned to from New York. 'This was a time of growing tolerance in the UK. I was a young editor, brought in the year after Blair was elected, and it was felt that an editor of my age could liberalise the paper and that would be fine.' He was 35 when he took the job. 'And it did happen. People forget that in the first Tony Blair term we did feel things could only get better.'

A sizable hangover from the Kelvin MacKenzie years at the *Sun* needed to clear. 'There is a generation of editors who have a very old-fashioned view of gay men and of male homosexuality. They really hate it. I personally have never understood how some straight men have this absolute horror at what people get up to in private.'

Yelland distributed some of the medicine, by sacking MacKenzie's most notorious anti-gay mouthpiece, the increasingly anachronistic Garry Bushell. 'The reason I fired him was that he had written a book, which was littered with deeply, deeply homophobic material.' His dismissal didn't go down well with Bushell. 'He launched a campaign against me and vilified me on many websites. For many years he was quite vicious.'

Wiping homophobia from the pages of the nation's best-selling newspaper was never going to be easy. 'It's very difficult, or it was then, to take a stand on an issue like this because people would assume that you were gay or you were bisexual or that you had a secret.' Yelland didn't care about such inferences, but there was a more entrenched British newspaper culture that did. 'There's nowhere in public life in this country where people are less self-aware than at the top of Fleet Street. There are senior people in the press who are gay and in complete denial about it. We all know that. There's quite a lot of that very unhealthy behaviour where people in the press think that they are campaigners for freedom and that they are working class, when in many cases they are the exact opposite.' On a more personal note, Yelland simply enjoyed the company of gay people. 'I find gay men and gay women have an appreciation and gratitude for life which makes them really interesting, because once you've come out you may as well be authentic in every other aspect of your life.'

With Bushell's services dispensed of, Yelland had another notorious voice of the paper, then reaching optimum popularity with a big proportion of its readership, to navigate. Richard Littlejohn, he recalls, had a favourite apocryphal rumour gleaned from the gossipy corridors of Westminster that he would repeat often. When Littlejohn talked of Tony Blair he would say, 'He's not gay, but he helps them out at weekends.' 'He was obsessed,' says Yelland. Littlejohn had heard, and more astonishingly believed, a rumour on the parliamentary gossip vine that sometimes Blair could be seen walking the corridors of British power with his little finger intertwined with that of his closest ally, Peter Mandelson. Yelland would try to explain to Littlejohn that this was nothing more than a ludicrous old wives' tale. 'What a load of bollocks,' he says. 'There are an awful lot of stories like that that people in Fleet Street believed.'

Yelland and Littlejohn would often come to blows over the columnist's copy when the writer aired his thorny views on homosexuality. Littlejohn was kept a close eye on by Terry Saunderson, whose Mediawatch column in the monthly magazine *Gay Times* had become the most detailed inspection resource for homophobia in the press. 'It would be incorrect to say that we argued all the time about it because sometimes I went along with it,' says Yelland, 'particularly in my early days. There were times when I didn't argue with him. There were times when I did with him and Bushell. I would refuse to run things. I would love to say that I was consistent, but I wasn't. You get like that when you're young. You compromise and go along with them.'

Under Yelland's early watch, a story made the front page that was at odds with all his brave – some would say foolhardy – attempts to modernise the *Sun*. 'There was a massive cock-up on my watch,' he admits, 'which was that we printed a front page that was very homophobic.' On Monday 9 November 1998 the paper printed the front-page headline: 'Are We Being Run by a Gay Mafia?' prompted by the outing of a fourth member of Tony Blair's cabinet, Nick Brown. Times had changed since Chris Smith stood on a stage at a campaigning rally in Rugby: the cameras were well and truly on now. The story followed those of Welsh Secretary Ron Davies's 'moment of madness' (his spin) cruising Clapham Common and the political commentator and *Sun* columnist Matthew Parris, when being interviewed about the Davies incident, outing Peter Mandelson on *Newsnight*.

He didn't like the tone of the Gay Mafia story one bit. 'I threw my toys out of the pram with the senior staff.' In an editorial leader column run in the Thursday's *Sun*, Yelland apologised for the headline and announced that the paper would no longer out anyone in future without their consent. 'We will not invade the privacy of gay people,' he wrote. 'Our readers are tolerant of private behaviour and find unwarranted intrusion offensive.' The *Sun* under David Yelland, contrary to every editor of the paper before him, 'would encourage gay people to feel more at ease.' This was a major statement for the paper. It felt radical, surprising and part of a genuine countrywide surge towards acceptance.

The Mandelson episode prompted a serious headache for Yelland. 'It was one of the big memories of my time at the *Sun*.' When the *Newsnight* story broke he was out for dinner with, 'of all people, Richard Littlejohn.' His phone began ringing immediately. 'And I had to decide what to do. I had Alastair Campbell ringing me and Peter on the phone, repeatedly, telling me, "This is not a story." I had bloody Richard Littlejohn in the background, who hated Peter Mandelson.' Littlejohn's favourite insult for gay men at the time was 'iron', the cockney rhyming slang derived from iron hoof (poof). 'I'm on the phone to Peter Mandelson, in this very posh restaurant, trying to work out what to do, and Richard Littlejohn's sitting in the corner singing, "Any old iron, any old iron," at the top of his voice. Mandelson says, "Who's that?" I said, "It's Richard Littlejohn." And he said, "Oh, you live together? I always thought so."'

Part of this scenario, surely, was the exact rush you desire from becoming a tabloid newspaper editor? 'I knew that what I ought to do was not report it, but it was leading me to one extreme or another.' The man responsible for outing Mandelson on *Newsnight*, Matthew Parris, was relieved of his columnist duties at the *Sun*.

He thinks the specific tone of reportage on Mandelson didn't change or improve after his enforced confession, from the broadsheets to the tabloids, and across each British broadcast network. 'He has a deeply homophobic press in a way that you could only have in this country. It wasn't so much that they attacked him. It was the type of language they used, with a nod and a wink, purely judgemental and belittling.'

Yelland forged ahead with his mission to rid the paper of this pernicious language. It became a defining mission, obsessive almost. His parents would ring him and ask what the hell he was doing when another pro-gay editorial leader appeared in the paper, then another, then another. 'They thought I was going a bit mad.' It's funny to think of a heterosexual *Sun* editor becoming a deliberate part of the LGBT equality vanguard, but David Yelland is a distinct man of his own mind. 'You learn quickly,' he says, 'when you are editing a tabloid that doing the right thing does not earn you any friends, at all. It loses you friends internally. It loses you friends among the proprietor and the hierarchy, not because they're homophobic, but because they assume you've got your own personal agenda and they can see that you're not putting the readers first. Then it loses you friends externally because no one gives you any credit anyway.'

For the many gay people whose lives were made even a fraction easier by the nation's popular mouthpiece retracting its house stance of bawdy, hang-'em-all homophobia, Yelland became a kind of ghost hero, the wizard tearing back the curtain on tabloid culture's very own Oz. 'I can't actually believe someone noticed,' he says, a crack tracing his voice. 'But there were people that came out because of the *Sun*, that took courage from the change of stance and thought, Well, if the *Sun* have changed their position then things must be changing for the better and I can come out. I got letters. Not many, maybe a couple of dozen. But that's a lot of people to me. They weren't readers. They were people who'd read about it in the news.'

The person who had begun this whole dialogue in Yelland's mind got back in touch. 'The most moving call I got was from Tatchell. He said that, if he remembered correctly, he'd sued the *Sun* five times, he hated everything it stood for and he'd never buy it for the rest of his life, but he thought it had made a huge difference in what it had done. It did make it impossible for the competition to be homophobic for a while. It changed a lot of behaviour.'

His decision to reform the *Sun* wasn't totally altruistic, however. 'There was another aspect to it, which was that I wore a wig when I was a kid.' Yelland's hair fell out completely when he was nine years old. 'I have alopecia,' he explains. 'I wore wigs for 22 years, until I was in my early thirties and I was living in New York.' The most famous men to suffer from alopecia in British cultural history are both gay: the actor, writer and artist Kenneth Halliwell, whose self-confidence was crippled by it, and the comedian Matt Lucas, who turned it smartly and adroitly to his physical advantage and incorporated the feature into much of his crowd-pleasing comedy work. Yelland likens the moment of personal liberation of divesting himself of the condition's disguise to that defining gay experience of coming out: 'I went into the editorial conference at the *New York Post* one morning, and I said, "You all know that I wear a wig and have done for a long time, but tomorrow I won't," and I took it off. That, actually, is why I have an empathy not just with gay people, but with anybody who is in a minority.' The next day at work, he felt like a new man. 'I know the relief and joy that comes with being honest.'

Anti-gay Legislation, the Fightback

Because of the infamous dinner that Tony Blair and Gordon Brown took at the voguish restaurant Granita on Upper Street to sketch out their plans for rebranding the Labour Party, Islington has always been the London area most synonymous with the Blair administration. The north London suburb was a watermark district of gentrification, and it has good gay history: its southern half was Chris Smith's constituency, and the first British Gay Pride march, in 1973, wended its way from Highbury Corner down Upper Street toward Angel Islington station.

In 1987 the gala performance of the film *Prick Up Your Ears*, a masterful biopic about doomed local residents Joe Orton and his partner Kenneth Halliwell, was held at the Screen on the Green, the boutique cinema halfway down Upper Street. The film made an unlikely star of Alfred Molina, as Halliwell, and cemented the irresistible early career trajectory of the British screen idol of the hour, Gary Oldman, as Orton. Halliwell and Orton lived and died in a single room on Noel Road, ten minutes' walk from the cinema. The screenplay for the film was written by Camden neighbour Alan Bennett. Chris Smith attended.

'It was almost certainly much easier for me to do what I had done in Islington,' Smith says, 'than it would have been for many of my colleagues in other seats around the country. There is a wonderful moment in *Prick Up Your Ears* when two elderly female librarians are coming out of the library.' Orton and Halliwell received prison sentences in the sixties for the artful, provocative and sexual graffiti they'd daub and paste into books meant for public usage. 'They've been talking about these defaced books,' he continues. 'One of the women says, "I understand that these are two homosexuals." The other one says to her, "Homosexuals? In Islington?" and the entire cinema roared with laughter.'

Prick Up Your Ears was released a year before the introduction of Clause 28. 'I didn't take it as a personal affront,' Smith says of the bill. 'I took it absolutely as an affront to me and many thousands of people like me and to the whole cause of humanity and decency. But there was one very revealing moment, I thought. It was one of the debates we were having on the floor of the Commons about Clause 28, which I think was still Clause 27 at that point. One of the Neanderthal Tories, Nicholas Winterton, was giving a speech, and I intervened to make a point. I sat down, having made my point, and he said, "The House has learned to listen to the Honourable Gentleman with respect when he talks about these matters." I was there, in the chamber. He couldn't just pretend that these were other people he was talking about, when there was one of them sitting right in front of him. And he had to pay due respect.' Chris Smith learned to graciously receive these incremental steps to equality in opposition. 'Even in those difficult days, when there was so much homophobia around, I thought that we'd made a tiny little bit of progress.' In government, he could begin to effect change in earnest, sincerely, from a position of truth divested of the idea of shame or victimhood.

He enjoyed his backbench years and subsequent entry to the shadow cabinet. 'On the whole, yes. They were infinitely frustrating because we were miles away from power and there was this horrible government that was doing all these wretched things to the British economy and society.' Because of his unique position in British politics for almost a decade, he occasionally crossed party lines when it came to admiring the work of his parliamentarian colleagues. He retained a special fondness for Norman Fowler's handling of the AIDS crisis. 'Fowler,' he says, 'played a remarkably noble role in all that. Partly because he convinced Thatcher and everyone else that this had to be taken seriously and the proper resources had to be devoted to it, and partly because he realised there was a job of public education to be done. I have my quibbles with some of the advertising that went along with that, but the principle of public education was a sensible one. Thirdly, he ring-fenced the money. It was absolutely the right thing to do.'

After his close friend and ally John Smith died while leader of Her Majesty's Opposition, Chris Smith voted for Tony Blair in the resulting Labour leadership election. 'I'd been very, very close to John. He'd been a very good friend, through the coming out and subsequently. History would have been very different had he lived. But I decided that I was going to vote for Blair, largely because I thought he had the best chance of winning us an election, though I had my doubts about his commitment to social justice.' In the event, Blair returned Labour to power after 18 years in the wilderness. Smith received the news at the Sobell Leisure Centre in Islington, where his vote was counted. When he was given the job of Culture, Media and Sport the next day, he became the first openly gay cabinet minister anywhere in the world.

Smith is disarmingly casual about the many firsts he chalked up as an MP. 'One of the fascinating things was that no one really noticed,' he says. He is neither a showy nor boastful man. 'We had actually made rather a lot of progress. It had ceased to be news that I was gay and that I happened to be appointed to the cabinet.' The story of British gay political equivalence is forever a snakes-and-ladders game of two steps up and one slippery slope back down. As an active member of a minority, you become attuned early to this frustrating method of progress, one in which battles must be lost in order to win wars. You get used to the slow drip-feed of information getting through, the centimetre by centimetre pushing of a sticking door until one day it creeks open and you manage to slip through. 'I think by that stage, for me, it was such old hat that journalists were no longer writing about it. It was an accepted bit of public fact. I had absolutely removed the news value from it.' The same was true of his constituency, where Smith's margin of victory upped from 363 votes in 1983 to nearer 15,000 in 1997's Labour landslide. If you think gay visibility doesn't matter, the hard statistics often prove otherwise. 'But then, of course,' says Smith, 'we had to get the government to start on a programme of reform.'

Homosexual equality was not achieved quite as effortlessly under Blair as history draws it. In the years of and since his premiership, Blair has become individually associated with a programme of liberalising homosexual legal reform that he was initially reticent to pursue. The constitutional programme for reform deemed most urgent by the MPs pushing Blair for change began with equalising the age of consent, the repeal of Clause 28, the provisions for the armed forces, and equal access to goods and services. There were adoption and parental laws to unpick. There was a whole raft of gender-assignment legislation to breathe into life. There were hate laws to draw up, and lastly, of symbolic and metaphysical significance, a government statute to recognise gay relationships as equal to straight, a fizzing new can of contention to open. 'There were a number of people who were arguing passionately that we have to get a move on with all this,' says Smith. Naturally, he was one of them. He mentions the banner names, Waheed Alli and Michael Cashman, outspoken advocates of the pressing and urgent need for reform. 'And, interestingly, Jack Straw, who was remarkably, strongly positive on LGBT issues, partly I think because a very close friend of his at school had been gay.'

Blair and Mandelson and the rest of the Prime Minister's inner circle, Smith says, were less keen to pull the change trigger. 'In the early period, the first year or so, Blair and his office at Number 10 were scared stiff of what the public and political fallout would be if they started to make progress on lesbian and gay rights.' He can remember specific discussions. 'We were pushing for doing something on the age of consent and they were very, very reluctant to do it.' The fear from Number 10 was that, having earned the backing of Middle England, they'd lose them all over again by endorsing radical social shifts that only ten years ago had cost them an election under Neil Kinnock.

It was not as if there wasn't ammunition being stoked from the opposition. 'William Hague – about whom no more need be said – defended Clause 28,' Paul Gambaccini notes. 'Even when it was clearly a dead duck. He was leader of the Conservative Party when the Commons had voted to overturn it. Entrepreneur and gay-rights campaigner Ivan Massow told me he was at a Conservative fundraising dinner where William Hague said, "I've had great news. the Lords has voted to retain Clause 28." I mean, he did not have to do that. You do not have to champion discriminatory legislation.

So to me, William Hague is always a villain. Whether you wish to put the name hypocrite to him too is up to you.'

Chris Smith says Blair was terrified of anything that could potentially lose him popularity. 'What will the fallout be? Will we lose swathes of pensioners voting for us who will decide to vote for the Tories instead? What will the tabloid newspapers do?' A compromise was struck with the MPs leaning heavily on Blair for LGBT equality, with the full backing of the pressure group Stonewall. 'And so the bargain that was done was that a a test case for the equal age of consent would be brought to the European Court. If the European Court ruled on it that would then force the government to do something, and the government could say, "It's not us, we're being made to do this." That is precisely what happened. A case went to the European Court, a decision was made, the government then said, "We've got to change the law," and they changed it. All through that time we had to push and push and push to get this done.'

The public mood afterwards was almost entirely as Smith, Cashman, Alli and their allies had predicted. 'Having achieved it, the roof didn't fall in. The tabloids didn't go berserk.' David Yelland was setting the temperature in those quarters. 'Pensioners weren't in the slightest bit worried about what had happened.'

Tasting the intoxicating liquor of public popularity, Blair's attitude to relaxing LGBT laws quickly shifted at home-affairs meetings. 'And suddenly, Blair and his office became completely relaxed about moving further in the direction of LGBT equality,' says Smith. 'That first bit was really difficult to get them to agree to do, but after that everything else came pretty easily. Now, of course, he will and frequently has advanced a lot of what the government did as being the triumph of the government.' Are you suggesting that wasn't the case? 'Oh, I think it was, but in those initial stages it was much stickier.' And it might not have happened? 'I think there

were enough forces within the party pushing that it would have
happened anyway, eventually, but they were much more nervous
about it than I'd hoped they would be from the outset.'

Chris Smith is mindful enough not to point out the fact that
he could have expected some reticence from New Labour's inner
caucus given an earlier experience with its chief cheerleader. In
rhythm and tempo, Peter Mandelson's outing on *Newsnight* was
almost the exact opposite of Smith's in a Rugby meeting hall 14
years previously. 'And, of course, the Mandelson response, which
was, "How dare you!" then phoning the director of programmes
and whatever else happened.' Ringing the editor of the *Sun* and
asking him to suppress the story. 'But, of course, Peter has never,
ever been open about his sexuality.'

The frustration of a figure like Peter Mandelson from a gay-
rights perspective is not his hesitance to talk openly and divest
homosexuality of its shame. That is his business, a step under the
microscope not all feel the need to take. What is so frustrating is
that for him personally, with so much rumination and catcalling,
his entire media profile may well have shifted had he taken up the
idea of transparency that was directly suggested to him earlier.
'Mandelson had come to see me,' says Chris Smith. 'He'd sought
me out when he was still working for the Labour Party as the
director of communications. He came to see me because he was
about to start trying for the Hartlepool nomination. He wanted my
advice about how to handle issues about sexual orientation.'

On this subject, Chris Smith was unequivocal. He was the only
person with any real, irrefutable evidence to offer. 'I said, "Look,
be as open as you possibly can be. It's the only way in which you'll
ever be able to handle this." I did think that, and this was even
back in the 1980s, in Hartlepool people are going to respect that.'
Mandelson furrowed his own path instead, opting to keep quiet
until forced out of the shadows on *Newsnight*. 'He took no notice

of my advice at all. I think his life would have been an awful lot happier and easier if he had decided to do that.'

For Chris Smith, it was not the umpteen Labour triumphs in equalising LGBT rights that is sharpest in his memory from the story of gay equality in Britain. 'The most gratifying thing of all, of course,' he says, 'is to see a Conservative government bringing in equal marriage. Completely astonishing. If you'd told me 25 years before I would have thought you were completely bonkers.' The period between *Jenny Lives with Eric and Martin* and David Cameron's coalition cementing the last equality right for gay men and women in the Marriage (Same Sex Couples) Act was one of tangible cultural metamorphosis. 'If you'd told me,' he qualifies, 'that the majority for equal marriage was greater in the House of Lords than it was in the House of Commons, I would have thought you were even more bonkers.'

Over his 22 years in parliament, Smith developed a casual acquaintanceship with *Sun* editor David Yelland. 'There was a wonderful moment,' he recounts. 'Mary Ann Sieghart had done a long piece about me and my then partner in *The Times*. It was a full page and a photograph of the two of us at home, a long and very positive story about the two of us.' Murdoch towers had begun its proper atonement for the Andrew Neil AIDS-story debacle. 'And this was picked up by the *Sun*, who reproduced it almost word for word – except any word longer than three syllables was shortened.' Yelland's staff, as Smith recalls, took only one liberty with the story. 'It was labelled a "*Sun* exclusive". At the bottom of this piece – this page or maybe page and a half in the *Sun* – there was a poll asking the reader to "tell us what you think" of this, what they called, "open relationship".' He forgave them the slightly odd phrasing, and waited nervously to see whether Yelland would be proved right on what he thought about the all new *Sun* reader. 'I thought, God, this is going to be terrible, and they're going to publish the results and 90 per cent of people will say this is dreadful, irresponsible and evil. About three weeks later nothing had appeared in the paper about it. I met David Yelland at a reception, and I said to him, "You know that poll you ran at the bottom of the article?" And his brow furrowed and he said, "Oh yes, virtually no one responded."'

The final piece of Chris Smith's parliamentary firsts jigsaw slotted into place in his last year in office. In 2005, the year after the Civil Partnership Act and 21 years since he had come out publicly in Rugby, Chris Smith became the first parliamentarian in Britain to come out as HIV-positive. 'They knew about my HIV status about two or three years beforehand,' he says of the *Sunday Times*. 'I had specifically asked them, partly because my mother was still alive and partly because it's actually quite a difficult thing to do to say something about your health status, so I said to them, "Look, at some stage I will want to say something about this and I guarantee I will say this with you, but I would rather you didn't now."' The editor honoured his request. 'This is a tribute to the *Sunday Times*; they respected that right the way through.'

Occasionally, the editor would phone and ask if the time was right to run the story. On 6 January 2005, Nelson Mandela's son Makgatho died of AIDS in Johannesburg. 'Mandela made this speech about how we have to stop hiding this and we have to be open about it,' says Smith. 'I sort of thought, Well, perhaps I should. And so I decided I was going to do it.' He called the *Sunday Times* editor and said he was ready to talk about his HIV status, but asked that he be afforded the kindness of writing the piece in his own hand. 'They ran a big thing on the front page and I did a thing on *ITV News* the following morning.' The reaction was swift and dramatic. 'There was endless stuff in the papers over the next couple of days, almost all of it really constructive, positive stuff, with the exception of one opinion piece in the *Mail*.'

Of the piece he carefully scripted, Smith says, 'I was sort of saying two things. One was that I hoped I'd been able to demonstrate that you can have HIV and lead a very full, contributing life as a really good citizen. The second, in a really perverse kind of way, was that I had been lucky, because I had this thing in a country where there is a national health service, where the medical response is very good and there are an awful lot of people around the world who have been nowhere near as lucky. That all seemed to go down very well.'

The crowning moment came when he returned to his parliamentary office the following Monday morning. 'There was a note on my desk,' he remembers, 'saying "please can you call Mr Mandela", with a phone number underneath it. So I rang this number and there he was at the other end of the line. For ten minutes we chatted. He said, "Well done, thank you. It's terribly important that you've done this."' It was a rather moving moment.' On 22 June 2005, Chris Smith was given his life peerage, becoming Baron Smith of Finsbury. His work continues.

7. POSTER BOYS AND PINUPS

Express Delivery

At the end of 1999, I interviewed for a job at *Attitude* magazine. The meeting took place in a small room on the ground floor of the publisher Northern & Shell's office suite, a waterside glass construction one stop south of Canary Wharf on the toytown trains of London's Docklands Light Railway, opposite the Olympic-sized Isle of Dogs Asda. I'd freelanced on and off for the magazine for a couple of years and met the editor, Adam Mattera, one night a few months earlier with a friend. He had an encyclopaedic knowledge of black music and a rivetingly witty and idiosyncratic turn of phrase. He called everyone 'doll'.

One of the rites of passage for aspiring *Attitude* writers was to pen an 'Icons' column, in which you'd pay tribute to a particular gay hero in 1,200 words. I did mine on Stevie Nicks, and in my interview Adam mentioned an aside I'd written about her being carved into Mount Rushmore: 'If only you could crimp stone.' This appealed to his exact humour. I learned quickly upon arrival that the office vernacular was two parts Jacqueline Susann to one part *Brookside*. It was a working life I felt happy to aspire to.

For almost a year prior to *Attitude* I'd worked at the *Daily Express*, my first London job. I was the deputy editor of XY, the first men's section of a British newspaper, started as a response to the phenomenal success of men's magazines like *Loaded* and *FHM*. The *Express* was a baptism of professional fire. Every Monday morning in the conference room, after the news editor had relayed the latest events in Kosovo, I had to speak about the launch of a fancy new cologne or why Gail Porter mattered, bullet points I could only ever mumble through on account of my never quite getting over the fact that I recognised the editor off the telly. Rosie Boycott was a famed seventies feminist charged with modernising the *Express* for the new millennium. Office apocrypha had it that she'd taken the senior editors from the paper on a tour of its heartland in the north of England, where it was most widely read by senior citizens. At one event in a Yorkshire village hall, Rosie had apparently stood up and delivered her opening speech about how the paper was being made 'by people like you, for people like you', only to be rebuffed by a nice old fellow at the back of the room who stood up and said, 'I don't think so. There's no one called Topaz Amoore round here,' referring to one of the senior feature writers sitting by her side. The tour didn't last much longer.

Dotted around the editorial floor in a grand building on Blackfriars Road were other famous faces with big opinions: Andrew Marr, Andrew Pierce and Peter Hitchens. My boss was an almost inconceivably bright and handsome man who spoke in a perfectly composed strain of RP, dressed like a character from a John le Carré novel at 27 and was later long-listed for the Booker Prize. I was surprised by how young some of the senior staff were and once asked a friend there how the features editor had got such a high-powered job so young. 'His mum plays tennis with the editor' came the reply, delivered without exclamation, as if nepotism was the most natural professional asset with which to be blessed. I heard someone being laughed at because of a particular college they'd attended at Oxford, and that ex-Cambridge graduates were allowed to dismiss those from Oxford on grounds of intellectual inferiority. This was all news to me, an alarming set of new pecking orders I could never have conceived of before witnessing them first-hand, but ones that helped me disentangle some of the more preposterous ways Britain is run.

It turned out that these strange hierarchies weren't all that was going at the paper. Rosie had employed a lot of formidable women in senior positions. The managing editor was a woman. The paper employed two black women in important roles – including one on the sports desk – which on an editorial floor of over 100 may sound like paltry tokenism, but for the fact that they were two of only three black women working in senior editorial positions across all of Fleet Street at the time.

Unlike the tabloid culture David Yelland talked about stepping into at the end of the eighties, the *Express* had a strong, positive and vocal gay presence, from star voices like Pierce's right down to graduate trainees. The showbiz desk was manned by Ben Summerskill, who later became head of Stonewall. His right hands were John Lyttle, the first gay columnist to write specifically in his own voice on a British national daily during Rosie Boycott's earlier appointment at the *Independent*, and Simon Gage, the editor who revolutionised the free gay press into something witty, knowing, sexy and proudly working class during his anarchic time at *Boyz* magazine. There were at least two gay men on the books desk. Rosie's finest journalist by several streets was Ros Wynne-Jones, the war correspondent who later decamped to the *Mirror* to script brilliant, pioneering work on social justice.

These were the days Fleet Street was just turning digital, when email felt exciting and the cuts room was starting to gather dust. The favoured office pub was still a wine bar. There were expense accounts, fax machines and long lunches dotting a culture of excess, alcohol, fights over bylines, and some more serious backstabbing. Our two-man team at XY had a pitiful four pages to produce weekly with the help of an allotted secretary. One day, a pre-fame S Club 7 arrived in the office to lip-sync and dance to 'Bring It All Back' for the showbiz desk. Two weeks later they were number one. The clash between a progressive editor with neat modernising touches and S Club 7 interviews didn't quite match the elderly readership. Sales didn't spike, but morale was good. Nonetheless, whenever I walked through the elaborate glass gateway to the *Express* there was the nagging feeling at the back of my mind that I had just arrived in London in my twenties and was working for a paper talking mostly to folk aged 60-plus back home.

The first cover star of XY was David Beckham, at the time with Manchester United and on his way to securing the treble – the Premier League, FA Cup and UEFA Champions League – an achievement not seen before, and likely never again. We did some other good work that year. My favourite commission was interviewing author Bret Easton Ellis, a long-standing hero of mine, then promoting *Glamorama*, a masterful, prophetic novel about a male model that served as a precursor to both reality television and Zoolander. We did the interview in the lobby of the hotel One Aldwych, and it was one Ellis suggested we continue upstairs in his room once his PR had disappeared and the sun had set, an invitation that caught me quite off guard (we didn't).

I'd been taken cautiously under the wing of Chris Williams, the paper's deputy editor, when I heard about a job freeing up at *Attitude*. At the interview, Adam and I got along quickly and well. I said I'd like to take the job. He looked at me as if I was mad to leave the *Daily Express* to work on the magazine. Chris echoed his reaction when I told him I was leaving the paper to work at a small gay title, before sending me to the managing editor to be offered a substantial pay increase. At *Attitude* I would earn £800 a month. But I was young, impulsive and had a council tenancy on a two-bedroom fourteenth-floor flat in front of the Arsenal ground which cost £240 a month to rent.

On the same afternoon I handed my notice in, I attended a features meeting at the *Express*. I'd been offered an interview with Miuccia Prada, the Italian fashion magnate and designer of whom I was and still am a big fan. (I'd bought a grey Miu Miu cagoule for £180 from Selfridges with my first pay cheque from the *Express*, comfortably the most money I'd ever deposited in a bank account.) I mentioned it – the interview with Miuccia, not the cagoule – to the features editor, and he thought she was too esoteric for the readers. He brought up the Bret Easton Ellis cover of XY. These people, he implied, not unfairly, are figures you are interested in. You are not thinking of the readers. He offered me an interview with the daytime TV gardening expert Alan Titchmarsh as penance and acquittal, which I politely declined.

It was at that moment that I understood that the *Daily Express* was probably not the right full-time home for me. So I packed up my belongings and moved for four hilarious years into the new heart of the gay media, from one prevailing mood of manhood to quite another.

The Journalist

Attitude launched in May 1994 under the editorship of Tim Nicholson, a straight man. Tim and his wife, Jane Phillips, had spotted an opening in the market for a high-end, glossy gay lifestyle magazine and taken their proposal to Richard Desmond, the head of

Northern & Shell, for whom they'd already worked. Desmond was then most famously publishing the celebrity bible and heavyweight seller *OK!* magazine, as well as a portfolio of lightly dusted top-shelf and satellite-TV porn. Tim and Jane had some pedigree in the prospective market after launching *Only Women* magazine, a crossover titivation aimed at women and shared by some gay men.

In 1994, the buzz phrase 'the pink pound' had been passed around the London offices of advertising conglomerates, describing the emergence of a cash-rich, time-rich gay demographic with no dependants who were buying into the high-end dreams of luxury holidays, booze and retail. Tim and Jane had consulted heavily with two gay frontmen for *Attitude*'s launch, Pas Paschali and Paul Burston. The latter was the editor of the London listings magazine *Time Out*'s gay section, the only man in mainstream British media to appear under the words 'Lesbian and Gay' every week on the newsstand.

Burston was friends with Tim and Jane. 'I was frustrated with the way that the gay press was at the time,' he says, 'and wanted to do something a bit more ambitious. They were the people with the publishing know-how, which I didn't have. We went to Northern & Shell together as a team. One of the things with Richard Desmond was that if we'd gone to a more mainstream publisher they'd have seen a gay magazine as a bit embarrassing, whereas to him we were the respectable magazine in the family. It was quite the reversal of fortunes.'

'When *Attitude* came along,' says Adam Mattera, 'I think what Northern & Shell did, quite wisely, because their interest was purely commercial, was to spot a burgeoning gay shift in culture and the pink pound. They saw that a new socio-economic group that had money was being defined. Therefore, there was an opportunity to make money off it. The people that were first involved were a great editorial team who could translate that into something new.'

Attitude chimed with more significant societal shifts than commercial opportunism. Straight men and women were going to lauded gay clubs which had been renewed with fresh energy and vitality. TV had started responding. 'There had been *Out on Tuesday* on Channel 4,' explains Mattera, 'and a little later Tony and Simon on *EastEnders, Beautiful Thing* at the theatre, then the cinema. It was an opening up of something that had previously been ghettoised and marginalised.' Confirming the indelible imprint the gay world was having on the mainstream, the comic Julian Clary interrupted the British Comedy Awards with an apology for his lateness with the appendage, 'I'm sorry, I was just fisting Norman Lamont.' It was a gripping moment of live-television aggravation that could well be gay culture's Sex Pistols moment of pure, unapologetic punk righteousness delivered to British heartlands.

Out on Tuesday was Channel 4's politer weekly gay magazine show. The first episode was presented by Paul Gambaccini. 'Abseil Productions, an independent production company mostly run by lesbians, called me up,' he explains. 'They said, "We have this series on Channel 4 on gay and lesbian themes. Will you present one of the programmes?"' He liked the sound of it. 'I said, "I will, provided it's the first." I thought, OK, whatever happens, this programme is going to make history.' There were obvious sections of the British TV audience and its religious watchdogs who would object to the programme. 'We all dreaded a response from Mary Whitehouse types – possibly from Mary Whitehouse herself – saying stop this dreadful programme.'

This was virgin territory for British TV programming. 'There had been a Grace Jones party programme from Heaven broadcast before,' says Gambaccini, 'which was the only nationally broadcast programme with a gay theme. So I thought, OK, this one is going to be serious. Programme number one is going to make history. Let's be there.' He kicked off the show with a to-camera piece filmed on Westminster Bridge, standing square and proud in front of the Houses of Parliament. 'My intro to the show was, "Never before have I lived in a country which has voluntarily taken a step backwards in human rights." Most of the first programme was about Clause 28. Can homosexuality be promoted? To me there was a moral imperative to speak truth to power.'

Paul Burston says there were two imperatives to the launch of *Attitude*. 'There was a whole load of people out there who wanted a gay magazine that was a bit more outward-looking.' *Out* magazine, America's closest equivalent to *Attitude*, was already on the market. 'It was a difficult balance to strike in some ways because we did get some quite pissed-off readers, straight away. They wanted more scene coverage, but that stuff was already out there.' The second imperative was more combative. 'We really wanted to fill that gap between traditional gay magazines and the closeted-ness of men's style magazines. I was quite annoyed at how *Arena* magazine always addressed its readers as if they were straight. It really, really angered me, knowing very well that at least a portion of their market would be gay. We had a real agenda. We did go out to ruffle feathers.'

Burston had form for contentious editorial at *Time Out*. He was a troublemaker from the outset, upsetting sacred cows in the gay world, sitting closer to the equality politics of the gay pressure group OutRage! than the more establishment-friendly Stonewall. He had written a blistering excoriation of Ian McKellen, for calling out the behaviour of gay protestors in Parliament Square when the age of consent hadn't been equalised. 'It was just after Derek Jarman had died,' he recalls. The director of *The Last of England, Jubilee* and *Sebastiane* was the start of a new visual conversation in Britain, one spread-eagled across and informed by the epochs defined culturally by punk and socially by AIDS, passed on 19 February 1994, aged 52. 'It was all very emotional. When it came out that they'd voted to lower the age of consent to 18 and not equality, there was basically a riot. I felt that was the dignified response. McKellen came out and made this speech scolding the crowd and blaming us for the vote going the wrong way. I thought that was disgraceful and told him at the time.' The missive didn't go down well. 'He went absolutely ballistic, got my home phone number and pretty much told me I wasn't entitled to my own opinion.'

Burston delivered a searing attack on the London gay scene, the exact opposite of the bells-and-whistles positivity of the free gay press necessitated by the need to please advertisers. 'I had written a piece about how I didn't identify with what was now being passed off as gay culture. I found it demeaning, patronising and infantilising.' The first issue of *Attitude* he remembers being received with a heated mixture of celebration and vilification. Boy George was the cover star. 'There was some absolutely vicious bitching. It was quite extraordinary. It wasn't a gay magazine in the sense of what had come before it. A large part of what *Attitude* was about was blurring the lines between what men's magazines and gay men's magazines were.'

To this end, there were several suggestions Paul made to Tim and Jane concerning the magazine's editorial content. 'I wanted a column called 'Straight Talking', where there'd be a straight person writing, again to blur these boundaries of what gay and straight was. For the first or second one we had Suzanne Moore. It was a way of getting some big-name writers into the magazine. Julie Burchill was going to write something for us but told us she couldn't because she found out it was owned by a pornographer. She sent me this sweet message saying, "I'm really sorry, I can't do it and it's not homophobia, it's just *him*."'

Paul introduced the important and emerging voice of Mark Simpson, whose recently published book *Male Impersonators* was setting up the tenets of a new discussion of male desire and consumerism, and who would coin the term 'metrosexual'. In his review of the book, another gay Fleet Street voice at the *Independent*,

Philip Hensher, described Simpson as 'the skinhead Oscar Wilde'.
Simpson was adept at redrawing masculinity into something bespoke
for shifting times. 'He wrote about those blurring boundaries
between gay and straight exceptionally well. He was very spiky. You
would always laugh out loud at his copy. It was sharp and pointed
and people would talk about it.'

Mark Simpson's was the beginning of a debate beyond
acceptance and equality, foraging in the undergrowth of male
desire. 'He said things about the gay scene in a way that hadn't
been said before,' says Adam Mattera. 'We were free to actually
begin to articulate a voice critical of mainstream gay culture. We
were free to ask what it meant to be gay. You didn't have to be
gay in one narrow definition of the word. Mark would write an
article about, say, going to a gay sauna, subjects that you'd never
read people being so honest and frank about before. He wasn't
just writing about the superficial side of that, but the psychological
inner questions that people would ask themselves as a gay man. And
he'd ask them in a really exposing, honest way that would put him
directly on the line. I don't remember ever reading anything like
that before him. I don't really remember anyone going beyond the
surface. There was no editor imposing constraints on Mark to tell
him how to speak to a mainstream audience.'

The Godfather of Metrosexuality

Mark Simpson cannot even remember if he was given a brief for
his inaugural *Attitude* column. 'I said I'd love to write a column,'
he says, 'but it wouldn't be about gays. I'm not interested in gays.
So it's going to be about the straight world and how it's not so
straight, really.' It was christened 'It's a Queer World', an ironic
riff on Disney utopianism. 'It was not about the queer world as we
know it, but about all those naff things that I specialised in.'

The origins of the word 'naff' are tricky to define and include references from way before it found a home in the tricksy, campy gay vernacular Polari, which emerged in the late fifties. Decades later it was accepted to be an acronym, or backronym, gay men used to refer to straight men, meaning Not Available For Fucking. One of *Attitude*'s early editorial obsessions, and certainly one of Simpson's, was the newly termed demographic 'strays', straight men that sometimes sleep with gay but do not identify as bisexual, widening further the remit of whom overt and covert gay culture took into its embrace.

Simpson's It's a Queer World was given two pages. His specialty was to peer between the cracks of local social reportage. 'I'd go to shopping centres and bingo halls and watch daytime TV, and bring my own perverse faculties and sense of humour, such as it is, to bear on it.' He would meander through the changing patterns of masculinity at his own tempo. 'Everyone was getting very excited about untucking their shirts and pretending they liked football at the time. Hence why Oasis were so important. I'm not saying they weren't incredibly important to and popular with people in the north, but they were totemic of that strange search for authenticity in the white middle-class male media of the time.'

Simpson had noticed a shift in masculinity in the early, forward-thinking straight men's style magazines *Arena* and *GQ*. 'They had pioneered the men's lifestyle market but had never significantly broken out of the circulation figures of the gay magazine market. You could talk about blokes in the early nineties in a way that you couldn't really talk about blokes now. The idea of a regular bloke, I'm not really sure what that is anymore. But back then, most blokes did not want to be seen reading *Arena* or *GQ* on the train because they would be thought a bit of a poof, a bit poncey.'

He saw in *Loaded* and *FHM*, the less elitist, more commercially minded and successful offspring of *Arena* and *GQ*, a sharpening of the market. 'The formula for taking men's lifestyle and the gayness of it and the metrosexuality of it to the masses was to hysterically assert its heterosexuality, to the point where it was actually very camp. This formula was eventually perfected by *FHM*.' At its peak, FHM was shifting close to a million copies a month to men divested of the shame of trying something women had been doing for years: buying into the glossy dream of the fantasy version of themselves. 'They were called *For Him Magazine*!' says Simpson. 'You couldn't get any gayer.' In their presentation and marketing, these magazines specialised in the worship of modern men, engendering a new form of boys' own tribalism which played directly to their times. 'It inoculated men's lifestyle magazines and also the down-low metrosexuality that new-lad magazines stood for. Buying glossy magazines wasn't gay. This was what lads did. The whole idea of "new lad" was a marketing concept anyway. It was a way of selling something new and non-traditional as traditional, blokey and normal.' There was an unfortunate side effect of all this redrawing of gender boundaries for women, one which would eventually pollute the heroic sales spikes of the defining men's magazines in the nineties. 'Of course, when those magazines were accused of sexism, this was music to their ears, because sexism is about as traditional as you can get. You were perfectly entitled to attack them for sexism if you wanted, but it was precisely what they wanted.'

The advent of *Loaded* and *FHM* had coincided with a major surge in male objectification, a new twist for British culture that *Attitude* rode hard. Male beauty had been a cause for quietly acceptable celebration in the old media since Elvis first curled his lip and swung his hips. Male beauty has always enjoyed an unspoken role in documenting its age. The male pinup was not new, but conversation about him, particularly among men, was.

The advertising industry has an especially coercive sideline in male beauty. In the seventies aftershave adverts, a clone-like, hairy-chested idol emerged in the figure of Burt Reynolds, a look later capitalised on by Tom Selleck. By the early nineties we reached a new peak with the imagery shot by Herb Ritts for the Calvin Klein underwear and fragrance campaigns, debuted in Times Square and sent around the world to conspicuous billboard ubiquity and a pulverising effect on how men would reappraise their own and other men's bodies.

These adverts, a thrilling new line in the sand for public displays of male sexuality, cemented Kate Moss's place as a generational icon. Her co-star, 'Marky' Mark Wahlberg, was an uncommon body beautiful with a blue-collar New Jersey background, a brother in New Kids on the Block and a pocketbook full of petty convictions. 'It was a stirring in the underpants moment,' says Simpson, 'but it was certainly a watershed. That moment is still very much with us and continues to be more and more extreme.'

Mark Wahlberg for Calvin Klein was the start of authorised male objectification. 'I was more interested in that than metrosexuality,' says Simpson. Getting men to have another man's name clinging to their waistband, circumnavigating their most erotic entry zones, was Klein's masterstroke of consumerism, one that would ripple across the world of high fashion for decades to come and has not been rivalled before or since in terms of selling the male body back to itself. 'The weird thing,' says Simpson, 'is that even though that campaign got a lot of attention at the time, because it was the first campaign of its type with that degree of explicitness – as some US chat-show host said at the time, "He's got a hold of himself and he's on the side of a goddamn bus!" – what's really odd is that in the couple of decades after that so many people managed to pretend that male objectification wasn't happening.'

It was Mark Simpson's duty to point out what the straight eye self-selected not to see: 'Of course somebody like me is going to notice male objectification.' He mentions an editor he once encountered. 'It was a progressive, liberal, right-on *Guardian* writer who once said to me, "Well, Mark, the thing about you is, you see what you want to see." What that meant was, because he's straight, he sees things as they are. Actually, because you're straight, you don't see what's in front of your fucking face, because straightness involves not just a way of seeing the world, but a denial of certain possibilities. If you are gay, you're very well aware of how the world is supposed to work and of what you're supposed to look at. The fact that I am gay doesn't disqualify what I see, but it does make it more difficult for some people to swallow.'

He mentions another incident, at Radio 4 when he was invited on to *Woman's Hour* to talk about the homoeroticism of rugby. 'Before we go on air,' he says, 'I get a voice in my ear saying, "Now, Mark, I need to remind you this is a family programme, so please bear that in mind." I was then presented with the point-blank refusal of the presenter and her chum from Radio 5, a sports reporter, to accept that there's anything homoerotic about rugby. How could you talk about rugby for a living and not have noticed? They were completely unbelieving. I do think that straightness can be a form of blinkered vision. I don't blame them.'

Mark Wahlberg's casting by Calvin Klein was a deft sleight of hand, introducing stark new lines of the gay gaze into the straight world. He was Eva Herzigová for Wonderbra in reverse, page 3 with a packet. Wahlberg's career is a concise lesson in the commercialisation of the male body. He's a smart and funny family man, the star of possibly the most tender male love story of the twenty-first century, *Ted*, the anti-*Brokeback Mountain*, in which the leading man chooses his talking teddy bear over his girlfriend and everyone lives happily ever after. 'But back then, with the dim-witted background and the criminal record which came out,' says Simpson, 'there was a sense that his was a classic kind of hustler situation.'

The Calvin Klein adverts could be seen as being part of the ritualistic romanticising of rent boys in culture, coinciding as they did with queer director Gus Van Sant casting Hollywood heartthrobs Keanu Reeves and River Phoenix in his Shakespearian hustler road-movie *My Own Private Idaho*. Hollywood's interest in male prostitution is a storytelling tradition that dates back to *Midnight Cowboy*, and it's an interest shared on British screens, first in the Frank Clarke scripted 1988 film *The Fruit Machine* and then Neil Jordan's Oscar-winning *The Crying Game*. In the television series *Prime Suspect*, Helen Mirren's Jane Tennison investigates a group of rent boys played by future stars Jonny Lee Miller, Danny Dyer and David Thewlis.

Advertising has forever followed cinematic blueprints. This rich strand of storytelling became subliminally transposed and ingrained into an obvious new home, the common or garden underwear ad, the seat of so many young men's awakenings. Wahlberg became a cross-pollinating international poster boy. His most recent modern equivalent is Channing Tatum, the cheesecake actor who made his personal and professional crossover into heavyweight material by playing a male stripper. Divesting himself of clothes for money was part of the actor's own rich backstory, and he was happy to talk about it, candidly and at length. 'Not only would the kind of stuff Channing Tatum talks about now have been totally unacceptable,' says Simpson, 'but Calvin Klein probably wouldn't have wanted it either. Because Mark was all part of what was being sold. He had to be completely heterosexual for him to be desirable in that way.' He had to be Quentin Crisp's great dark man.

Mark Simpson's travels in search of material for *Attitude* took him frequently to America. He witnessed the blue-collar, buff-body tradition equating a release for young jocks in the same way football and pop music did for men in Britain. 'Back then, most British men with bodies were escorts.' The male body was not part of our national temperament. 'Bodies require infrastructure: gyms, lots of protein, sunshine, the right kind of food, readily available. Lots of these things were not available in Britain in the nineties. People were still huddling into smoke-filled pubs with no ventilation, drinking and smoking, eating chips. Oh, and now you took drugs as well. None of which is conducive to upholding body culture. In California, beach culture, the climate, the porn industry and the other, smaller porn industry – Hollywood – meant bodies had always been more important.'

The body culture Wahlberg championed and made so desirable in his jockey shorts began to trickle over the Atlantic. It became first and most evident in gay culture during the bacchanalia at Trade, the east London nightclub which rampaged into life in 1990, shifting the time patterns of the nightlife into the day by opening during the early hours of Sunday morning and closing that afternoon, sending a teaming mass of half-clothed, saucer-eyed gay party lunatics, muscles bulging, out of Turnmills nightclub onto Clerkenwell Road to buy party supplies from the bemused petrol-station attendants opposite. 'AIDS has an important part to play here,' notes Simpson. 'You'd seen so many people waste away. So fitness, as well as looking fit, becomes even more valued and fetishised. Gay men had always tended to be interested in idealised bodies and muscle, but had tended, for the most part, to think of it as something they would consume rather than embody.'

These shifts were not being registered and noted in the mainstream. Simpson was there to document it all. 'We're these isolated individuals so we need a strong rampart or castle to hide behind,' he says. 'But it's also a bouncy castle for the eyes. It's not about withdrawing or retreating from the world; it's about selling yourself.' The idea of the body as brand percolated through gay culture and would later be observed through religious levels of devotion to perfecting the perfect shape, first on the pioneering gay sex app Gaydar, then on social media portals like Instagram. 'A long time before Grindr, Gaydar taught gay men how to turn themselves into porn. Not that they needed much encouragement. This pornographisation of yourself is something that happens on a mass scale now.'

Towards the end of the millennium, certainly by the time I'd arrived there, *Attitude* became a home for a watered-down version of Mark Wahlberg for Calvin Klein, a place where straight pinups and poster boys went to strip for the titillation of the gay eye. Part of the impulse was drawn with a commercial necessity from both sides, for the simple purposes of securing work from a guaranteed audience and shifting magazines. But I went on enough of those shoots to recognise a part of it as a simple desire to be physically adored. In all the four years I worked at *Attitude*, the one ongoing discussion that returned each issue was the tricky mathematics of weighing up how many of these men you could anoint as cover stars a year, to maintain balance between addressing ideas of gay identity and desire and keeping the magazine commercially afloat. A scantily clad man would always result in a commercial spike that could, at its best, double the sales figures and cleanly outsell a niche straight rival.

The most vocal gay critics of *Attitude* always objected strongly to this gay-for-pay model. The first letter of complaint about the magazine publishing too many naked issues arrived in the office postbag the day after the first naked issue was published. 'Well, of course this still goes on today,' says Simpson. 'How dare you put a straight man on the cover of a gay magazine? But magazines are dreamy things. They were about selling dreams, sometimes nightmares, and they are full of glossy ads selling the desire for something mostly unattainable. Even if you want to be meticulously or pedantically political about it, I don't have any problem – surprisingly enough – with young straight men taking their clothes off for gay magazines. I think it's great. The personal is very much political there. Not only do I think it's great aesthetically, but this is possibly the biggest statement you could make about where we are today, that so many straight men are not only willing but eager to objectify themselves, bending over for gay men in public, symbolically.'

Once upon a time, and not very long ago, the very suggestion that gay men might be looking at you with a rapacious eye was something straight men had to respond to with violence, verbal or physical. 'You had to prove your heterosexuality by telling the world that you hated those poofs,' says Simpson. 'And now it's a part of your career portfolio. That does go back to Marky Mark. But unlike Marky Mark, you don't get the feeling that this is simply a hustler move, that this is rough trade who would quite possibly in other circumstances knock you over the head and steal your wallet, which may have been part of his appeal.'

The Story

The first story to break *Attitude* out of the margins and feed a genuine news line to the tabloids was the decision of Pet Shop Boys singer Neil Tennant to talk openly about his sexuality for the first time. Reading the piece back now, it is a perfect record of its moment. Paul Burston interviews him, beginning by explaining that he has heard rumours that Tennant may want to talk on record about being gay for the first time, to set a decade-long assumption straight. The writer goes on to challenge the singer about the covert messages that have been woven through Pet Shop Boys' back catalogue without rubberstamping their gayness head-on. Tennant fires back with complicated, convincing arguments, saying the band had always hidden in plain sight, making perfectly obvious their homosexuality without having to spell it out, assuming that a gay audience would enjoy specific resonance in their work. The exchange is so far from a media-managed, pre-ordained modern celebrity coming-out tale that it reads rather uncomfortably, if valiantly, from both sides. It is tense and nervy, underpinned with the fear that, even in the changing world of modern masculinity, saying 'I am gay' is still a very real risk in terms of public perception. Burston wants a hero; Tennant refuses to be it. It is a charged and sometimes antagonistic exchange that strangely manages to embolden both sides of an argument about public transparency.

Tennant has since said, at length and often, that he regrets the interview, the only sad addendum to a story that delves into so much uncharted new territory, reframing coming out as an interior rather than exterior action. Sooner or later, public outings had to get wrestled back from the shame of tabloid headlines cooked up by Kelvin MacKenzie, with Richard Littlejohn the writer by his side. These are private, personal stories that necessitate being told from the inside to honour them with their full detail.

Pet Shop Boys were then completing promotional duties for their album *Very*, for which they sported a new uniform of orange jumpsuits and dunce hats. The record featured a male voice choir singing a Village People song and opened with a married man being scorned by his wife for effeminacy. The gay cultural references, which had dotted Pet Shop Boys material for the decade prior to its release, were no longer deftly, slyly positioned as the punctuation points of their art, but by now were a crystal-clear creative bedrock. The tension between what Pet Shop Boys were and what they said they were throughout their previous ten years of astronomical global success looked like it had started to chafe internally, bubbling towards public self-combustion. That Tennant remains so collected during their public declaration feels stoic.

Burston says he was not thinking about the interview as a direct reversal from tabloid stings, in which public figures had been forced to come out with their stories told on straight men's terms. He went into the interview as a Pet Shop Boys fan and remains one. He understood that the band embodied a very specific fear about coming out in the eighties (there is an argument to be made that Pet Shop Boys were the best pop act of all time at being in the closet, right up there alongside Liberace, Barry Manilow and Freddie Mercury). 'But I don't think it's very easy to do what Jimmy Somerville did, to marry politics and pop music, and most people who do it, do it really badly and it becomes shrill. There was nothing shrill about Pet Shop Boys. The messages were there but they weren't done in an explicitly agitprop way. I do admire that.'

Jimmy Somerville had repeatedly criticised Pet Shop Boys for their previous stance of forever dangling a suggestive foot from the closet door without ever quite making the leap. This public-perception opacity later became known as the 'glass closet', a cut-throat game of semi-revelation in which a star will live a gay life without declaring it directly, one mostly popular in Hollywood where there is a tacit agreement that questions about the personal lives of stars like Jodie Foster and Kevin Spacey are off-limits. 'He didn't like being pigeonholed,' Burston says of Tennant, 'and I did understand that. But I was also quite irritated and shared some of Jimmy Somerville's criticisms of them, that they had used gay culture so explicitly in their work without saying where that interest came from.' This, he says, was the central tension during the interview. 'There was a sense of him wanting to have his cake and eat it, really. I'll do a coming-out interview but suggest that it's no big deal because everyone knew all along.'

The interview was a big deal for the readers of *Attitude*. 'We did have letters which were incredibly eye-opening. I think we even published one in the next issue, with someone saying, "Neil's not gay, no, no, no. You stitched him up." With fans, of course, you think they must work out what's going on and read the signals and read the lyrics and know. But often people don't see that until you actually state it. There is a refusal to want to read the signs from some fans unless it is in their face.'

Tennant's outing was the first significant gear change in the magazine's history. 'It did a lot for *Attitude* in that people would then see us as the place to go to.' The most notable consequence was when Robbie Williams gave his first solo interview to the magazine during the hysteria around his leaving Take That, a problem considered so endemic at the time that phone lines were set up for grieving fans.

The PR

Caroline McAteer began her professional PR life working for the Outside Organisation, the London agency that managed the media profiles of a string of household names, including David Bowie and Paul McCartney. Until she began representing the most famous man in Britain, David Beckham, Caroline's clients included Boyzone and the Spice Girls. One of her first dealings with *Attitude* magazine was on behalf of Boyzone's Stephen Gately.

Caroline had a particular fondness for Stephen. When she talks about him she wears the protective armour of a sister doing everything she can to keep her younger gay brother from being thrown to the wolves of everyday antipathy, because she knows he's one of the special ones. 'Everyone close to Stephen knew that he was gay,' she says. 'And it wasn't a secret in any way. He had been with his boyfriend, Eloy de Jong, for a while. At that time, and people do forget this, it wasn't done to be out, gay and in a boyband, because as far as everyone was concerned your audience was young teenage girls.' Industry thinking was that to come out would harm sales.

One day Caroline took a phone call from a journalist at the *Sun*. 'Someone had got pictures of Stephen and Eloy and they were going to sell them to the paper and out him.' A little rooting around – Caroline is nothing if not meticulous in the charge and guidance of her clients – and she discovered that it was a venue security guard on one of the Boyzone world tours. 'I had to make that call to Stephen, which was hard because he was a very sensitive individual anyway. He took it quite hard. For his family and his friends this was not a secret, but I think he was more concerned about what the impact would be to his fans. Would people accept it or would they not? He was scared of the public's reaction.'

At the time it was a story without precedent, not only because of his commercial cachet in a premier-league boyband, but because of the religious conservatism of his home of Ireland. 'The *Sun* agreed with us that they would pretend they were negotiating with this guy to do the story, to buy us a bit of time. Obviously, Stephen wasn't going to just say "I'm gay" the next day. I went to Dublin, met with Stephen and tried to work out what he wanted to do.'

Prior to sitting down with Gately, Caroline had several other conversations, with management, other band members and the heads of Boyzone's label. 'They were all involved in this,' she says. 'No one had ever come out before in a boyband and they were at the height of their success.' The faltering start and crash landing of the boyband 2wo Third3, the joke of whose name was that two of the three members were gay, and the glass-closet success of Steps was fresh in the industry mind. Caroline took an alternative view. 'I said to Stephen, "Listen, I don't really care about that. I am looking at this from a personal point of view because this is your life."'

She offered him options on how to proceed: 'Either this guy goes and sells his story and outs you, and then we respond to it afterwards and deal with the fallout. Or we try to stop the story, which is near impossible. I said, "You're going to live your life paranoid, always looking over your shoulder, wondering who's watching you. Every time you're out at a restaurant or every time you check into a hotel. Do you want to live your life like that? Or the third option is you just take control of the situation yourself and say you've got nothing to hide."' At the end of the conversation, she told Stephen to go away and think about it, to talk to his family and Eloy, and that whatever he decided she would be behind him all the way. There was a parting note. 'He said, "What do you think?" And I said to him that for me, I'd want to take control of it and live my life.'

The *Sun* ran the story on 17 June 1999 under the headline 'Boyzone Stephen: I'm Gay and in Love'. The singer was on a sold-out European tour with Boyzone. 'I was with him a couple of days before the gig. He performed with Pavarotti and he was petrified about the story coming out. We were on the phone late watching Sky News when the front pages of the papers with him on went up,' says Caroline. 'The rest of the band were really supportive and had his back, which was incredible for them because they could have thought his coming out would destroy their careers. They were completely, 100 per cent amazing. The label was really good as well. It was one of those moments where everyone was great. To be fair, the *Sun* were too.'

The story was written by deputy editor Andy Coulson and showbiz writer Rav Singh, who was Adam Mattera's closest tabloid ally while at *Attitude*. 'Rav was smart,' says Caroline. 'Being on the side of the client rather than the person who's selling the story is a smarter move than trying to shaft someone. They knew what they were sitting on. It was a massive story. It was a big story for the broadsheets, too. The usual practice for newspapers was to try to make anything gay seedy. It wasn't with Stephen. He was in a relationship with nothing to hide. We knew what the media reaction would be, what his personal circle's reaction would be and what the label's reaction would be. But no one knew what the fans' reaction would be. He was overwhelmed by how positive it was – girls writing to say they still loved him, boys saying how much his coming out had helped them – he had sackloads of letters.'

An *Attitude* cover soon followed. 'Stephen Gately was a pivotal cover for us,' says Adam Mattera. 'It's easy to remember all the big names that came out before and after, but there was a whole substrata of people after Stephen, the most famous of whom I suppose was H from Steps. Mark Feehily came out towards the end of Westlife, then there was Darren Hayes, then Ricky Martin. Stephen did it at the height of his success. He did it right.'

When the Irish people defied the campaigns of the dominant religious right in the same-sex marriage referendum of 2014 and voted overwhelmingly for equality, it is perfectly reasonable to assume that the country's isolated, popular and brave gay role models Stephen Gately and Graham Norton had played a significant role in changing the texture of national thinking toward inclusivity and progress. In 1999 bands would still receive physical fan mail, letters and annotated gifts, which Caroline says arrived for Gately, 'by the sackload. From everyone. It was amazing. He was like a different person. He was so happy and free. It really upsets me to think about it now.'

Gately died young, at 33, of a congenital heart defect on 10 October 2009. 'He was always going to be loved,' she says. 'He got so much love. You would not believe it. That was the thing that meant so much to him, you know? It was so amazing, even thinking about it now. I find it very hard to bring myself to talk about it.'

The Editor

Adam Mattera began his professional life as a writer at the black music magazine *Echoes*. During his tenure there he interviewed major international stars such as Mariah Carey, Janet Jackson, Prince and Luther Vandross, 'because the other people that worked there at the time were specialists in just reggae or hip hop or specific areas, and the areas I was interested in I got first dibs on.' While at *Echoes* he began freelancing for *Attitude*. His first piece was an 'Icons' feature on the camp *Thunderbirds* mannequin Lady Penelope. By 1998 he had been made editor.

His major challenge from the outset was negotiating how to talk to gay readers directly while appeasing the commercial demands of Northern & Shell, who had clocked major commercial spikes from exclusives like the Robbie Williams story. 'To be fair to them, it's difficult if you don't have detailed knowledge of gay culture. I remember doing Aiden Shaw on the cover of the magazine, and of course the publisher didn't have any idea of who that was.' Shaw was the defining nineties gay porn star, known not just for his 11-and-a-half-inch phallus and prodigious workload, but artsy, poetic sidelines in writing high-minded literature, making abstract art and performing with Leigh Bowery's countercultural pop wing Minty.

Aiden Shaw's reach in the gay world was extensive enough to later have a character named after him in *Sex and the City*, albeit with a slightly different spelling (Aidan instead of Aiden). Carrie Bradshaw's alternative to Mr Big was given his name as the show's creator, Darren Star, was such a fan of the real Aiden Shaw's work, as Shaw found out when an invitation to a series premiere of *Sex and the City* in New York landed without prior notice on his doorstep.

'Richard Desmond would say, "Why are you putting this bloke on the cover?" And I get that. They had no context for it. Whereas if you did Robbie Williams, they got it. There were certain points when Robbie would be a default position as a cover. Get Robbie on the cover, that'll sell.'

Mattera had registered the significance of the Neil Tennant interview. 'It was great that someone like Neil Tennant would want to share their voice in there. When they were being interviewed by an intelligent gay journalist and challenged, they knew they were speaking directly to their gay audience. That would have been the only direct link to their fans in a way they wouldn't have if they'd gone on television. It wouldn't happen in the mainstream press, either.'

He had to learn quickly and on the hoof how to maximise exposure for the magazine amid the mainsteam, straight press.

'The first big thing that I worked on was the Spice Girls cover.' After the departure of Geri Halliwell, midway through a coast-to-coast tour of America, the Spice Girls were undergoing a rebrand. They were comfortably the most popular musical phenomenon in a generation. 'I remember staying late in the office and waiting for faxes from America where the shoot was happening. There were lots of late-night phone calls about things that had to be dealt with, and I'd stay behind in the office to take them all.'

The creative for the cover was to reimagine the four remaining Spice Girls as the Village People. Baby was the construction worker, Posh the cop. 'Not only were they into it,' he says, 'they went beyond it. The girls were having a lot of fun, playing around with props onset. One particular photo had Victoria putting a gun into Mel C's mouth. A toy gun, obviously. She's a cop. It was funny and playful and stupid.' Dealing with an international team on a cover shoot was all new territory for Adam. 'The journalist was out there, who subsequently went totally AWOL with her copy, though it turned out to be brilliant when we did get it. She wrote a great piece and got them to be really naughty and funny and slightly outrageous. She really pushed something in them. The images, particularly that one with the gun in the mouth, pushed it even further.'

When it hit the shelves, the tabloids wanted their pound of Spice flesh. 'It was before I'd learned how to PR the magazine, which was really by a process of trial and error.' The press went for the Girls in a big way. 'One headline was "Sick Spice". The implication was that the pop stars of the nineties were now so desperate that they were doing anything to get attention, appearing in gay magazine *Attitude*. Their fans will be outraged, they're pulling out guns and talking about sex. They made a really big thing out of nothing really. But it was a really interesting lesson for me.'

Thanks to the Spice Girls, he witnessed the magazine's reach at close quarters, counting the column inches and news broadcasts to determine how much cross-media interest it could generate. Mattera began developing relationships with showbiz editors at the tabloids, Andy Coulson at the *Sun*, Ian Hyland at the *Mirror* and particularly Rav Singh at the *News of the World*. 'It was all really good for spreading the brand.' This was not just about kowtowing to the dominant celebrity and tabloid culture. It was about making a gay magazine as good as you. 'Culturally and politically, it was absolutely breaking down the lines between what people see as a ghettoised community that should be left to look after itself in the corner to being given a voice in the national conversation.'

The problem with gay issues in the national media is that they will always remain a minority. The assumption will always be that the majority of readers are straight. So when a breaking story like the eventual equalisation of the age of consent happens, it is a news story that reaches the cover of every newspaper. It is a massive societal shift. But it has a finite news life. The story will almost certainly finish there. It happened, let's move on. There is no consequence in a news sense, because it enables people's lives to get incrementally better, not worse. What I loved about working at *Attitude*, under Adam, was that we could facilitate a magazine that went on to record the consequences of that legislation, to build a world in which it lived and breathed and affected readers' lives. 'Some of the criticisms *Attitude* would get at the time,' he says, 'you know, I heard them all. I would often hear back from people about *Attitude* being superficial and obsessed with celebrity and fashion, but what I always thought was that when you went beyond the cover there were some hard-hitting stories in there, about male rape or body issues, prostitution, HIV, really in-depth, decent features and columns, of which Mark Simpson's was the most well-known, that questioned what it meant to be gay. We started addressing issues in an accessible way underneath those celebrity covers.'

'You're in it and you don't process it at the time,' continues Adam. 'You're a gay man, discussing work with other gay men as a team and discussing what you'd do next, what was important to us. There were strong, conflicting agendas at the magazine of what we all wanted it to be. We were so lucky. Peter Tatchell launched a campaign against the magazine because it was published by Northern & Shell. I got where he was coming from. I also think that he was wrong, because *Attitude* was doing its own job, in isolation, competing in a mainstream market. By targeting that and asking people to boycott it, you denied it that significance. Yes, the publisher was breathing down my neck in terms of sales. But in terms of actual content and what we got to put in the magazine, to be honest we were given absolute free rein.'

By doing the youth issue, something that couldn't have happened when I started at the magazine as being under 21 and gay was illegal, you could take a yearly temperature of this incredible confidence that was building in young gay men across the country. We could watch it blossoming in real time. These things didn't have to happen. Whenever I think back to my time working at that magazine, there is always one salient point that kept me there. It was never the best-presented magazine in the world. It never had the biggest budgets. It was never the slickest, glossiest or coolest title on the news stand. But what it did have was a uniquely intimate relationship with its subscribers and supporters, which saw us receive letters from the readers that would reduce the staff to tears. Just to have been a little part of that as it happened felt like enough reason to leave the *Daily Express*.

8. POPULARITY CONTEST

The Control Room

In early 2005 I was approached to write a book to accompany the upcoming sixth series of *Big Brother*. It would mean having a desk up at Elstree Studios, just off Borehamwood high street, in the studios named after *Star Wars* director George Lucas, and attending each weekly eviction of the reality show on a Friday night, snooping about behind the scenes then catching up with the housemate put out to pasture at the weekend. I'd write a chapter a week, and the book would come out three weeks after finishing the winner's epistle. The book commissioner was gay, I was gay, the director of the show was gay and so were many of the production staff. *Big Brother* had, by this point, comfortably become the most useful, cross-class, -race and -gender arbiter of LGBT representation British TV had ever seen, with a proud inclusiveness not just of the Ls and Gs, but the Bs and Ts, too.

The early noughties were marked with a succession of noble gay men winning talking-point prizes across the high and low arts in the UK. If it was just a coincidence that these big trophy wins timed with the repealing of draconian gay legislation, it never quite felt like it. Kicking off the decade, the exceptional German artist and ideologue Wolfgang Tillmans won the 2000 Turner Prize. Tillmans worked light years ahead of his time in honing a sensitive eye that seemed to predate digital photography.

In 2001, Ryanair steward Brian Dowling won *Big Brother*, joining his fellow gay countrymen Stephen Gately and Graham Norton in the spotlight. In 2002, Will Young took the crown in the inaugural season of *Pop Idol*, the reality-show singing competition that would beget the landscape-changing cultural monoliths *The X Factor* and *American Idol*. Then, in 2004, Alan Hollinghurst won the Booker Prize for *The Line of Beauty*, his sprawling story of Thatcher's Britain and homosexuality, a wonderful study of friendship and loss that earned symbolic comparison with Evelyn Waugh's *Brideshead Revisited*. The day after Hollinghurst's win, the *Daily Express* ran with the surprising and slightly alarming headline, 'Gay Sex Wins Booker Prize', a homily Hollinghurst himself laughed long and hard at.

If Alan Hollinghurst and Wolfgang Tillmans were clear cases of gay men at their most exceptional, blessed with almost otherworldly talent, Brian Dowling earned us our right to be ordinary, too, as important a distinction in the equality narrative, and one that is apt to get lost between the cracks.

In retrospect, given the microcosmic puddle of alternate stardom that TV's reality strand has turned into, it's easy to forget the technicolor glow that a real-time house-share incarceration drama, screened nightly and streamed minute-by-minute digitally onto computer screens, could cast over the country. Now it has been reduced to the inarguable essentials of human contact – sex, drinking and fighting – and, once agents got involved, it all became too familiar, the rot set in and the genre lost its early determinist sparkle. But at least until Nikki Grahame screamed 'Who is she?

Who is she?' to her omniscient confessor in a locked room while entertaining the idea of falling in love with a soft-edged crusty with Tourette's syndrome, *Big Brother* was at the vanguard of the millennium's new TV wave. It elegantly and anarchically filled in the nuance, detail, unforeseen storylines and exciting twists that soap opera was wrestling to keep hold of by virtue of taking ever bigger and more implausible fictional liberties. With early reality TV, you didn't need three families with convicted murderers living on the same street; you just needed the queasy threat of someone who'd double-cross their granny for a fiver or a fumble.

A Friday *Big Brother* eviction was the noughties mirror to the cross-generational, round-the-telly excitement of a new episode of *Top of the Pops* – itself a braying and argumentative public popularity contest – 20 years previously. Predating the digital democratisation of fame on social media, *Big Brother* marked a shift in interest from a star's exterior talent to their interior life. In some peculiar way, below the vanity and preening of the housemates, it predicted our current obsession with mental health, bullying and body image, too. Week after week the show would throw up new British archetypes both familiar and recognisable, of a kind the curated worlds of old stardom and fiction could simply not keep up with. It coincided with the fourth wall being smashed to smithereens by assistants telling stories for free on the website Popbitch that they could have been paid handsomely for by gossip columnists. Those early *Big Brother* contestants that prepared to expose themselves for our empathy and vilification, to slot into a more people-like-us version of the star machine, were rewarded well for their trouble. If a Friday *Big Brother* eviction was touched by the hysteria of vintage *Top of the Pops*, it had its own *Smash Hits*, drawn by the whip-smart editors and writers at *Heat* magazine.

The previous season, *Big Brother 5*, was its most gripping yet. Just as Boy George had asked direct questions about gender and otherness two decades previously without so much as a clear word on the subject, Nadia Almada strode onto screen, immediately anointing herself in the grand tradition of busty screen starlets, to take that particular conversation one step further. She became the first transgender winner of the show. Not only was Nadia a whirlwind of fragrant, empathetic starriness, a Diana Dors for a new screen medium, she overcame two beacons of old-fashioned masculinity during 'Fight Night', a contentious, compelling experiment in broadcasting a fracas and one that saw it temporarily taken off air for the first time ever.

Big Brother's triumph was to present LGBT people on TV in a brand new way. It gave us our happy ending, presenting us as victors, not victims. So I took the commission. It was the jolliest summer. The money was great, the production staff on the show were funny and clever, and I'd given up drinking for a year, so having something to do on a Friday night other than getting smashed was handy.

One Friday early into the run, series director Tony Gregory invited me into the production van to watch the action take place from his bird's eye view. A bank of screens lined the far wall. Twenty seats were assembled, cinema style, to watch over his performance. There was modest catering. Everyone but me sported a headset; I had a notepad and pen. It felt like being in a hub at the centre of the universe, a control room from which everything that dropped out of friends' mouths the next day could be carefully aggregated and prejudged.

That year was the peak of *Big Brother*'s casting wand being waved across the sexuality spectrum: Derek Laud, the black, gay Tory spokesperson; Craig Coates, the Norfolk hairdresser, and Anthony Hutton, the buff, preening, straight object of his affection; Kemal Shahin, the bisexual Muslim who chose to enter the house in a traditional wedding dress to betroth himself to *Big Brother*, and later transitioned to being female; Makosi Musambasi and Orlaith McAllister, the glamour girls who'd smooch in the hot tub; and bisexual Lesley Sanderson, the 'Udders from Hudders'. British TV had seen nothing like it before. These audacious figures, drunk on their hunger for fame and fortune and desperate to escape their nine-to-five existence, joined the other early *Big Brother* housemates in presenting Britain and its fresh new youth as something curious, confident and uninhibited, something that didn't need pop stars to cling to in order to guide their identity issues toward real self-esteem. British youth, for a spell there, looked like something fit for purpose, and *Big Brother* felt briefly like its boot camp.

That night, Tony Gregory commanded the control room like a fighter pilot entering a war zone. He unleashed all his alpha qualities to ensure that what went out on TV, with no delay mechanism, was worthy of the conversations it would spark the next day at the bus stop, the chippy, the hairdresser waiting rooms and on the front covers. He rose to the challenge like a man possessed. With a big, booming voice and acute physicality, he charged around the tiny caravanette that was *Big Brother*'s nerve centre. Executives from the production company, Endemol, and from the broadcaster, Channel 4, would occasionally make a suggestion, but otherwise the role was his to own. He showed a liberal predilection for the use of every profanity and expletive to hand, deploying them for maximum effect, shouting down a mouthpiece into some poor production hand's ear. He demonstrated the controlled rage of an orchestra conductor in charge of a Wagner symphony. Multimillion pounds' worth of production money rested in his hands. A constructed universe was subject to his instruction. In these situations, you need someone in charge. He was it. In the form of Tony Gregory that summer, that night, I saw for the first time an entire workforce absolutely terrified of a gay man for all the right reasons. Of course *Big Brother* would present LGBT people as champs. It was run by them.

The Reality TV Saint

I was an early convert to reality television as a viewer. The beginnings of my interest in this third wave of television storytelling – neither fiction nor documentary, but something tenser, more volatile and immediately reactive – cast back a decade before Nadia Almada's prom-queen coronation. During the summer of 1994, MTV aired the third season of Mary-Ellis Bunim and Jonathan Murray's *The Real World*. In the show, eight strangers are holed up in a fancy loft apartment in a new city and filmed 24 hours a day while learning to navigate their new lives together. Because season three was in San Francisco I'd tuned in from the start, and the show's duty to honour the city's gay heritage was played out to heart-wrenching emotional effect. *The Real World: San Francisco* would turn out to be a new watermark for gay representation, finding us an international martyr in the form of reality TV's first patron saint, a truly wonderful human being called Pedro Zamora.

Zamora was a 21-year-old AIDS educator of Cuban descent. During the filming of the show he found a boyfriend, Sean Sasser, with whom he would enjoy a commitment ceremony on camera, a first for American TV. It was easy to understand what Sasser saw in Zamora. He was lovely, kindly, handsome, clever and equipped with an acute emotional intelligence. Quite aside from what would happen during the show, Zamora was loaded with backstory. He lost his mother to skin cancer when he was 13. His father, Hector, confronted Pedro at 14 about his sexuality after uncovering a secret boyfriend. Hector was supportive and concerned about any potential homophobia his young son might face in their home in the Miami suburb of Hialeah. American AIDS education was not in the hands of a Norman Fowler figure, and Pedro had thought he was not at risk from the HIV virus as a teenager because he was neither a prostitute nor an intravenous drug user. As a result of the flimsy and futile message the government sent out, directly attributable to the Reagan administration, Pedro tested positive for HIV at the age of 17 on 9 November 1989.

Pedro Zamora's story was unflinchingly brave not just because he had tested positive for HIV five years previously and used a reality TV show to wear it entirely free of shame and enlighten America. His relationships with his housemates reflected other accuracies fiction could never have dared broach. The previous year the straight actor Tom Hanks collected untold plaudits for his decision to take a plum role in a film bound for glory, the first AIDS Hollywood blockbuster, *Philadelphia*; Pedro Zamora lived out its reality in front of TV cameras. Casual homophobia was upended in his wake in the loft. Antagonists became allies. Each episode brought a new, insightful hand played by Pedro in redressing assumed prejudices, reframing a new version of the American dream. A new dialogue around the disease emerged for young America, one untouched by finger-wagging, blame-apportioning and endless rounds of misunderstanding. His roommate attended lessons Zamora gave on HIV awareness in San Francisco. He felt like a metaphor for the whole of the country.

Halfway into filming, Pedro Zamora's medical condition dramatically worsened. He made it clear to the producers that he wanted them to tell his story to the end. It became one of the most arresting in American television history, earning him honorary tributes from *Time* magazine and a special commendation from President Bill Clinton. *The Real World: San Francisco* began airing in June 1994. Two days after its final episode in November that year, Pedro Zamora died, aged 22. He has since had a street in Miami named after him, a succession of charitable foundations spring directly from his work, and an award-winning graphic novel by former *Real World* roommate Judd Winick and a feature film made about him, *Pedro*, written by Dustin Lance Black, the scriptwriter who would go on to win an Oscar for writing Gus Van Sant's interpretation of the Harvey Milk story. In the canon of gay American screen heroes, the ones who really broke the mould, Pedro Zamora is as close as you'll find to peerless.

Cabin Crew

When he was offered a job on the first season of *Big Brother*, TV producer Paul Osborne was not directly thinking about watching *The Real World: San Francisco* as a 21-year-old, seven years earlier, though his memories of the effect the show had on him were lodged somewhere at the back of his mind. 'I do remember being very emotionally upset about it,' he says. 'They followed Pedro's story so sensitively. He came out first as gay. Then he came out as being HIV-positive. Then they must have put it all in the can, edited it and by the time it came out he died. That was incredible. There is the power of reality TV, right there.'

Paul Osborne had a tricky relationship with working in TV during the nineties, interconnected with his tricky relationship with sexuality. His last job before *Big Brother* was on *The Big Breakfast*, a show that shared much of the same production team and some of its borderline-lunatic screen energy. Paul was charged with cheerleading families into unnatural states of telly-friendly hyperreality in the early hours of weekday mornings for a slot called Family of the Week. He became increasingly drained by the process: 'It just all felt so false.' So he decamped to Australia for a year to rethink his future in the business and to get his head around some more pressing personal matters.

'I didn't come out until late,' he says. 'I was certainly gay before I came out. I didn't come out to my parents until I was 30.' Paul grew up in working-class Glasgow. He knew well the power of the television set long before his professional life brought him to it. 'I think it's incredibly important. From my perspective, I'd spent that year prior to *Big Brother* in Australia navigating every conversation I had with everyone around my gayness. Do I come out to this one? Do I let this one carry on talking about girlfriends as if that's a given? We all know how long it can take to process your sexuality. Coming out over and over again, yes, it is tedious, but I felt there was also a certain anxiety attached to it as well.'

This was inculcated young. 'Any portrayal of gay men on TV, going all the way back to *Dynasty*, is important. That drip, drip, drip effect of sitting watching television, in that room with my family, and there being a gay man's story – not a particularly positive one, but it was a gay man's story nonetheless – was hugely important to me.' Familiarity had softened previous reactions he'd heard to stories about HIV and AIDS on the news. 'I was very nervous about coming out to my parents because of all those reports and my dad's reaction. I thought he was super-homophobic when I was younger, because of the way he would react to those news reports. He behaved to type, as a classic working-class Glaswegian of the time: "Just fucking round 'em up."' This was not what his son wanted or needed to hear. 'So yes, TV was really important in so many ways.'

On the plane back from Australia, Paul read a news report about *Big Brother* in the *Daily Telegraph*. It was clear to him that something exciting was happening on TV back home. 'That hadn't existed before, an appetite for people like us on television and on the cover of magazines. In whichever working-class town you lived, the idea of people like you on television was pretty much unheard of outside of soap operas.' A spark began to ignite in his mind about possibly returning to his old professional life. He touched down to an offer from Ruth Wrigley, executive producer on *Big Brother*, to step in and produce the tasks that kept housemates minds' active in their confined voluntary imprisonment.

The first prominent LGBT casting on *Big Brother* was Anna Nolan, a figure no fiction-writer had yet thought to invent. For the inaugural psychological experiment of locking up a group of strangers in a house for the summer to see what transpired, Anna, an Irish lesbian and former Catholic nun, was the most immediately endearing. Wendy Rattray, another early *Big Brother* producer, says, 'Anna was just extraordinary.' Anna's accidental subversion was to upend any preconceptions one might instantly form about an Irish Catholic lesbian nun. She dressed well. She was coolly engaged in popular culture, with opinions to spare. As an extra tick on her subculture scorecard, she could skateboard. Anna Nolan was the first *Big Brother* contestant to be mentioned in *The Face* magazine, then the most useful gauge as to where the margins were likely to cross over to the mainstream.

'That combination of an Irish Catholic lesbian nun,' says Wendy, 'is probably not that unique. But her openness made her absolutely unique. Just the decision to go on TV and be open about that was incredibly brave of her.' Anna was a quick and firm fan favourite. 'From a viewer's point of view, she very quickly completely normalised what might seem extraordinary on paper. As soon as you saw her on TV she was just Anna, a really decent person that you couldn't help but love.'

Anna Nolan was a symbol of goodness, a new curveball for gay usefulness on British telly. In the tabloid explosion that erupted around her fellow housemate 'Nasty' Nick Bateman and his skulduggery in attempting to win the first *Big Brother* crown, Anna stood apart from the rest, a first example of the new feudalism that earmarked *Big Brother* as must-watch TV. For me personally, Anna was the first time I had seen Catholicism and homosexuality cohabiting together plausibly on screen, spoken in language I could directly relate to, not presented as shocking bedfellows riven with guilt, catastrophe and rejection. She reconciled the eternal tussle instilled by the faith between biblical damnation for something entirely innate and that simple old Christian premise of loving your neighbour as yourself. Anna Nolan was the opposite of all that disquieting, incalculable, unnecessary Catholic hysteria which seems so utterly nonsensical when you live in the middle of it. She was calm and soothing. Faith and sexuality could chime in her with harmony, cordiality and respect, without being boring.

'Some of the conversations that Anna had from a gay perspective were very politically astute,' says Paul Osborne. 'They were educational to me. She was sophisticated. She was dry, sarcastic and funny. She was also incredibly popular.' Aside from his subterfuge in vote rigging, Nasty Nick had been antagonistic to Anna on numerous occasions on the topic of her sexuality. He'd derided the recently outed pop goliath George Michael, who had undergone the kind of entrapment police sting in a Los Angeles lavatory that Miriam Margolyes performed against in earnest at the Pretty Policeman's Ball. Nasty Nick had conflated gay men with paedophiles, a dwindling but still not uncommon prejudice as the millennium turned, one that the boxer Tyson Fury would later invoke to add to his personal spreadsheet of futile prejudices. 'Anna went off about that,' recalls Osborne. 'That whole exchange between Nick Bateman and her about George Michael was important. I hesitate to use the term, but for me Anna was the first time I'd ever seen a 'normalised' gay person on television.'

By the time of casting for *Big Brother 2*, enough frenzy had built around the show for a price tag to sit on the head of anyone holding the keys to who was going into the house. Endemol were way ahead of Lord Leveson with regards to underhand newspaper practice. Their senior producers and the attendant commissioners at Channel 4 had been instructed on how to prevent their mobile phone calls from being intercepted, a common tabloid ruse to prise the names and personal details of housemates from their gatekeepers. 'The phone-hacking scandal didn't come as any shock to me at all,' says Wendy. 'We just took that as an accepted press practice. If they wanted to find something out, they'd tap your phone.'

Between seasons, Endemol sent senior producers over to *Big Brother*'s homeland in Holland to be taught new techniques. 'Nothing had ever been done like that in the UK,' says Wendy. 'I don't think I'm overstating the fact when I say that *Big Brother* changed the face of TV, not just in Britain, but across the world. The whole system they had in place, the way the gallery worked, the way that they filmed it, the editors that had to work in such a short space of time.' A Dutch employee of the company gave individual lessons on how to be the voice of *Big Brother*, to maximise the storytelling potential of the housemates. 'I was trying it one day and she said, "No, no, no, no, no. You sound like a sex-line operator." She told me off for being a bit saucy, which was something *Big Brother* would never be.'

The role of *Big Brother*, as mentor, confidante, confessor and safe haven, worked therapeutically for young gay housemates who might not have been previously privy to a sympathetic, wise and non-judgemental adult on whom to lean at home, school or church. 'To keep the purity of the experiment you couldn't ask them specific questions about an incident,' says Wendy. 'That would stop them behaving in a natural way.' *Big Brother* was not there to tell anyone off for being gay or make a judgement about what that would behaviourally entail. He or she was there to allow them to be themselves, to encourage them to be the most honest version of that thing. 'It was a slightly counselling role you'd take with them, without being too interfering.'

The contestants for the highly anticipated second series included Brian Dowling. 'Anna begat Brian, for sure,' says Paul Osborne. 'Not just gay, but both Irish Catholic as well. She probably inspired him to audition.' Wendy Rattray doesn't remember any particular box-ticking initiatives involved at the casting stage, one that would involve sifting through tens of thousands of audition tapes and then a rolling tour of the country to meet designated individuals who'd caught a particular producer's eye. 'I don't necessarily think that we were looking for somebody who could top Anna,' she recalls. 'We weren't as crude as thinking, OK, what's the top-line of the characters that we're looking for? Brian didn't necessarily have a USP as an Irish gay man. That wasn't a headline for him. There was no real headline for us as far as I can remember. I think we all just loved him, his energy, his enthusiasm and the fact that he was so very, very funny.'

She says that when it came to producing the show, the staff would have to edit down so much more than they could use of Brian's natural showmanship, and that they could have easily made that series into *The Brian Dowling Show*. Paul Osborne was given the job as care producer, responsible for the housemates' welfare within and immediately out of the *Big Brother* house. He was involved in casting from the start. Brian's tape he remembers lighting up the room whenever it came on. Brian had not come out to his parents at the time, and the only caveat for his entrance to a house he was clearly born for was that he had to tell them first. It would protect their reaction and his from the public gaze. Reality television could be quite an innocent endeavour in its younger years. Moral, even.

The Hostess

Besides the high ratio of LGBT folk forming a gregarious, disorderly queue to become housemates and the inclusiveness of its staff, *Big Brother* had other instant attractions for a gay audience. For season two, *Big Brother's Little Brother* was introduced, an early evening spin-off show that would bring homespun LGBT issues, without ever quite labelling them as such – a relief in itself – forward to the teatime slot. Its thick-set, crop-haired presenter Dermot O'Leary was an instant favourite with gay men. The public anchor and face of the show itself, Davina McCall, had an even more enduring and entrenched relationship with the gay community, one which stretched way back beyond Davina's immaculately blossoming TV skills.

Davina McCall slices through to the centre of warmth and glamour with an unusual effectiveness on screen. She comes from an unequivocally good place. Davina attended her first gay club, the Lift in London's West End, when she was 16 years old, in 1984. 'I remember thinking then,' she says, 'first of all, this is the best music I've ever heard in my entire life. Secondly, there was an atmosphere in there not just of heavy sexuality but of really good fun, too. I thought, Yes, I'm going to have a bit more of this, thanks very much. As I got older, obviously, I carried on going to any kind of gay club I could find.'

She attended Michael and Gerlinde Costiff's fabulous London night Kinky Gerlinky in the early nineties, 'in a sequinned skirt with masking tape crossed over both of my nipples. My friend Stu went in a pair of shoes, a top hat and a belt, and that was it.' It was all part of the street theatre of the night. 'Nobody batted an eyelid. It was so liberating, exciting and freeing, and I think we felt like boundaries were being crossed all the time. It was a time when we were making incredible advances in women's rights and gay rights. Race, religion, creed, sexuality, suddenly everything was OK.' At least it was in the night-time metropolis, a place she felt most at home.

Davina began running her own clubs in the late eighties. She learned to mix her naturally maternal manner with the waspish dialect of drag queens while working club doors with a headset and clipboard. She ran a night at fashionable west London club space Subterranea with Patrick Lilley, the bon viveur nightclub promoter who had done most to open the door of racial inclusivity in London gay nightlife with his sensationally enduring garage basement party Queer Nation. McCall was a regular there, too.

There was something about the spirit of gay clubs that appealed directly to Davina. '"Heterosexual female" doesn't feel like a label I'm entirely happy with,' she says. 'I may not always be a heterosexual female. Who knows? Nobody knows.' She has battled addictions and a complicated relationship with her own mother, which shares some similarities with the rejection gay children can feel within the family home. 'I think that my life has made me realise lots of different things; importantly, that acceptance of myself and of others is definitely part of the key to happiness.' She recently saw a post on social media that chimed with her. 'It said, "Thou shalt not judge because thou hast fucked up also." That is so true of me. I've led a very colourful life. I've done some pretty awful things. I've got myself into some pretty dark situations.' Throughout it all, there were friends, a non-biological family of allies, of which gay folk know all too well the importance. 'I've got people around me who have seen me through some pretty terrible times. They still like me and I am so grateful for that. Acceptance that judging is such a negative thing to do has made me a much happier person.'

She took this egalitarian aspect of her youthful adventures in the night into phase two of her professional life. 'I like to think that *God's Gift* and *Streetmate*,' she says of her pre-*Big Brother* career on TV, 'laid a bit of the groundwork for what was to later happen.' *God's Gift* was a late-night response to the declining success of Cilla Black's *Blind Date*. It was a racier version for a more accepting age. 'We did the first ever gay game show on it,' she says proudly. 'We did, I think, four or five episodes that were just gay, with girls and boys in it.' The director was Tony Gregory. 'Yorkshire Television actually wouldn't air them for a bit,' she recalls. 'It's amazing looking back. The heads at Yorkshire Television were horrified by the idea of a gay game show. And they were such good fun. Obviously, *God's Gift* went out in the middle of the night so we just made the show with the assumption that nobody was watching it. Anything goes, do what you like, say what you like.'

Her next appointment was for Channel 4's dating show *Streetmate*, where she continued in her endeavours to deliver to gay men and women exactly the same 15 minutes of fame afforded to their straight counterparts. 'Taking a guy out on the street to look for another guy felt completely normal to me because it was only an extension of what I was doing with friends anyway.' She says that, occasionally, the production would hit problems, like when they took a man out on the streets of Dublin to see who took his fancy. 'We had a chat and he said, "I'm single, but look, I'm gay." I was like, "And? Let's go and find you someone." We spent the next few hours in the streets of Dublin going up to well-turned-out boys in tight T-shirts and asking them if they were gay or not.' Even to a kind face like Davina's, the response was far from positive. 'I was like, "Mate, this is not going to work."' They decamped to a gay club, to everyone's satisfactory conclusion.

Another episode of *Streetmate* hit further problems when they filmed in the executive gay paradise of Mykonos, the Greek island summer nirvana that ritzy gay men have flocked to for decades. 'I literally had to tell the boys there, "Please, please, please, can you be a bit more picky? We do have to make an entire programme out of this. We can't just say, 'Right, who do you fancy?' and you say, 'Him, him, him and him,' and then get off with them. That isn't going to work."'

By the time Davina McCall was employed as the presenter of *Big Brother*, she was ready to become the face of a heavyweight TV revolution. 'Everything about it was groundbreaking,' she says of the first series. 'Just the fact of how much we relished coming back every night to see the same people and to know what had happened to them that day, how disgusted we were that somebody had cheated. It was just fascinating going through that first series with the nation and knowing how gripped by it we all were.'

The show taught her lessons about the changing national temperament, how roles of gender and sexuality were now up in the air and realigning, moving towards something closer to what she had seen in eighties nightclubs. 'The biggest thing I learned from it – and I would say that if I learned it then the nation learned it too – is that we cannot judge a book by its cover. You might say to yourself, "Oh, I don't really like people like that. Ugh, God, no, no, no, they're the kind of people that I really hate." But then they do something really sweet and touching, and you'll go, "OK, I am completely wrong about that type of person."'

To watch this happening in real time was a magical experience for the presenter, one she hadn't anticipated when first entering the world of telly. 'Reality TV is different now, and it is so salacious that there's not actually much room for kindness or compassion in it anymore. It tends to now be vanity, fight, vanity, getting off with someone, vanity, fight again, more vanity. And that's fine. I don't judge it at all. But I think we did actually learn quite a lot in those early series of *Big Brother*, and that was that we were becoming more accepting, more all-encompassing and a bit more liberal, really.'

Davina loved Anna Nolan. 'She was cast because she was an enchanting person,' she says. 'That's what I loved about *Big Brother*. It wasn't about quotas. It was about people and how much we wanted to see them on screen.' By Brian Dowling's turn on the show, she was in full control of her speeding new vehicle, racing through its gear changes and setting a special reserve of affection aside for her people. She presented the final of *Big Brother 2* pregnant with her first child. Her most maternal performance was yet to come. 'What you get in a gay club is a collective feeling of love for each other when you are all in the moment. Let's not forget that during the eviction nights at *Big Brother* it was like that. We were all collectively in the spirit, together, unified.'

The Only Gay in the Village

From the production gallery at Elstree, it was clear to Wendy Rattray that Brian Dowling was becoming the star of the show. The executive producer sent an email round the producers telling them to cut back on Brian, not because he wasn't coming up with endlessly entertaining, usable material, but because it would potentially compromise *Big Brother*'s impartiality, positioning him at an unfair advantage in the audience vote over weaker housemates. Brian may well be the only person on TV to be edited down for being too good on it. 'You could just keep on filming him,' Wendy says. 'He really was quite the star.'

Big Brother had a trick up its sleeve. To introduce a touch of tension to proceedings, a second gay man was interred at *Big Brother*'s behest. Josh Rafter was cut from a very different cloth to Brian Dowling. Metropolitan, built, in full control of his physique, he had a very gay job, working for the booming gay flat-share agency Outlet, at a very gay address, Old Compton Street. Josh came tinged with a recognisable millennial gay aspect that seemed to operate from the hips and eyes. Where Brian was alcopops, G-A-Y bar and 'who's your favourite Spice Girl?', Josh was protein shakes, upscale gym memberships and hard house. His entering the *Big Brother* house shone a spotlight on Brian's naïvety. The man who had prided himself on being the most popular in the house and was building up a massive fan-base outside of it was suddenly derailed and possibly even scared by another gay man's presence.

Paul Osborne had been part of the selection committee for Josh's casting. 'I liked Josh and thought he was very attractive. I thought it would be very interesting to have two different kinds of gay men in there.' If he had any expectations about how Brian might react to Josh, he thought it would mostly be admiration. 'I certainly wasn't expecting Brian to deal with it in the way he did.

Maybe I was just very naïve. I didn't think there was going to be any kind of romance because they were very different people, but I thought, Surely he's going to fancy him? His reaction was so the opposite of that. I guess it was jealousy. He was the only gay in the house, and his role was suddenly usurped and all the girls in the house were fawning over Josh. I did feel guilty about it.'

Wendy Rattray remembers his entrance similarly. 'Here was Brian,' she says, 'this incredibly young and probably quite inexperienced guy. You'd think he'd like another gay man who was a bit older and good-looking coming in. We thought he might look up to him, even.' Which was exactly what didn't happen. 'He really did not like Josh being in the house. I think he felt intimidated by him. Here he was, blossoming in the house in many ways. Suddenly, here's somebody else who's not only gay, but is also really quite together and confident and comfortable about himself.' Josh's reaction to Brian was equally telling. 'I think Josh quite liked Brian,' says Wendy. 'But he also quite liked the idea of the effect he had on Brian, who would almost behave like a little kid in front of him.'

Big Brother had turned into William Blake's *Songs of Innocence and Experience*. Until that moment, Brian was allowed to be the star of his own show. He had to grow up overnight and learn how to deal with not being the special one anymore. It was fascinating to watch. In scenes that are wincingly recognisable for any gay man ever to have faced a tougher, stronger, more alpha counterpart, Brian deals not only with the realities of what being performatively gay means, live on air, but also the stark realities of attraction. The new territories crossed for mainstream British storytelling of the gay experience here were manifold. Brian and Josh was an anti-love story, one that carried with it universal characteristics of jealousy, one-upmanship, personal development and competitiveness.

The distracted air of Brian Dowling at Josh Rafter's appearance was later used to acute comic effect by the double act of Matt Lucas and David Walliams, who transposed Brian's behaviour at having his crown toppled into the *Little Britain* favourite Daffyd, the only gay in the village. Brian was the reference they mentioned in all their press about the character. 'Women know that feeling,' says Davina McCall. 'With us it would be if a girl comes in who is prettier or sexier or more intelligent. We're all the same. I think people could identify with Brian on every level.'

What was interesting from a gay perspective was to watch how Brian was slowly unfolding and rinsing out an old seventies television stereotype that still remained cognisant in the memory of older viewers. Rather than seeing the desexualised gay man like John Inman on *Are You Being Served?* or Larry Grayson on *The Generation Game*, we were bearing witness to the presexualised model. Brian Dowling was a wonderful comic character, living on his wit and approachability. He could be bitchy without it hurting, was sharp with a one-liner and knew how to position his hair just so. He had every attribute of honest local gayness, except the developed sexuality at its core. It was a spectacular new nuance to watch the man argue this out with himself on the TV and the rolling digital platforms accompanying the show. 'That made us all fall in love with him so much, didn't it?' says Davina. 'He turned into this sweet little boy when faced with an alpha gay male coming into the house, and what that showed everybody was that it doesn't matter whether you are gay or straight. We really are all the same. We go through the same insecurities.' What it showed a gay audience, more directly, was the pecking orders you quickly attenuate to in gay life, lessons that school can never prepare you for because there you are always the minority.

'It was the turning point in terms of Brian not just being a clown, too' says Paul Osborne. 'He might have just floated down the river on this comedy card. Because Josh went in, I guess that was a chance for him to show that he had real feelings. You'd get those moments when he was a little upset. The raw details of his sexuality were more in the forefront, rather than just his playful "gayness". Brian's reaction to Josh was to shut him out. It was full leakage. His heart was on his sleeve the entire time. It gave Brian a bit more depth than being the funny little guy.'

A straight writer would never deploy that complexity and sensitivity in the tale of two gay men sharing an enclosed space. When he came out of the *Big Brother* house, Brian Dowling was subject to a succession of interviews, in some crowning him the temporary deity of the reality genre, in others fishing for simple old gossip on how he'd reacted to Josh Rafter. 'I'm so not Josh's type,' he told Simon Gage in *Attitude*. 'He's got a lot of charisma, whereas I'm just up for a laugh and a joke. The thing with me and Josh was that people assumed that we were going to get along. As soon as it was announced that Josh was gay, all the cameras in the house were like, "Whomph", and zoomed in on me.' It can be a funny experience watching the version of yourself you've presented to reality TV in the aftermath. 'I think Josh is good-looking but we had nothing in common. There's nothing more. Everywhere I go it's "You like Josh, you like Josh" and it's like, "What? What more can I tell you?"'

Brian's eventual triumph, winning this crazed new national popularity contest, was a win for all gay men. He wasn't just us at our most vocal and stereotypical; he was us at our most vulnerable and innocent, too. In the house, he was boy and man. Those awkward shifts played out on screen. 'Brian's moment was huge,' says Davina McCall. 'A gay man winning a show like that, which was so high profile at that time, was incredible. And the fact was that, even if you were slightly homophobic, he was such a great guy that he won everybody over and everybody loved him. All the broadsheets, the tabloids, all the magazines that got involved – that made me really happy. I remember saying to friends and family that this is a big moment. This is groundbreaking. This is new. In our own little way we may have made a difference.'

Wendy Rattray says that the great gay television turnaround effected by *Big Brother* was not planned. 'TV is a unique working environment,' she says, 'in that there are a lot of gay people and a lot of women in high-powered positions. It doesn't feel like it's a very straight-male-dominated environment in the way that it is in other workplaces, like the corporate environment where you can talk about glass ceilings. Honestly, I don't think that *Big Brother* was very different from any other TV show's staff. We, as producers, operated in an environment where it didn't feel like there was any discussion to be had. Representing people on TV didn't feel in any way out of the ordinary for us, it just felt completely normal. I do not recall any of us thinking this was a great moment for gay progress in Britain. I just remember us all being really happy that Brian won.'

For Paul Osborne, this was more than a personal triumph for Brian; it was a symbolic moment for Brians everywhere. 'I suppose it was quite similar to the Will Young and Gareth Gates final of *Pop Idol* the next year,' he says, 'when no one thought that Will was going to win.' Because the gay man, prior to his relationships being validated in statute, was ever destined to be the bridesmaid, the accomplice, the Mandelson to his Blair, the Watson to his Sherlock, the Norris to his Rita. For Osborne, a gay man becoming the winner for once mattered deeply. 'He had to win,' he says. 'I remember Davina was behind Brian the whole way. When she brought him out as the winner it felt almost like she was a proud mother; it was that joyous moment, the one we all want when we come out. She was pregnant at the time, heightening it all, making it all really quite hormonal.'

From his position in the crowd, Paul could see Davina whispering in Brian Dowling's ear. Through some sense of heightened telepathy, and a little lip-reading, he could make out her words. 'She just pointed to the crowd and to the fireworks going off in the night and said to him, "That's for you." It felt genuinely moving. She was explaining to him that life was going to be all right after he'd come out, in both senses of the words. It was amazing. The audience was joyous. It was very pure, that feeling that he deserved it.'

Reality TV, the Case for the Defence

Of the early noughties gay popularity-contest winners, Will Young felt like the connecting tissue between them all. He was the reality show star who would go to a Wolfgang Tillmans exhibition at the Tate, read an Alan Hollinghurst novel and vote for Brian Dowling to win *Big Brother*. If Dowling and the rotating cast of *Big Brother* LGBTs were challenging the fictitious types drawn on *Coronation Street*, *EastEnders* and *Hollyoaks*, it was as if Will had stepped in from a recording of *The Archers* to take his unexpected place in the Saturday night TV spotlight.

'Two of the most thrilling covers I remember doing,' says former *Attitude* editor Adam Mattera, 'were Brian Dowling and Will Young. They both felt like a sea change for gay culture. Everybody was talking about them and everybody was voting for them, and they had a huge tabloid price on their heads. At the time when Brian won, I can remember all the staff sitting down and watching the show together and feeling like something was changing.' The role entertainment plays in popular preconceptions being questioned cannot be underestimated. 'There's politics with a capital "P" and politics with a lower-case "p", and those kinds of people, those representations, whether it was somebody winning a reality TV show or somebody on a soap opera you see every day or a TV presenter that acts in public life without shame, knowing that they are gay and out in their lives has a huge significance to a generation of young people.'

The fallout of their wins would turn old light-entertainment habits on their heads. 'There was that marvellously complicated time,' says Russell T Davies, 'when Brian Dowling came out of *Big Brother* and was presenting children's television alongside H from Steps. One out of the closet, one in the closet, the closet probably relevant to both because it's children's television and it was all so ripe with the complications of visibility.' These tangles had to be unknotted in public in order to have consequences. Only ten years previously Gary Hailes had been turned down for a job presenting children's TV not because he was gay, but because he had played a gay character on *EastEnders*. 'The fact these people existed should be celebrated,' continues Davies, 'it was so joyous. *Big Brother* was so important. Nadia and Jason, I was so involved in that storyline and Fight Night that I was voting for her in it.' Davies once saw Jason Cowan, the former housemate and ringleader of Nadia's threatening straight antagonists, on a train. 'I didn't say a word, of course. I just sat there hating him.'

'It's easy to look back and think, Oh, it's just some guy who won a reality TV show,' says Adam Mattera, 'because of what that genre became later. It's easy to assume that those things were trivial. But Brian and Will, their being accepted helped form a tapestry of different representations of how it is to be gay. These faces are accepted by the public and endorsed by the mainstream media. They are loved in that moment.' Russell T Davies thinks reality TV was 'enormously important'. He sat and watched gripped by the biggest gay *Big Brother* storyline to emerge post Brian and Josh, another *Brideshead* narrative in which young hairdresser Craig Coates fell hard for his straight housemate Anthony Hutton. 'Those are the glory days of *Big Brother*,' he says. 'Anthony and Craig is one of the most complicated gay stories I've ever seen portrayed. The brutality and honesty with which that was laid out. As gay men we all hated that man and kind of loved him.' We all saw something of ourselves in Craig Coates, for what gay man can really put up his hand and say he has never fallen head over heels for the great dark man at his social side? 'Yes, it's the foolishness of it. Absolutely. Crying in the diary room, scintillating. In reality shows you can see a depth of detail that no drama could hope to replicate.'

'My favourite ever scene in *Big Brother* was in the diary room,' says Paul Osborne. 'When Makosi realises that Craig is in love with Anthony. She's sitting in the middle on the diary-room chair, Craig on one side and Anthony on the other. They're all talking away to Big Brother. She turns to Craig and he's literally just staring at Anthony, while Anthony's staring at her tits. She says, "Stopping looking at my boobs, Anthony," and Craig just fires up, absolutely whacks him across the face and says, "Oh, get a fucking grip!" It's astonishing on so many levels. Craig is totally expressing himself, Anthony gets riled up, Makosi excuses herself from the diary room and walks straight into the bedroom and announces to everyone, "I think Craig likes Anthony." Oh my God, that storyline, that whole interplay was just incredible. And it lasted for seven or eight weeks. Anthony hung out with Craig the entire time.'

The effect these stories have on gay and straight audience alike is the sinew of cultural acceptance, learned, registered and understood young. Wendy Rattray says that she will sit down with her children and explain to them the relationship of the gay Brighton hairdressers watching TV on the audience's behalf on *Gogglebox* who can trace their lineage back to Brian Dowling. 'I had to explain,' she says, 'that they used to go out together but they don't live with each other anymore. They were asking questions about them still being friends, which is a really good conversation to have with your kids. At its best, reality TV does reflect the way life is. The gay characters on reality shows are just part of life. When culture, in whatever form it takes, starts reflecting the changes that are happening in real life, it can normalise and make sense of the life you see around you every day.'

The Pop Idol

For Exeter University history undergraduate Will Young, Brian Dowling's *Big Brother* win was a watershed moment. 'The thing about the early days of reality TV was that it was so democratic,' he says. He would watch the show religiously, not just as a diversion from the serious business of studying, but because it fell precipitously into the moment that he began the tricky reconciliation between being publicly and privately gay. Will had spent the first year of his degree in a not dissimilar situation to the one Craig Coates found himself on *Big Brother*; he was in love with his straight best friend. 'It's OK, we're still friends now. He was wonderful about it. He lives in America and is married to someone from *Glee*.'

   Will didn't like the look of the Exeter University gay society, 'because they all wore Buffalo shoes.' He learned his gay life lessons the hard way, on the hoof, deep in love. 'I was the self-hating gay, the only gay in Exeter,' he says. Will and his friends watched *Big Brother* together, and seeing what happened next in the everyday kitchen-sink saga of the life of Brian would provide nightly respite from all that heartache. 'He was amazing, because I didn't know many gay people back then. For a gay guy to win it was incredible. Me and my friends just thought he was hysterically funny and quite real. He was an air steward. He did a Tina Turner dance with his friend Narinder, who was a bit of a bitch. Then he had that mental thing with Josh.' This recognisable behaviour all appealed. 'I was at a very parochial, bourgeois university, and he did loads in terms of cutting through with people.' Will Young's history degree was bookended by a first year watching Russell T Davies's *Queer as Folk* and a final one engrossed in Brian's *Big Brother*. 'It was good to know that gay people were not *just* bumming all the time.'

A win for a gay man on a national popularity contest is, he thinks, as revolutionary as it is conciliatory. 'A mirror went right up to the audience. People had to ask themselves questions about what they thought about others. You fuckers voted for me, know what I mean?' With his own experience of winning a reality TV contest on *Pop Idol*, that reflection went back into the family home. 'My dad had to look at the things he had said, and he wasn't even particularly homophobic, but he had to look at the language he had used around us and face that guilt. People suddenly had to look at that, en masse. That's why I think reality TV was such a unique experience.'

The first thing Will Young's mother said to him when he came out was, 'You're going to get beaten up.' Disappointment doesn't begin to cover his reaction. 'Really? You can't think of anything else?' He can forgive the warning if only because it didn't quite square with Will's understanding of a new gay world, one largely gleaned from the TV screen. 'Gay people had got to the stage where we were seen as the people you could go handbag shopping with,' he says, instantly conjuring up the figure of Stanford Blatch, Carrie Bradshaw's plump, bald, wisecracking and neurotic GBF in the smash millennial hit *Sex and the City*. 'It wasn't ideal, but it was at least something other than being a person to beat up. Brian was so important because he was being voted for. It was about a gay man being liked.'

Will would take his extracurricular education while studying for his degree where he could find it, mostly on Channel 4. 'They'd do a gay season, which would probably be one night between midnight and 5am, and I remember watching those things and being blown away, just because they were the only things I'd seen. There was a film where someone had really raw sex, this one guy fucked the other one who was HIV-positive.' He hadn't engaged in any gay culture previously as a teenager, for fear of it betraying to others who he really was. 'I was so repressed I just wouldn't go there, at all.'

His one outlet was singing. Because he had a fine, high voice – another indicator he was fearful of anyone misinterpreting – at boarding school he would lock himself in a dark room to sing. He became so obsessed with the idea of giving off clues to his gayness that he hid a box-fresh pair of red New Balance trainers just after purchase for fear of anyone thinking he was gay. Why didn't he buy blue? Or grey? These are the loopy questions you ask yourself when figuring out the acceptability of your sexuality in a world that seems in that moment ludicrously censorious. Will picked up a copy of *Attitude* magazine – with Chris O'Donnell, the actor playing Robin in the new Batman movie, on the cover – from the supermarket shelf one day. 'My mum turned round and said, "Do you know that's a gay magazine?" Clearly absolutely mortified. I'd only picked it up because I liked the haircut on the cover.'

After leaving Exeter, Will did a term at Arts Educational, the west London drama school with a speciality in musicals. There wasn't a boyfriend, but he began his physical gay education in earnest. 'Obviously, there was a bigger mirror in the boys' dressing room than there was in the girls' there.' Was there anyone straight in his class? 'Not many. There were a few that started off straight, but I later found out they certainly didn't end up that way. Went in straight, came out crooked, as they say.' He interned at Sony Records in the publishing department and saw an advert for *Pop Idol*, the new talent show cut from the same cloth as the Saturday night successes *Popstars* and *Popstars: The Rivals*, the entertainment vehicles that took a peek behind the curtain of the pop industry and threw out one burst of success for Hear'Say and a more enduring lifespan for perennial gay pop favourites Girls Aloud. Will Young harboured artistic ambitions of becoming a recording artist and didn't feel there would be many avenues open to him. 'I entered

Pop Idol because I couldn't see any way of my getting into the industry, because I was gay. That was one of the major reasons. There were no new, out gay people signed at the time. I'm posh, I'm not cool and I'm gay. Who the fuck is going to sign me? It was a major concern.' He took the plunge.

Will's great musical hero was George Michael. 'The only person to come out that I had personally been such a huge fan of was George,' he says. 'I was and still am a massive fan.' During his commercial supremacy in Wham! and the astronomical success of his solo album *Faith*, George had kept his sexuality hiding in plain sight. Wearied by a level of success he could neither cope with nor maintain, he swung into the nineties with his masterpiece *Listen Without Prejudice*, on which he proceeded to write, sing and perform with deft detail about the gay male experience. 'It was my first musical awakening. It's seminal, it really is,' says Young. 'I have definitely subconsciously modelled a lot of my singing on him. He was my first number one singer, basically. The emotion in his voice is peerless.'

The title *Listen Without Prejudice* could hardly have been any clearer for George's intentions with the record, to start afresh his artistic journey in a voice true to himself. In a series of audacious masterstrokes, he reconfigures himself artistically not in the hip-swinging model of Elvis, his *Faith* touchstone, but in that of John Lennon (on 'Praying for Time'), the Rolling Stones (on 'Waiting for That Day') and Stevie Wonder (he covers 'They Won't Go When I Go'). *Listen Without Prejudice* sounded like the closest a British artist had come to fashioning a gay *Songs in the Key of Life*. If his lyrics rippled with unguarded honesty ('I think there's something you should know … There's something deep inside of me/There's someone else I've got to be'), his accompanying press portfolio remained closeted. Those three little words – I am gay – remained unspoken.

For his next album, *Older*, George Michael penetrated even deeper into the gay male experience. On 'Fastlove' he forged a dramatic disco tribute to cruising. 'Spinning the Wheel' alluded to the Russian roulette nature of unsafe sex. On 'Jesus to a Child' he scripted the perfect eulogy to the partner he was then grieving, Brazilian clothes designer Anselmo Feleppa. George Michael had opened his artistic hand with Wham! as a teenager bristling with youth, sex, beauty, freedom and fun. These solo records were his official entry into adulthood.

George Michael's public coming out preceded Young's private one by a year. One played directly into the other. 'It was glorious,' recalls Young. 'Even now I remember how cool it was.' Having been arrested for importuning an undercover policeman in the restroom of the Will Rogers Memorial Park in Beverly Hills, he turned the potential public shaming on its head when he released the single 'Outside', a rabble-rousing call to arms in celebration of public gay sex. The video featured disco balls coming down from the ceiling in a public toilet and hot cops wielding their truncheons suggestively in time to his immaculate ear for dance-floor pacing. He turned a victimless crime into a one-act disco symphony that remains one of the great watermarks of gay pop insurrection and will likely for all time. 'Just so cool,' says Young.

Will worked out the *Pop Idol* audience immediately ('Mrs Miggins in Southampton') and found a persona close enough to his own to fit expectations while staying true to himself. As his popularity began rising in haste, his full intention was to officially come out at the end of the process, effectively making him the first British pop star to open his mainstream artistic hand gay and proud since Jimmy Somerville and the Frankie boys in the eighties. 'I think this is why I was quite a good character for the show: I was sexually neutralised of my own doing.' Amid an unusual year of strong characters, including the overbearing singer, Darius Danesh and Gareth Gates, the council-estate kid who could sing through his stammer, Young earned early notoriety by answering back the impressive overlord figure of Simon Cowell, already on his way to owning British Saturday night TV.

'In terms of being gay in the competition,' he recalls, 'I had made a decision from the beginning that if someone asked me, I would never deny it.' This ran contrary to the show's press office, who advised against doing anything to compromise his popularity in the public vote. When he was asked on finals week who his ideal date would be, Will answered, 'The Queen.' Not only a quick retort, but one that rang quite possibly true for this classy character who was breaking down a considerable amount of the target audience's preconceptions and inverted snobberies towards plummy public schoolboys. Will Young didn't just break the working-class code of reality TV stars, he formed a new archetype: the gay man smart-thinking mums wanted their sons to end up with.

Though as discernible a triumph as Brian Dowling's on *Big Brother* from gay viewers' perspectives, Will's winning *Pop Idol* felt rather different from the inside. 'I was just so glad that it was almost over, to be honest,' he says of the final. 'I thought, It's good, I'm here and I've not been thrown out early. I had a really stressful soundcheck for the final. All the judges would watch it and they weren't allowed to say anything. All the keys of the songs were written for Gareth. Darius and I would sing them and we'd say to each other, "Have they really done this?"' He could see the business logic. 'I didn't blame them. Gareth was more in the ilk of a solo Westlife star, and I mean that with respect. He was in that pop lineage and looked of his moment, and I wasn't and didn't at all. He'd sing 'Unchained Melody' and I'd sing the Doors.' Will doesn't regret the experience for a moment. He never looks back on it thinking, What the hell was I doing on that show? 'No, no way. It's more like, Wow, I did it.'

Will Young's debut single was 'Evergreen', an anodyne Westlife album track. His recording career would markedly improve from thereon in, and he has since developed a similar love/hate relationship with the tune to the one Kylie Minogue has with 'I Should Be so Lucky'. 'Evergreen' became the biggest-selling single of the decade, shifting 1.8million copies, including a record-breaking first-week tally. The music industry was still capable of shifting new music at the time, and the *Pop Idol* contestants were paid a flat fee of £60,000 straight into their bank accounts for the spin-off arena tour, which Young would bring to a climax with his winner's number. He remembers that one contestant didn't have a bank account and kept her money under her mattress, so a hired hand at the production company was assigned to help her open one. Even for Young, who came from a financially comfortable family, was aghast at the amount they were making from the outset. 'The statistics all became a bit dizzying.'

As part of his winner's deal, Young was given former Spice Girls impresario Simon Fuller and his team at 19 Entertainment to handle his management. Fuller cannily passed on the two lucrative sponsorship deals tied up with Young's winners package, with Pepsi and Wella hair products, turning them over to the runner-up, Gareth Gates, for fear that this kind of commercial deal at the outset would dog Young's career later down the line. He saw in Will a good voice, talent, songwriting ability, a performer and popularity. He wanted to play the long game and find him the right audience. Will says Fuller was a genius at thinking about the broader picture, what might happen two or three albums in. He insists that Fuller had no issue with his deciding to come out. 'With someone like Simon it would be like, "Who really gives a shit?"'

Will wanted to go with a broadsheet to declare his sexuality, preferably *The Times* or the *Telegraph*, with him writing the piece. 'That got scuppered because the *Mail on Sunday* were going to print a story. So we went with the *News of the World*.' He was advised to keep the tabloids onside if he wanted any chance of career longevity.

The *Mail* retaliated with a string of outrageous accusations. 'The things that the *Mail* wrote about me, homophobia to the point that they were implying I was pretty much a gay rapist at boarding school, with a gang of gay friends. Who? I have no idea. What friends? A litigation lawyer had to read it to me and at the time all I would get told was, "Don't take on the tabloids because you need your career."' The allegations and implications bore no relation to his time at boarding school. None of it tallied with the boy hiding his trainers and singing in the dark, crippled with fear at being outed.

'At school I ran a very sensible self-preservation programme, which was not to come out until uni. To be called gay at a boys' school was the worst slander ever. Fucking hell, you might as well choose your own social death.' After a breakdown in 2012, Will Young spent six months at a rehabilitation facility near Oxford, where he attempted to undo some of the damage caused by his early years at boarding school under an intense programme designed for post-traumatic stress disorder. He has done a lot of work on his gay shame since, facing up to a succession of mental-health and addiction issues so often related to institutional rejection. You can see why incorrectly sourced or made-up tales of debauchery at school hurt so much.

Young first saw his coming-out story in the *News of the World* at a Tesco checkout and promptly had the most serious of a succession of panic attacks, the old words of his mother ringing in his ears. 'I honestly thought that I would get beaten up for it. I was in this superstore thinking, Fuck. It wasn't so much about feeling self-conscious as being about the labelling. For a long time afterwards it was "gay Will Young", which at least took over from "posh Will Young."' He was taught by his press officer how to steer a conversation away from the gay issue and back to the music for daytime TV interviews. 'I think half of it was very positive and healthy, and I think half of it – and I don't know whether I'd had this conversation with her – was a hangover from the nineties where you just don't talk about this. There were people like Jon from S Club 7 she'd handled, but that would have never come out at the time. They were different sets of fans, very much in kiddie land.'

Having exempted himself from the admonishment of the closet, Will had a brief, three-night fling with a member of the upper-tier pop coterie of the time. Because this person was closeted, they had to invent an elaborate ruse to distract the waiting paparazzi outside Will's Notting Hill home for his partner to make a hasty escape. Will found a toy kitten and started flinging the toy around by the tail outside his house to distract the press while his overnight adventure slipped out of view. 'There was never a question that I wouldn't come out,' he says. 'I was 20. I'd waited such a long time to do this. I'd been at frigging boarding school since the age of seven, and no way was I going back in the closet. I always said that if there is a kind of people who wouldn't buy my music because I'm gay, well, I don't want them buying my music.'

Young's record label had to draw up a plan of action to make his outing work. He found strong allies who would help protect and facilitate his identity, keeping a firm grip on mid-market commercial success while going just far enough in terms of playing with the idea of himself as a gay artist. For his second video, Fuller's creative right-hand at 19, Katia Drummond, introduced him to the exemplary filmmaker Baillie Walsh, who fashioned a love triangle inspired by Edie Sedgwick film *Ciao! Manhattan* to accompany Will's reading of the Doors' 'Light My Fire'. The video commissioner at his label, Michael Keith, would keep directors engaged with ideas that kept Young honest to himself without scaring the horses. 'It was about coming up with ways of sexualising someone who people don't necessarily want to know about their sex. That was really interesting, and I think we had real fun with that. The swimming pool video, for instance, with me learning how to swim but standing there in Speedos.' An image open to alternate readings, which had been utilised way back for Bronski Beat's 'Smalltown Boy'. 'There are things you can do as a gay artist that you can't as a straight artist. When I did the *Top Gun* video, it took on a whole new meaning with a gay artist in the middle of it. It becomes instantly even more homoerotic. That is what we presented.'

Will had to remain temperate about the delivery of his music to a Marks & Spencer audience. When the director Wiz handed him an early treatment for a video with a scene featuring him kissing another man, Young felt it might be pushing his audience slightly too far, with too literal a representation of a self he'd fought hard to protect. He favoured the suggestive approach. He says it fills him with joy to watch an artist like Olly Alexander, the Years & Years singer, who is now able to fully express his sexuality in pop videos, without shying away from the actual sex. 'There is a climate and it changes over generations. Young kids don't give a shit about the way that Olly presents himself. They love him for it. I love him for it.'

In some respects, Will thinks that his gayness created some artistic opportunities that otherwise would have remained shut. 'I did get access to people once I came out that maybe was because of it. People like Baillie – brilliant, brilliant people who were interested. I think I and the people around me had a lot of fun playing around with what it could mean to be a gay artist at that time, and we got some really good help along the way. They all embraced it. Michael Keith embraced it, Katia embraced it, and then slowly the press embraced it, too.'

His career has not been without incidents of casual homophobia, however. There was the famous time the then-omnipotent Radio 1 breakfast show presenter Chris Moyles imitated his voice in a campy, derogatory manner, an incident that in the long run did more to outmode Moyles in his audience's mind than it did Young for his. Will says that an executive at Sony asked him to repeatedly rerecord his vocal for his signature hit 'Leave Right Now' because he sounded 'too gay' on it. 'Hello?' Then there was the incident at a photo shoot for *GQ*, when the magazine was about to anoint him as one of their men of the year and he was instructed to put his top back on for a photo. 'I was dancing a lot and was in good shape. We were about to do a shot with my top off and they stormed in and said, "Yes, but you might look too gay." If you're a straight bloke with your top off, fine. If you're gay, not fine. You are de facto camping it up.'

If Brian Dowling was British reality TV's pacesetter, Will Young was its accession to the establishment, fitting in everywhere and nowhere. For the British pop landscape he became another bellwether in the march toward acceptance, opening up the shires and *Telegraph* readers to the broadening reach of LGBT representation. He looked a little like Merchant Ivory redrafting a gay Robbie Williams, and he belonged in the esteemed lineage of a class of stately homo that includes Rupert Everett, Stephen Fry and Clare Balding. Will Young was George Michael reconfigured for an age of transparency and openness. His massive blue-eyed soul sales predated Sam Smith's auspicious transatlantic career by a decade. He bucked the reality TV trend by improving sales as his career continued. He gave lower-case 'c' conservative Britain an icon all of its own to sit proud in the heritage of gay artistry. He says he could not have done it any other way. 'I don't think I could have sustained a career that long without coming out at the start,' he says. 'For one thing, that lie would have sent me loopy. Can you imagine?'

Reality TV allowed Will Young to be famous and gay. He continues to nurse his mental health the best he can. Only one worry remains. 'Being agoraphobic, clubbing isn't quite my thing,' he says, 'So you go on Grindr.' The gay dating app can involve the exchange of intimate visual information. 'I'm amazed that, given the amount of people I've sent pictures of my cock to, that it's not become famous, too. Maybe there's just not enough interest in it?' He pauses. 'I'm partly offended.' Then he laughs. 'God knows why it's not out there somewhere.'

9. PENALTY SHOOTOUT

The Terraces

I grew up in a football family. Not an obsessive football family, but a football family with its own peculiar and occasionally fractious dynamic (Dad supports Manchester United, brother supports City). Nonetheless, it was one where masculinity was synonymous with an interest in the beautiful game. In this respect, I couldn't quite work out where a ten-year-old who preferred listening to Dollar cassettes on a shiny red Walkman to watching 90-minute kickabouts interrupted by a mug of lukewarm gravy every Saturday afternoon fitted into all that. It soon made sense.

When it came to football, I was the absolute gay-child cliché. Last to be picked for the team in games lessons, entirely uninterested in getting my hair messed up when I did, then later preferring to loiter at the top of the playing field, gossiping, smoking or both, to taking part in any kind of team sport. By fourth year at high school I just didn't bother turning up. The school at the top of Sharston Mount was being demolished the following year, when we would all be chucked out anyway, so the teachers had a mostly last-days-of-

Rome attitude to our education. That suited me fine. Nobody really cared if you didn't show up for PE. The only time I remember any authority figure getting aerated at school in those last two funny years I attended was when one of the pupils in my year, the last kids standing in a virtual ghost space with the odd smashed window and a permanently faulty heating system, broke in to the school one night and a rumour circulated that he'd defecated in the water tank (he had). We all got sent home for that. The conversations at the bus stop were like something straight out of a Willy Russell play.

Yet by some strange form of osmosis, connected to a strong sense of civic pride I felt early and hard about being Mancunian – a feeling instilled by so many local characters telling you that to be Mancunian was to somehow be better than the rest – football seeped into my blood with the recurrence of a soap opera, an interest that spiked as I moved into my teen years because of football's twin associations with music and fashion. I still wasn't necessarily interested in what was going on on the pitch, but I was in the terraces, where all the best-dressed lads with the best taste in music were hanging out. There is nothing to be proud of in any of this, but still ... the thought of all that raw, pent-up masculinity, the immaculately shod hooligans going to hang around, have a fight and follow a team of fit young men they were personally devoted to and hung every inscrutable surface tenet of their identity on, carried with it a hauntingly erotic overtone.

There was no antipathy between the PE wing of the school and the few kids who couldn't be bothered to play their games. A nice gym teacher with shaggy blond hair and the best Adidas tracksuits, the closest the girls at the adjacent building got to having an onsite heart-throb, cornered me one day and asked about my English project, which he'd heard was on the Smiths. He sat me down and let me ask him questions about Johnny Marr and Andy Rourke, the band's guitarist and bass player, whom he'd taught at our school some years earlier. He brought in his copy of *Meat Is Murder* for me to copy out accurately the lyrics I wanted to quote. It was the first time I'd ever interviewed anyone and it felt really good, unearthing this big raft of personal information and writing it down the way I wanted it to be read.

My brother got his first job at the high-end Piccadilly casualwear shop Hurley Sports, then responsible for cladding the best boys on the terraces at Maine Road and Old Trafford. There was a 40 per cent discount involved. A whole world of football casuals' gear, of Lacoste, Diadora, Fila, Lotto, Kappa, Ralph Lauren, Stone Island and CP Company, started casting its spell. The politics of purchasing trainers was way easier to follow than the offside rule for a young boy in absolute thrall to the kind of argyle sock or shade of Pod shoes his big brother deemed acceptable. Dressing in the manner of a footie fan wasn't about trying to look straight or fitting in. It was about trying to look sexy, in that ravishingly buttoned-up way that still exists in the men of the north of England and probably always will on account of the weather.

The culture around footballers – the booze problems, the glamour models, the perms, the sensational managers smoking cigars in shearling overcoats, the flash car stereos pounding out Alexander O'Neal tapes – and their immediate local influence interested me way more than the game. I liked the pack mentality and the shared hope and tears. I liked all that outpouring of contained male emotion, which was constantly at the teetering precipice of overspill, pouring back and forth between the teams and their fans.

The sums began to add up. I realised that turning my back on football at a young age was nothing to do with escaping into another world, but probably a rather more innate fear of what it was I found attractive in the beautiful game. It took me a while to work out quite how hot I find football and everything that goes along with it. I didn't even fancy individual footballers. I fancied football – the realm, that catch-all space that still seems to carry the entirety of a certain type of British masculinity manfully on its shoulders, directing their dreams like air traffic control.

For gay men in the eighties, football was one of the most conspicuous worlds to which you were not invited, rendering it as a realm all the more appealing to sneak in through the back door. At some point in the last 30 years you might think someone – an industry overlord, a clever chap who'd perhaps noticed what had happened in terms of advancement in culture, even someone in successive British governments when they welcomed LGBT folk to the table – the obvious commercial spike of inclusivity and opened the front door for a brand new demographic to step through. Yet somehow they never did. I never did get an answer to the question: why?

Mothers and Sons

Just before Christmas 2013, Los Angeles Galaxy footballer Robbie Rogers took his mother out near his home in West Hollywood. 'I was sitting in Soho House,' he says, 'and we were just having dinner and talking about marriage.' Same-sex marriage, that is. The meal sounds like a scene from *Brothers & Sisters*, the TV drama about a wealthy American family presided over by Sally Field as the loving matriarch with a special fondness for her gay son, the most seemingly stable of her sprawling clan. Robbie Rogers would make a perfect casting for the kind of handsome, well-dressed, well-groomed and well-adjusted gay son of whom any modern mother could stand proud beside. He looks like Justin Timberlake's more sensitive younger brother.

Robbie was 26 years old, at the upper age bracket of a fledgling new generation, a subset of picket-fence gays defined by social and political winds that had pushed marriage to the top of the gay news agenda. 'I was saying I definitely did want to get married,' he says, true to type.

'I asked her how she felt about that,' he continues. 'And she said, "I'll definitely be there and your grandma and grandpa will be there, too."' It was not the first time the subject of gay marriage had been broached in the Rogers family, who called the idyllic suburban Californian coastal nook of Palos Verdes home. Robbie came out to his family in November 2012, just in time to ignite fireside discussion on the state split over Proposition 8, the bill which enshrined in law that marriage should only be between a Californian man and a woman.

Robbie understood that his mother was discreetly fishing over dinner for information about her son's love life, in the exact manner that the Sally Field character in *Brothers & Sisters* might of hers. Perhaps there was a serious young suitor looking to whisk her offspring down the aisle, even? Because he had been out to her less than a year and courting his first boyfriend less than six months, Robbie deflected the inquisition back and turned the personal political. '"I have a lot of friends that can get married now,"' he explained to his mother, '"which is awesome because some of them would be separated through visa problems."' She was satisfied with the response. 'She said, "I'm really happy for you and your friends."'

Robbie Rogers talked about his coming out a lot in 2013, the year he became a reluctant, complicated figurehead for gay sportsmen, particularly footballers in the UK. Getting to this point with his mother had been hard won. 'She's sweet and very smart. She had an open mind when she realised everything that I'd been through.' Convoluted by the early realisation that he was gay, Robbie Rogers's childhood was distracted. 'I'm from a very conservative, Catholic family,' he says, 'so whenever there was stuff in California regarding same-sex marriage, they were on the wrong side. They were just homophobic. But that's probably because they never thought that they had a gay son. I never gave them a chance to know that.' Like the country's laws, they changed.

As a teen, Robbie was a good boy, in the obedient sense of the word. 'I mean, I wasn't looking for gay life and I didn't find it. I was definitely being careful with that. I was in such a whitewashed, conservative community. Everyone wanted to be the same. Everyone's parents were competing. It was just weird.' When he speaks like this, his upbringing sounds more like an episode of *Desperate Housewives* than *Brothers & Sisters*. 'It was exactly that. I didn't know anybody that was gay in Palos Verdes.' He didn't even try the internet.

Robbie would try to organise his thoughts in a manner respectful to his household culture and Catholic religion. 'Like, OK, yes, God created me to be gay, but if I act on it? That's the thing.' He practised the double-bluff tomfoolery of loving the sinner, hating the sin, and by his teens his physical life was devoted to sport. Unusually for a Californian surfer, with the wind in his hair and beach on his doorstep, he followed the English football team Arsenal, and developed a special talent for the sport. In keeping with the culture of that sport, he dated women from high school through to his very public – and very out of keeping with football culture – coming out, at 25. 'I was ashamed. But then I think a lot of gay men deal with a lot of different kinds of shame.'

Two years prior to his full disclosure, one whose effects should have rippled hard around the institution of English football and beyond, Robbie Rogers began to reconcile himself to the double-narrative he'd threaded through his early adult life, one in which the surface didn't quite connect to the substance. 'I thought, This is just a waste of a life,' he says sadly. 'There is no way that, just because you're a gay man trying to love and live your life and be open and have relationships, someone can judge and say, "Oh, you're going to hell because you're born this way or that way." That's insane to me. Absolutely insane.'

Part of his attraction to football was a professional life that might take him far from home, to work out the sort of man he was going to allow himself to be. 'Subconsciously, I wanted to be close to my family, but not too close. So I ended up studying at the University of Maryland.' His talent did the trick. His first professional footballing appointment was in Holland, then Columbus, Ohio, then Leeds, before eventually moving to the home counties. He would spend his off-seasons in New York or Paris: 'I'd find places away from my family.' In light of this, the dinner conversation with his mother struck a poignant, redemptive note. 'It wasn't really me having to persuade her or anything,' he says. 'It was just about her or anyone in my family being exposed to it. I think that's the best way, really, just to expose people to it.'

In the course of just over a year, this nice, athletic American everyman became an important addition to a very British problem: gay men's relationship with football and football's relationship with gay men. The most interesting complication around him turning into a new poster-boy for gay football was that his main problem regarding sexuality was not being a gay footballer, but being gay itself. The hurdle he had to leap was personal, not professional or political.

Robbie joined Major League Soccer side Columbus Crew in 2007. He enjoyed booming professional highs, including winning the MLS Cup (the American equivalent of winning the Premier League). 'The year we won the championship, it was the same year I made my debut for the national team. I was 21, 22.' These highs were compromised by crashing personal lows, however. 'I think when you're having the most success you can kind of forget about your other struggles. But there were so many times after we won the league that I remember, when my teammates would all be going out and partying and hanging out with their wives, and I just went home depressed and thought, Why am I not happy? In my career there were so many times when I struggled with my mental health. That affected the way I played.'

He played for the USA Olympic team at the Beijing Olympics in 2008, the same year Proposition 8 came into effect in California. He signed for Leeds United, playing in the Championship, the second-highest division in the English football league system, at the start of 2012. The intensity of British football culture came as a surprise to him. He was genuinely shocked by the banter in the dressing room and filled with self-loathing by it. No one had explained to him the strong tradition established over the previous 20 years in northern English cities welcoming gay men, of the gay villages that were blossoming in Leeds, Liverpool and Newcastle, complementing the enormous, city-defining strip in Manchester. But then he never asked.

Robbie only managed to play a limited number of games before injury scuppered his first season at Leeds. He was loaned to the less prestigious Stevenage. The club's proximity to London meant that he could start exploring the city and find his place within it. 'I became myself there,' he says. He met a gay stylist on a publicity photo shoot and became buddies with him and his boyfriend, without telling them that he too was gay. It was here that he began formulating plans to leave football because of his sexuality. 'I didn't want to be the guinea pig,' he says.

It's not quite fair to call the British gay football mess a last taboo. There are still plenty of other important national institutions that have yet to embrace a gay figurehead, and over whom the antiquated shadow of 'the closet' looms. The royal family only managed to unearth its first gay member in 2016, when Lord Ivar Mountbatten, a cousin of the Queen, came out and broke an unspoken rule in the family in which gay men, from the Queen Mother's attendants to Diana's couturiers, were forever cast in a damningly servile role. But the subject of gay men and football had by now become such a matter of symbolic urgency and institutional shame for British football that there were more openly gay bishops than there were active professional gay football players, of which there was a round number of zero.

Any institutional change introduced by the Football Association to rectify this anachronism looked pitifully superficial, clumsy and ineffective. A placebo initiative for Premier League players to wear rainbow-striped laces at games as a display of support for closeted gay players, introduced by the pressure group Stonewall, felt well-intentioned if tokenistic. Buried on the FA's website, the banner 'Football v Homophobia' points to initiatives that never seem to result in a practical end, of finding that needle in a haystack: the gay footballer that will be accepted on the pitch and supported by the sport's professional governing body.

Football in Britain has talked a type of talk about the problem around gay footballers coming out, without much direct action in assisting them to do so or anyone taking responsibility for sorting the mess out. The disgraced publicist Max Clifford, who once ruled the roost on these matters, said that he would tell gay-footballer clients thinking of being open not to bother. In lieu of any direct action on the subject, a common argument floated through the ether that the fans couldn't cope with a gay player on the pitch. Yet that argument ran counterintuitive to the same fans listening to Nick Grimshaw waking them up on Radio 1's breakfast show or having Evan Davies take them through the news of the day on *Newsnight* without feeling the urge to shout 'poofter' at them every time they appeared. If a gay man is good at doing something, Britain has long since found its mechanism for embracing them doing it their way. The outsourcing to fans of an untested problem feels like blaming payday loans for ruthless employers or housing-benefits claimants for rogue landlords. Social media hardly helped, incubating a transitional, bleating anger culture in which we were more likely to shout about the symptoms of a rotating wheel of problems than address the problems themselves. Given that football is such an obscenely commercial industry, the most obvious place to start tackling homophobia in dressing rooms, on the pitch and on the terraces would be where it really hurts football clubs, in their stuffed wallets.

On 23 February 2013, Robbie announced that he was gay in a nicely worded missive on his web page. It is worth repeating in full.

For the past 25 years I have been afraid, afraid to show whom I really was because of fear. Fear that judgement and rejection would hold me back from my dreams and aspirations. Fear that my loved ones would be farthest from me if they knew my secret. Fear that my secret would get in the way of my dreams. Dreams of going to a World Cup, dreams of the Olympics, dreams of making my family proud. What would life be without these dreams? Could I live a life without them?

Life is only complete when your loved ones know you. When they know your true feelings, when they know who and how you love. Life is simple when your secret is gone. Gone is the pain that lurks in the stomach at work, the pain from avoiding questions, and at last the pain from hiding such a deep secret.

Secrets can cause so much internal damage. People love to preach about honesty, how honesty is so plain and simple. Try explaining to your loved ones after 25 years you are gay. Try convincing yourself that your creator has the most wonderful purpose for you even though you were taught differently.

I always thought I could hide this secret. Football was my escape, my purpose, my identity. Football hid my secret, gave me more joy than I could have ever imagined ... I will always be thankful for my career. I will remember Beijing, the MLS Cup, and most of all my teammates. I will never forget the friends I have made along the way and the friends that supported me once they knew my secret.

Now is my time to step away. It's time to discover myself away from football. It's 1am in London as I write this and I could not be happier with my decision. Life is so full of amazing things. I realised I could only truly enjoy my life once I was honest. Honesty is a bitch but it makes life so simple and clear. My secret is gone, I am a free man, I can move on and live my life as my creator intended.

The words that really stung for me were 'football hid my secret'. It was another twist on the exclusion so many young men experience with a shared collective energy around the game. What a way for a professional institution to behave.

Robbie says he received no professional or PR instruction on how to write the letter ('sometimes you hear people make a big announcement one way or another and you can just tell that it's not genuine, and you wonder what the motivation behind it is'), but had been moved by the content of the brilliant musician Frank Ocean's similarly themed open letter dropped onto the internet the year before, around the release of his Grammy-winning album *Channel Orange*, which dealt with similar issues of shame and a further direct narrative journey of unrequited love for a man. 'I didn't realise how big of a deal it was going to be,' Robbie says. 'I didn't have any idea that it would reach people around the world or the impact it would have, especially on younger people. I mean, I'm happy it happened that way, but it wasn't my master PR plan.'

At the age of 25, during what should have been the peak period of his career, Robbie Rogers quit football in order to live his life fully, turning his coming-out prose into a document the very definition of bittersweet. He was already well into forging a second career in the fashion industry. He interned at *Men's Health* magazine on the fashion desk, began attending the menswear shows at London fashion week, worked for a notable fashion PR firm and accepted a place at the London College of Fashion to study technical menswear design, intending to pay for it with the money he'd saved from his football career. He had come out to his stylist friend and boyfriend. He had the armour to live a gay life and was beginning to assemble the professional wherewithal to find a job that would let him. He was living in east London and tentatively stepping into gay spaces. 'My first taste of a gay community,' he says, 'of going out to bars and partying and whatever, was in east London. I'd go to the Nelson's Head or East Bloc. So grungy, but so fun. It was really cool.'

On a personal note, his tale reads close enough to that of any other visiting overseas fashion student brought up in a rigorous Catholic household to make it quite unremarkable. But the professional football aspect of it made Robbie Rogers's a story symbolically irresistible to unzip. This was a rabbit hole the FA must have seen itself falling down at some point as it moved in the opposite direction from contemporary British culture and politics, as it stayed rooted in an old-fashioned machismo its most famous and popular player of recent times, David Beckham, has done such a magnificent job of smashing to pieces. It is only because Robbie Rogers started to engage in some form of gay life in places without Leeds United or Stevenage fans present that he didn't get involved in tabloid scandal and have ownership of his already tender move to personal acceptance robbed from him.

Robbie named and shamed the aggressive homophobia of football's dressing-room culture as being part of the reason for turning his back on his sporting gift. If the Football Association and the international football body FIFA emerged blushing from his outing, his premature retirement made it brisk-enough business for them to sweep under the carpet. Nobody from either body made a prominent statement saying that this shoddy state of affairs would be dealt with in the future or that a gay footballer who wanted to come out would be supported, in full, by their employers forthwith. It feels almost comic to have to point out that, in the twenty-first century, men should not be disqualified from doing the job they ought to be doing on account of their sexuality. It is farcical to point by comparison at the inclusivity of the England women's team, one unencumbered by the commerce and dictatorial rule of their male counterpart. It feels even a little cruel to look at their relative levels of success, to highlight the shoddy workmanship of an England men's team bound by a culture of denial, regression and money.

Endemic attitudes at the FA and FIFA throbbed through Robbie's tale. Their silence became noisy. He says he didn't feel comfortable going to his bosses at Leeds or Stevenage, or to the FA, to enquire if they would support a decision for him to come out and stay on the pitch. 'No, I never asked those questions. I was so afraid.' Leeds United made some headway in the aftermath to shoulder any responsibility they had for Robbie's inability to be himself at work, and began work on real, recognisably useful local initiatives to combat any future problems, including inviting Robbie to play as a moment of empathetic symbolism and supporting his work with his charity in sport and sexuality. Still, Robbie saw his resignation as a fait accompli. 'My thing was that I was done and I was going to do it on my own terms, away from a football club. I was going to take some time to myself and no one was going to try and persuade me to do that while I was back in football, and no one was going to persuade me to do it in any other way.'

His industry had failed his gift. It had form on this matter. When Robbie Rogers arrived at Leeds United, he caught a programme on television covering a story he wasn't familiar with, but was enshrined in the doomed parochial legacy of the Football Association's treatment of gay players, one that set a tone that is yet to be broken. 'There was a documentary talking about Justin

Fashanu,' he says. His teammates were talking about it the next day. 'I heard for the first time guys saying, "Yeah, there will never be an out footballer in Britain." Little did they know I was having lunch right next to them.'

The Player

'I hope the Jesus I love me welcomes me home,' read the final sentence of Justin Fashanu's suicide note, left by his side in the Shoreditch garage he was found in, having hanged himself, on 3 May 1998. Dead at 37 years of age. Fashanu was being pursued for a same-sex sexual assault claim in the USA, one he thought he would be found guilty of because of the astronomical scales of antipathy towards him after coming out in the *Sun* newspaper in 1990. On the night of his death, Justin had paid one final visit to Chariot's gay sauna, half a mile down the road. The mating grounds that Robbie Rogers first experienced gay life in, the Nelson's Head pub and East Bloc nightclub, were a stone's throw from where Fashanu's body was found.

Justin Fashanu is not just the homophobic shame of the Football Association; he is the homophobic shame of Britain. Justin was born to a Nigerian barrister father and nurse mother in London in 1961. When his father left to return to Nigeria and his mother was no longer able to cope, he and his brother John were fostered young, eventually to a couple in Norfolk. They were both promising athletes as kids, and it was thought for a while that Justin had a promising future ahead of him as a heavyweight boxer. He became a professional footballer with Norwich City in 1978 and was bought by Nottingham Forest in 1981, becoming the first black player in Britain to command a million-pound price tag.

At Forest, rumours of strife with manager Brian Clough abounded. A story in Clough's autobiography about a locker room interchange between the manager and his player pinpoints the casually offensive heart of the culture his outing fell into:

> 'Where do you go if you want a loaf of bread?' I asked him. 'A baker's, I suppose.' 'Where do you go if you want a leg of lamb?' 'A butcher's.' 'So why do you keep going to that bloody poofs' club?'

A tabloid sting forced Fashanu to sell his story to the *Sun* in 1990, making him the first gay British footballer to declare his sexuality. The story was maximised for full lascivious effect, emphasising Fashanu's claim to have had an affair with a Conservative MP, though whether it was one rushing through anti-gay legislation in the form of Clause 28 at the time was never asked by the paper's inquisitor. A torrent of abuse and disgust followed Fashanu onto the pitch and bled into his fractured family life. His brother John never seems to have quite reconciled himself to Justin's life or the actual cause of his death, beyond the noose. He later told the *Daily Mirror* that he had paid Justin £75,000 to keep quiet about his sexuality, though John's daughter Amal filmed a beautiful, sympathetic documentary about her uncle Justin later for BBC3, which refused to sugarcoat her father and instead cross-examined his latent prejudices to moving, intergenerational effect.

Justin Fashanu was the bluntest end of a culture not just reluctant to budge out of an arcane, bloody-minded homophobia, but one that seemed almost delighted with its decision to entrench it. The farcical aftermath of his revelations, including the barely plausible story that he had an affair with bisexual actress and *Coronation Street* fixture Julie Goodyear did not deter from his martyrdom.

For Robbie Rogers, freshly arrived on British turf, football's spiritual home, the Justin Fashanu story was all too much. 'I think a lot of gay men deal with a lot of shame,' he says. 'I know I did. I think that's why ultimately he took his own life. There are a lot of moments in a gay man's life when they maybe feel really unconfident and that the only way out of this dark hole is to take your own life.' He does not specify whether he ever went to those darkest recesses. 'So that, first of all, was so sad. That the football world was not supportive of him was sad. That his own family were not very supportive of him was incredibly scary. I thought, Wow, what if my family is like this? There were a lot of things that touched me.'

Football is England's epic, shared national romance. The game is arguably as pivotal to the shape of our culture as the Bank or Church of England. Key tournaments bring the country together in a manner political parties would shed blood to mirror. 'I know that the Professional Footballers' Association have counselling stuff that you can reach out to,' says Robbie, 'but it's crazy to me that they don't have some kind of a campaign or an organisation that is at least trying to create an environment that makes it possible for athletes to come out. Maybe they're working on it? I don't know.'

Maybe the problem runs deeper still, to the top tier of the football industry. Internationally, the world of football is opening itself up to criticism through FIFA giving the 2018 World Cup to Russia, whose record on LGBT rights has been the subject of controversy, and then a whole new level of farce through awarding 2022's World Cup to Qatar, a country where it is both illegal to be gay and, due to the extreme climate, may well prove physically impossible to play football. 'They shouldn't have to think about that,' says Robbie. 'It's really sad. And you wouldn't think that at this time we would really have to be dealing with this stuff, especially with the strides we've made elsewhere. Men can get married in California and here. There are so many places where they can, but there are, I think, 80 countries in the world where it's illegal to be gay. We live in these bubbles. So many changes need to be made. Then for younger people that are closeted, they see that it's illegal to be gay in Qatar and they know that the World Cup's going to be there – and maybe they're football fans? That's so damaging on their psyche, on their mental health, where, yes, they want to be a footballer, yes, they realise they're gay, and the World Cup is in a place that doesn't permit that. It is something that people should not have to deal with.'

Two announcements shortly after Robbie's appeared to move matters slowly forward at grass-roots level. Former Aston Villa player Thomas Hitzlsperger, capped 52 times by the German national team, came out the following year, announcing that he wanted to talk about his sexuality 'to further the debate about homosexuality in sports'. He, too, retired, in September 2014. Just a week after Hitzlsperger, semi-professional player Liam Davis, of the practically unheard of Gainsborough Trinity, announced that he was gay, and he carried on playing, opening a real dialogue in the lower divisions of the game. Former Liverpool striker Robbie Fowler went on record to apologise for his schoolyard homophobic behaviour towards straight former Chelsea player Graeme Le Saux, a silly on-pitch event that happened all the way back in 1999 and had clung to thuggish football mythology over the years.

These were still baby steps. 'In the end, the only way to change it is when footballers come out,' says Robbie Rogers. 'That's the only way to do it. But the FA's role is to create an environment where it is possible and to educate the fans and the clubs that it's OK. That any kind of inequality is unacceptable, and when it happens, to punish the clubs. If it's racial or if it's homophobic or whatever, there has to be consequences. So that's the next step that I think they need to make.'

The National Hero

'Dreadful,' says David Beckham's former PR Caroline McAteer about the treatment of Justin Fashanu. 'And you wonder, how could that happen – it's sad really, but you hope that attitudes have now changed.' She says that if a British player came to her now and asked to handle his coming out, she would probably take the gig. There would be enough professional intrigue to engage in new territory after her immaculate handling of Stephen Gately's outing. 'I would say it's very different to the music industry. I think that, because you have this whole thing with banter and the rival teams, it makes it a very different environment. I know people say it's going to be weird in the dressing rooms and whatever, but I don't think other players would have an issue with it. I think it's more that terrace culture.'

She points out that when Victoria Beckham began dating David she would get all sorts of abuse jeered at her from the stands at United games, often when she was sitting with her mum and dad. Elton John stepped in to lend a supportive hand, and told her that when he was the owner of his beloved Watford FC he would get worse. 'He told her they'd sing to him, "Don't sit down while Elton's around cos you'll get one up the arse." That's what they'd chant. For 90 minutes.' Would the mob mentality of football make coming out impossible? 'Not impossible, but I think that's what makes it different. If a tennis player comes out it's easier. For individual sports, it is always easier.'

Caroline thinks this is part of what made the diver Tom Daley's outing that much sweeter. 'Who knows about any other divers' lives? There has not been a single negative comment towards him. People respect it because he's just being who he is.' Because new media is surpassing old as a way of controlling news stories, Caroline says that she would instruct a player wanting to come out to follow Daley's lead. 'He recorded a video and put it up on YouTube,' she says. 'You don't have to explain yourself to anyone. You can talk directly to people, unmediated. But I think it would be much more difficult, still, for a footballer. It would depend on the individual. You would have to be a very confident person in who you are to deal with it, just because you have to understand that, whether it's aggressive or good-natured, you're going to get abuse.'

McAteer now runs a sports media company and sees first-hand the other issues that are still left unaddressed in football stadiums. 'I look after a lot of African players, and a lot of stuff they have had shouted at them from the terraces, it really is disgusting. To see how they deal with that is how you're going to have to do it: "Can I handle it? Is it going to put me off my game?" For some people, it can really affect them. So I think you'd have to be a really strong individual to deal with it. Some slow progress is being made. Arsenal have got a whole group of fans called the Gay Gooners. For most of the players it's not an issue. Paddy Power teamed up with Stonewall and recorded an ad to support the rainbow laces campaign, which showed players all wearing coloured laces to support equality.'

She hears the rumours about some top-flight international football players and lets them go in one ear and out of the other: 'This one's gay, so is that one. Honestly, there are always rumours, and I don't know any that are.' This is not to say gay footballers don't exist. 'For a lot of players they don't do any publicity or interviews, they just live their lives. I could name you a whole bunch of players who you wouldn't know who their wife is or whether they have a girlfriend or not. They're not hiding anything, but they're getting on with living their lives.'

She thinks the old, unwritten don't-see-don't-tell rules of the music industry are probably applicable to the current climate in football. She can't see someone voluntarily choosing to tell their story unless, like Robbie Rogers and Thomas Hitzlsperger, they are about to retire, or it got to a situation where something was about to be exposed. 'It's awful to think about people worrying about having stories sold. Awful.'

It shouldn't have to be like this. A decade before Robbie Rogers and Thomas Hitzlsperger came out, national hero David Beckham had done his bit for challenging the inclusivity of gay men on the football pitch by agreeing to be shot and interviewed for the cover of *Attitude*, an unprecedented act of personal bravery for English football. David Beckham was not, however, the first footballer to appear on the cover of a gay magazine. 'Oh, the Vinnie Jones cover has a whole other story to it,' says Adam Mattera. 'Vinnie was in fact the first footballer to appear on the cover of a gay magazine. But David Beckham was the first footballer to willingly appear on the cover of a gay magazine. That's a pretty crucial difference.'

When he began as *Attitude* editor, Adam had commissioned an interview with Vinnie Jones, then making headway in his post-footballing life in Hollywood, as a tie-in for a scent he was promoting. The interview came back and, liking what he read, Adam put the art director onto a picture search for appropriate imagery to illustrate it with, a photo shoot they could buy in with Vinnie that might work for the title. 'There was a shirtless image we could use for the cover, and there was another in the series of him looking at himself quite significantly in the mirror. It was a man looking at a man, which always has a certain homoerotic appeal. So, you think, this is absolutely going to be of appeal to certain gay men. Vinnie's a type. There's gay appeal there.'

A perfume interview was elevated to cover status and Vinnie Jones made accidental history. In the event, all hell broke loose. 'The people around him, his agent, the PR company, none of them knew it was happening. The tabloids picked up on it. So not only was it in the magazine, it was in the papers too. They were not happy. Vinnie was not happy. Vinnie was furious, in fact, which was relayed through his people and back to us. To be very specific, what came back to us was that Vinnie's son didn't want to go to school and have people taking the piss out of him because his dad was on the cover of a gay magazine. They said he'd be bullied because of it.'

This was the media temperature that *Attitude* attempted to work in. It was the perception at the time that because Vinnie Jones was on the cover of a gay magazine it would therefore ruin his career, everyone's going to beat up his son and people will think that he's gay. It all just got ridiculous. That's the context in which David Beckham decided to say yes to appearing on the cover of a gay magazine. He was either very dumb or very brave. I don't think he was dumb at all.

Adam Mattera cannot quite remember when David Beckham's name first started being bandied around the *Attitude* office, though one of my jobs during my first year at the magazine was to walk up and down Old Compton Street one evening taking a straw poll of which celebrity the readers fancied most out of Robbie Williams, Russell Crowe (then riding the international success of *Gladiator*) or David Beckham. I gave up after the first 50 split into 5 for Robbie, 2 for Russell (1 from me) and 43 for Beckham. 'I think it happened incrementally,' says Mattera. 'He was obviously a star within the world of football. That was a world that I didn't have any particular interest in and isn't necessarily of automatic gay interest. But when he started dating Victoria, their combined star power went into a different level.'

'It was a combination,' says Caroline McAteer of Beckham's emerging, Diana-level star wattage, 'of what he was doing as a footballer and how big she was, and when you put that together the doors that open for you are not like anything I've seen before or since. Both of them had a really intuitive understanding of it all. David's really smart.'

On a purely physical level, Beckham sent out signals beyond his natural good looks. 'The way he chose to represent himself,' says Adam Mattera, 'and the way they chose to represent themselves – where they would wear matching outfits, he would wear a sarong – started to challenge the ideas of what it meant to be a man, which tied to ideas at the magazine. He was questioning the traditional idea of masculinity. I don't think it can be overstated how, in that age of celebrity, when image became so crucially important, David didn't have to say anything, just his being was enough. Not long before that, if you thought of a footballer, you thought of Kevin Keegan.'

Only a few years earlier, another pretty, blond United player, Lee Sharpe, had resolutely failed to capitalise on his potential commercial reach. 'Lee could have been a superstar,' says McAteer. 'I totally agree. But there was no one at that time in the football world, which was very old-fashioned then, to make it happen. Those were the days when press requests were faxed to the club press office. There was no proactive courting of the media. There was only really fear of it. So no one ever took any risks. I can imagine with Lee Sharpe it was just about shutting down stories. All we did with David was choose carefully what we picked.'

Caroline says the decision to do the *Attitude* cover was made by Beckham himself. 'It was before the World Cup in Japan in 2002. We had maybe 150 to 200 requests on the pile from people wanting to talk to him. *Attitude* was one of the most interesting, so we picked that. No footballer had been on the cover of a gay magazine before. David was into it. He 100 per cent got the significance of it.'

The David Beckham cover of *Attitude* appeared on the shelves in June 2002. The cover line was 'To Dye For', in honour of bleaching his hair for the magazine. In the piece, he talks about gay fans and says, 'I have a big fan zone in the male area. I think it's a good thing. I don't think it separates me from other footballers, but it's not … you know, I do think I get a different sort of attention. I don't mind. I'm not unique, other footballers do but they wouldn't necessarily talk about it. It's part of me. To the outside world it probably makes me a little bit different, you know? It's not just about the football side of things. I think it's a good thing. It's never been an issue in my life. I've had people talk about me but it genuinely doesn't bother me. Why should it? Is it brave? No, I don't think it is. You shouldn't even think about it. It shouldn't matter what people are saying and it never has to me. It's just not an issue. That's the way that I was brought up and that's the way that it will always be.'

'His fans crossed over everywhere,' says Caroline. 'It wasn't a calculated thing in any way. It was just who he was and still is. To get first a big female following and then a massive gay following, there was no other footballer that had that. This was a bit of a moment for us. There are not many people who have got that appeal to men, women, gay, straight, young, old – everyone basically wants to know you. It's across the board with him.'

'A smart machine was in place around David,' says Adam Mattera, 'that was making the right positioning choices for him. But that doesn't detract from what he did. We wanted to do him on the cover. From our point of view, we want to be part of that. We want this man on the cover. We want gay magazines to be seen as parallel to other magazines he appears on the cover of. We want him to be in the magazine, interviewed, saying he has no problems with people being gay and him championing being gay, most importantly from within a testosterone-fuelled and very possibly institutionally homophobic industry that propagates the narrowest ideas of what it is to be a man, and may well have the blood of Justin Fashanu on its hands. So Beckham is part of that lineage, breaking it. He doesn't even have to say anything; he can just be an icon that represents change, represents a breakdown and challenge to that whole thing.'

'I think it was seismic,' says one of the founding *Attitude* editors Paul Burston. 'I've said this many times, but I think David Beckham's whole embracing of his gay audience and playing to them probably had as much impact in tackling very old-fashioned masculine values around sexuality as Peter Tatchell's entire career. It was massive. It sent this really strong message to young men that it was OK to be relaxed around gay people. That's a huge message to send out with a photograph. If you take that quote, which I've always really liked, that homophobia is the fear that men will treat you the way that you treat women, then there was Beckham saying, "Please, treat me like that. Please look at me like that, letch at me." It was quite an extraordinary thing for a straight man to do at that time.'

Mark Simpson, one of the early *Attitude* columnists, delighted at the cover. 'I've always considered football a game whose principal use is to prove your heterosexuality,' he says. 'But Beckham was using football as an enormous billboard for his fame, his celebrity. The paradox in so many ways is that without homophobia in football he would not have become the huge star that he did. It was precisely because he wore sarongs and loved his gay fans and tried on nail varnish, and he wasn't gay, he was married with kids; it was that which made it such a big story. He's pretty. But he's not that pretty. Nobody's that pretty. It was because there was a story attached, and the story was, Fucking hell, what a poof!'

David Beckham was at the vanguard of a new masculinity, one David Bowie had tried on for size before him. 'He's good at the drumroll moment,' says Simpson. 'That was his thing. He's the high street, football Bowie. He's the closest that we had in the noughties to a proper pop star. David Bowie deliberately outed himself as gay, when of course he had a wife. David Beckham did the noughties equivalent: he presented himself as a footballer, as a working-class hero, from London, like David Bowie, but right at the heart of the world of traditional masculinity he said he didn't care about being looked at by men. There's a whole host of them now, an entire generation of professional footballers who are Beckham-esque. A whole generation of men. I suspect the person who knows this best is Beckham himself. I suspect he's entirely aware that it was timing, and that if he hadn't done it, somebody else would have, and he'd be worth a fraction of what he is today. I don't wish to minimise his personal role. He was perfect for that role because his name makes people smile.'

The Final Whistle

Robbie Rogers's retirement from professional football lasted less than six months. He got his happy athletic ending eventually. He won. Just not in the UK or on behalf of one of its teams. Living in London and preparing for his first term at fashion college, he received an offer from David Beckham's old club, LA Galaxy. 'I was very afraid to go back, but I thought, OK, at least I'll go back to train and see if I can just get over that myself. And then after doing that I was like, How great would it be to make the statement and play in front of my family, in LA, where I started? So it just seemed like the perfect fit. But I'm not going to lie. I was very, very worried.'

This time he did take advice from a friend at Galaxy on whether he would, as a gay player, be accepted on the pitch and in the dressing room. 'The night before my first training day he sent me a message saying, "Actually, I don't think it's going to be weird at all. You know everyone here. Everyone knows you or they've read your story. I think they're going to treat you just fine."' His friend turned out to be prophetic. 'Going into a locker room is so different for me now because I can just be myself.'

Finally, Robbie Rogers can play football and acknowledge his life. One day, when the British gay football mess is flushed out, we will laugh about how ludicrous this all seems. Robbie Rogers will take his credit for redirecting our national game by shouldering the responsibilities his employers were not man enough to face. Having to move to America to do the thing he should have been allowed to do on British soil will become another part of football mythology, and some folk will look foolish for not letting him do it here. We know enough about gay culture to see how this works, at least in Britain, where gay men's astonishing transition from enemies to friends of the state nears completion.

Robbie Rogers's heroism may be obfuscated in his mind, but it is there. He learned to be a good boy by ditching the obedience. 'Things have just become really normal,' he says. 'Going to training every day, travelling to the games, playing games. I don't really think that the guys here on my team think of me any differently from any other guys. I might be the only gay footballer there is out there, but we just talk about it exactly like relationships they're in. The only weird thing about it is just how normal it is now.'

He says interviewers are no longer obsessed with the gay issue and will treat him as any other player. 'It really is about the game now. The first year back was really tough. Every question was about being the only out gay footballer, but now the questions are all performance-based and stuff to do with the season.' He felt the change coming a year after his first game. 'At first it was a little tough, and I really did feel like the outsider, being the only gay one and how I relate to everyone else, and then I realised I was being kind of stupid. Everyone here is different. Everyone has their own path in life. The thing that is unique about me is that I love men. I have a boyfriend. But everyone is so different. I just came to terms with it and found peace with being the only gay footballer. The guys from my team didn't treat me any differently. They were supportive of me.'

The seventies San Francisco political martyr Harvey Milk still has the final word on coming out. 'As difficult as it is,' said Milk, 'you must tell your immediate family. You must tell your relatives. You must tell your friends, if indeed they are your friends. You must tell the people you work with. You must tell the people in the stores you shop in. Once they realise that we are indeed their children, that we are indeed everywhere, every myth, every lie, every innuendo will be destroyed once and for all. And once you do, you will feel so much better.'

Forty years after the fact, Harvey Milk's words still resonate for Robbie Rogers. For the football industry, another of Milk's speeches: 'Like every other group we must be judged by our leaders and by those who are themselves gay, those who are visible. For invisible, we remain in limbo – a myth, a person with no parents, no brothers, no sisters, no friends who are straight, no important positions in employment.'

'I think it's exactly that,' says Robbie of Milk's words. 'If a whole stadium was chanting something homophobic toward me, it would hurt but I could still play. But if the guys in my team treated me as an outcast, going into the locker room every day and training with those guys and showering with them, that's where it would really affect me, and I wouldn't want to be a part of it.'

Football is one of the few safe spaces for openly shared male intimacy. It is a place men can hug, kiss, scream at and jump on one another without inference; where players can strip off and swap shirts by way of condolence or congratulation; where the raw, physical affection of sharing the ripe taste of perspiration and cleansing yourself of it communally afterwards is encouraged; where the body supersedes the mind. There is no reason it should not be a force for good, for everyone. The reason the football conversation is so important to gay men, like the army before it, is that you simply don't get any of that with another British national sport, like snooker or darts.

'There is a special way you can build relationships with guys in your team,' says Robbie. 'You go through such hard training together and you travel together, but it's more just about being able to build great relationships because you're with people so much and you're working so hard to win a football match. You come from different countries and learn to live in those places, with teammates helping you out. It's just a great way to build relationships.'

When he came out, first to himself, then to his family, then to the world, Robbie Rogers talked through his problems with a therapist. 'It helps just to realise why I'm a certain way in relationships or why I'm shy in certain ways or why I lack confidence in certain things.

And that's why, when people ask me for advice, that's the only advice I can give them. I say, "I can't help you, but you should speak with someone else." Or for closeted people, I cannot tell you to come out because I didn't come out until I was 25. But definitely speak with someone away from your family and friends that you can share these kinds of feelings with, these emotions, and try to work through some problems. Because I think if I had spoken with someone when I was younger, not necessarily come out when I was younger, but just spoken with someone, I probably wouldn't have the same kind of mental issues I have now.' He stops for a moment, before adding, 'Not that I'm insane or anything.' A sentence brushed with the possibility of what might have been had he not been afforded the kindnesses he was, unlike Justin Fashanu before him.

Robbie is still in the relationship he talked to his mother about over that lovely lunchtime in Soho House, West Hollywood. His partner is Greg Berlanti, a Los Angeles TV producer and writer who had a hand in, among other shows, *Brothers & Sisters*. They were set up by a mutual friend at a small house party in West Hollywood on the day of LA Pride 2013. Robbie says he wants to get married some day. 'Yeah, I do, which I never, ever thought in my life that I could do, or that I'd *want* to do. But then just coming across my friends that had families – you know, older guys – just educating myself, I was like, Oh yeah, I would love to do that. I had a gayducation. It's funny. In my family, my mom, who never believed in that stuff, now she prays that I have a family.' And the world still turns.

No British professional footballer approached Robbie to offer guidance when he came out in early 2013, but he sees things changing with a new generation emerging, for whom sexuality is not the issue it was once for his generation, for mine and for the ones that preceded us all. It begs the eternally unanswered question of what is so special about British football that it can't let anyone other through its turnstiles. 'It's a very masculine, macho culture in Britain. I'm not saying that the guys I played with were not very supportive of me after I came out. They were in many ways quite loving, but for some reason the stereotype, the tradition, the environments in football clubs are just really … it's a little backward.'

On 22 February 2016, Greg Berlanti announced that he had become a dad, to Caleb Gene Berlanti, born over the previous weekend to a surrogate. 'There is nothing I've wanted more or waited for longer,' Rogers's partner posted, unmediated, on Instagram, 'than to be a father.' He continued to thank family and friends, including Robbie, adding a note of humour by way of a sign-off: 'Check back in approximately 25 to 30 years for the tell-all about how I screwed it all up. Until then apologies for the over-posting of baby photos. My heart is full forever.'

Greg, Robbie and Caleb live together in West Hollywood. 'He's amazing,' says Robbie of Caleb. 'Such a little personality. We're just taking it day by day. It's great to get home every day from training and to see him smile. I took him down to the stadium and onto the pitch on the first day, when the season started. It makes us both really happy. I never would have imagined even going back to playing football. So much has happened in the last few years. It's kind of crazy.'

Robbie sees Tom Daley as the generational game-changer for gay sportsmen, by coming out exactly on his own terms, as a teenager, without apology or any vestige of shame. 'Tom's done an amazing job. He is such a positive role model.' Daley didn't have the locker-room banter to contend with, of course. 'But still, for him to have the courage to come out. He's probably one of the most famous athletes, everyone watches him in the Olympics and people are like, "Don't come out because your sponsorship will be affected," and this guy was like, Fuck it. He wanted to be happy. He wanted to be himself. I think that's absolutely amazing.'

For British football culture, he remains positive that change will eventually come. 'There have been changes,' he notes. 'FIFA has different issues they have to address, too. There are issues of sexism, racism, homophobia; there are so many issues because I feel like it is a boys' club, an old-school boys' club that hasn't moved on with the rest of our society, and things need to be done.' Reluctantly, he will take pride in his own part in the gay football story. 'I won't be able to play forever, but at least I went back to the Galaxy and we've won championships here. I've got to be a gay man around a bunch of straight football guys, you know? They'll take that story to other parts of the world and tell their friends because it's something to talk about, having a gay athlete in your team. It's all about education.' Robbie now has somebody to chat about his situation with. 'I've talked to Thomas Hitzlsperger about his experience and I have talked to a lot of younger athletes, who are a lot more open to changing their lives and don't want to come out late. Change will happen.'

Throughout his troublesome few years, right up to his happy ending, Robbie Rogers never lost his faith. Though he identifies as a Christian rather than a Catholic, he still feels most at home in Catholic churches. 'Yeah, I believe in God. I believe that there's a purpose for me here and there's a reason why I'm here on earth. People say, "How can you be religious and a footballer and gay and all these different things?" And I think, Why not? Isn't that the best thing about life? That you can be so many different things? So I think that there's a reason for all this stuff. All the struggles in my past I think prepared me for this moment.'

Occasionally, at training sessions at LA Galaxy, Robbie Rogers will bump into David Beckham, the most famous British footballer of his generation, possibly the most famous Brit, wandering through the corridors of his old club. 'Nice guy,' he says. 'He's always offered us a lot of support.'

10. BAND OF GOLD

An Equal Marriage

On the evening of the equal-marriage bill passing through parliament, I attended the recording of a new comedy show called *Vicious* at the ITV studios on the South Bank of the Thames. Westminster glistened in the distance in the twilight. *Vicious* told the story of a co-habiting gay couple in Soho who had been together just shy of 50 years. The show was shot like an old seventies sitcom with a live audience. It shared something of the tone of programmes I'd loved as a kid: *Robin's Nest, George and Mildred* and *Man About the House*. Suburban comedies that dealt adroitly with the minor stuff of life everyone forgets to put on screen now.

Vicious felt satisfyingly unfashionable. The central couple had been shaped not just from their gayness, but with the transcendent chorus of bickering that defined old married screen hands like *Coronation Street*'s Jack and Vera Duckworth. I always loved the Eminem quote on gay marriage: 'everyone should have the chance to be equally miserable'. It always made me laugh. At the end I turned to my boyfriend Dave, sitting next to me, and thought about the shared possibility of the couple we might one day be; one that, as children, we had both deemed pretty much unthinkable.

On a split stage – one for interior scenes at home, the other for exterior – the couple were brilliantly brought to life by two of Britain's most elegant elder gay statesmen, Sirs Ian McKellen and Derek Jacobi. They rose sensationally to the challenge, gifting each snarky, camp interchange a knowing plausibility you could never learn by observation alone. The original title of the show was *Vicious Old Queens*, a defining production note they injected into each scene. The programme was the brainchild of playwright Mark Ravenhill and Gary Janetti, an American TV producer who had previously worked on *Will & Grace*, the US sitcom which effortlessly brought upscale, metropolitan gay conversational broadsides into the American home, then networked them across the globe. By putting the gay men upfront in the story, *Will & Grace* changed the texture and reframed the landscape of American TV.

In *Vicious*, McKellen plays a cantankerous old goat tinged with Norma Desmond levels of self-delusion about his long-diminished acting career. He is thrilled to get an audition for a walk-on role in *Downton Abbey*, the loquacious costume drama that gave British drama its first gay butler pinup. Jacobi is McKellen's browbeaten other half, the kindlier, put-upon spouse who must indulge his partner's peccadilloes in order for the home to run smoothly, with the patina of acceptance, pride, resentment, delusion and joy that circulates around every beating heart in a lifetime love.

The audience implicitly understands that, like Jack and Vera, George and Mildred, and Terry and June before them, beneath their open veneer of antagonism there is only love. They cannot live without one another. The characters were called Freddie and Stuart.

The gender difference would have been small enough not to matter on any other day. At not yet a decade old, the Civil Partnership Act had eased into being without any discernible effect on the national character, other than making us feel a little warmer and more inclusive. The only real bugbear thrown up by the Act seemed to come from some straight couples who would like the option of entering a civil partnership rather than a marriage; they saw marriage as an outdated, outmoded institution and would rather engage in a less patriarchal legal acknowledgment of their partnerships, which all seemed fair enough.

Yet marriage was the last piece of statute necessary to give gay men and women equal legal status in Britain. Equivalence looks all the more irresistible when it's blinking just out of sight. Symbolically, it needed to happen. The country had come a long way in the past 30 years. As if some strange hand had guided Ravenhill, Janetti, McKellen and Jacobi, here it was being played on a stage for prime-time ITV. I spoke to the press officer in the green room afterwards, and we both noted how wonderful it was to see a show about two pensionable gay men in a relationship being laughed and cheered along not by a gay audience, but the kind of Middle England, *Daily Mail* reading, wash-your-car-on-Sundays family demographic that would have paid the same respect to a show with a straight young couple aimed directly at them, like *Gavin & Stacey*.

This wasn't any other day. The equal-marriage bill passing through parliament hung heavily over proceedings. No one really knew which way it would go. There was a discernible feeling from within parliament that the Prime Minister was using it as a sugar-coated liberal placebo for the atrocious targeting of the poorest British citizens for problems largely caused by its richest under his swingeing programme of austerity. Were LGBT voters now just a tactic, a pawn set to take bishop in the country's sometimes squalid, often incomprehensible short-term political chess game?

At the end of filming, McKellen and Jacobi stood at the front of the stage to take their curtain call. They bowed with unguarded theatricality. McKellen's mock-demure smile, his raised eyebrow, his great booming basso voice and slight shake of the head was now so embedded in British culture as to warrant him the position of a kind of grandfather figure to the country. Both actors had paid their dues, over and over again, in terms of charity and fundraising commitments, taking awareness of the improving British gay condition all the way to Hollywood and beyond. Both had a clear and tangible starring part to play in that transition, very possibly the roles of their lives. They'd obviously loved filming the show. It was a joyous occasion about to be made more so.

At 10pm McKellen silenced the audience's cheers and plucked a mobile phone from his pocket to make a more serious announcement. At that moment, the Marriage (Same Sex Couples) Act had achieved an overwhelming majority vote in the House of Commons, 400 votes to 175. What was even more remarkable about the occasion was that the coalition government had helped a Tory leader defy his own party to do it. Maybe we weren't a tactic, a strategy or a sideshow after all. The Tory vote was split, with 136 against it and 127 in favour. In victory, these are mere details. Some of these MPs were the deplorable men and women who had pushed through Clause 28 as a matter of urgency 25 years previously, denying school children access to the poetic and practical work of masters extrapolating lyrically on our essence. Denying us the good fortune and basic human right of becoming good as you.

Watching McKellen announce this to a cheering, mostly straight audience was spine-tingling. The auditorium erupted. He got down on bended knee, turned to Jacobi and popped the theatrical and theoretical question, 'Will you?' It didn't matter that Jacobi was already in a civil partnership with Richard Clifford, his partner of 34 years, only 13 years less than Freddie and Stuart's, or that McKellen was single. The comedy moment translated to its desired ovation.

I looked at Dave again. I thought, Every day is a first day when you grow up gay, in its own little way. Perhaps this would be the last first to look out for, the last big public signpost. Perhaps when schoolchildren today have seen their gay and lesbian uncles and aunties, their gay and lesbian parents, brothers, sisters, cousins and best friends walk down the aisle, and when that act has gone unquestioned, there will be a whole generation to whom life is inconsequentially equal. In that moment, I felt surrounded by and full of love.

Role Models

I've always loved the company of old men. I didn't really know my grandfathers; one died just after I was born and the other a few years later, a man I barely remember not being incapacitated, struggling to speak. My mum and her only sister would regale tales to me from an early age of their side of our fascinating family lineage. It included one matricide, mental illness, nervous breakdowns, suicides, an uncle who had gone to prison because he wanted to see what it was like, a serial philanderer, and another uncle who was best friends with the brilliant Mancunian writer Anthony Burgess, author of *A Clockwork Orange*. Burgess stole his teenage sweetheart. The stories came thick, rich and fast. Old sepia-tinted photographs appeared while they poured one another a tot of brandy. The past looked like an exotic foreign land and yet felt like exactly the same place: different years, same quandaries written on their faces; just people.

As a teenager, I had plenty to take the place of missing grandparental figures. I learned early that if role models are missing from life then it's probably wise to find some. When I was 14 I answered an ad in the local paper and started a Saturday job in a car park, collecting the tickets in a small booth where I'd spend all day doodling and listening to music. It was a great job. I learned about the Smiths splitting up in that booth. It housed my first heartbreak. I taught myself to write for pleasure, not for school, on the back of receipt pads, wiling away the hours to the conveyor belt of passing vehicles full of supermarket shopping bags, harassed mothers chewing Thorntons toffee and weekend lovers drink-driving after Saturday afternoons spent all over one another in the pub. All of life passed by. I did my last shift there at 22.

The car park was run by the Corps of Commissionaires, retired ex-servicemen working for pin money who wore immaculate uniforms to patrol seven storeys of suburban hatchbacks and share cranky chatter in the small catering cabin you'd clock in and punch out of. The buttons of their uniforms were buffed and shoes polished just so. They were funny, filthy, wise men. They had seen more of the world than I could comprehend existing at that time, and they had seen it all dotted with death, destruction and commensurate camaraderie. They had played their own significant roles in defeating an enemy that championed inequality by force and an unthinkable collective will. They'd fired guns and dodged bullets. They didn't bleat on about it. You just knew. I loved being let in to their company. It's not difficult in retrospect to work out what it was I found so quietly amazing about those fellows.

Some of them were like characters from a *Carry On* film, in constant reverie. Some were more insular, gently formed giants of a type you saw stooped at the bar of the local trades and labour club, one that might recall a snippet from their life in return for half a pint of bitter and a packet of Worcester sauce crisps. The small cabin where we'd take our breaks smelt of old cologne, chip fat, Benson & Hedges, tea the colour of fake tan and ink from the car park's printing materials. There was always a well-thumbed copy of the day's *Sun* and *Mirror* sitting on an old armchair, a conversation about the darts, a blue joke, a small manila pay packet, a half-finished crossword puzzle, a toilet flushing, a photograph of a new great-grandchild, a Gene Pitney song playing on the wireless, a tale of how much the wife's catalogue bill cost that month, a death. They were the proudest men I ever worked with. They treated me like a fellow worker, mercilessly taking the piss – the most traditional Mancunian form of saying 'I like you' – but asking about life, enjoying the flighty nonsense of youth, joining the dots between the generations and touching something close to universality between them. They were gentlemen.

I got my gay granddad figure a little later. Every home should have one. In 1995, I saw a slim volume called *As Luck Would Have It* sitting on the 'books for review' shelf at *City Life* magazine. The author was Samuel Lock. In the brief biography that fell out of the book it was mentioned that, though he had lived a colourful life punctuated by work in the theatre and documentary filmmaking, this was his first published novel, at 70 years of age. It doesn't seem so old at 45, but at 23 it felt like a lifetime away. Sam's writing was a fluid, confident and curious composition style that edged in and out of high literature, fussiness, outrage, serenity and gossip. He had scripted a full gay sex scene in one paragraph which glowed with dirty, effervescent control. It's easy to say that I sensed a new hero in my first reading of *As Luck Would Have It*, but by the time I read the opening two pages of the novel at his funeral 21 years later, that was exactly what Sam had become to me. He hated me for telling him on the one occasion I did.

The first time I met him was six months after reading and reviewing the book. He invited me to his flat for an interview, an artist's studio space on the third floor of a Chelsea low-rise opposite the English National Ballet School near Stamford Bridge, Chelsea's football ground. That he lived between a ballet school and football ground always felt perfect for Sam. The allotment of saved studio spaces at the top of municipal blocks was a hangover from the astonishing fifties commitment of the local council to the nascent art world that would explode in the area during the swinging sixties. Sam predated all that. He knew Kenneth Williams,

Beryl Bainbridge and Maggie Smith, and said he intended to one day write a memoir (he did, but it was never published) called *The Night I Danced with Sean Connery*, based on a true story he told often and well. One late afternoon, deep into our friendship, after we'd seen a matinee screening of the Iris Murdoch biopic at the Curzon cinema on the King's Road, he took me back to the studio and read me letters that the two of them had exchanged, kept in a drawer in a bureau at his studio.

It wasn't the casual starriness of Sam's past that interested me. It was his absolute dedication to living in the moment, right until the end. We would drink together at the Quebec, the London gay institution and public house for 'older men and their admirers' that, despite several cosmetic renovations in the 20-year lifetime of our friendship, still felt like it was beamed into Marble Arch from David Lynch's imagination. We ate outdoors at the Bluebird, observing everything changing and somehow staying the same in his neighbourhood, smoking cigarettes underneath a heated pillar on the snazzy forecourt. Sam's taste was always immaculate, but there was no snobbery to it. He liked *EastEnders*, deplored *Coronation Street* (the only thing we ever disagreed on) and was the only person I knew in London who understood *Mrs Brown's Boys*, which he described to me once as 'pure vaudeville' after a long discussion about that year's immaculate gay arthouse hit, *Stranger by the Lake*, which we both adored.

One day, not long before he died, I found myself returning from visiting Sam at the Chelsea and Westminster hospital. Walking along the gangway of my own third-floor municipal block, in east London, putting the key in the door, I thought, This is exactly the analogous area to Sam's Chelsea in the sixties. I realised then just how much I had followed his example; he was operating like a supernatural shadow over my shoulder. Something else we shared was favouring the idea of casual magic over coincidence or serendipity.

When I first met Sam there was, beneath his cascading and impish tales of a world that never seemed to end, a discernible undercurrent of concern, a little sadness, one he offloaded gently on this nosy stranger interviewing him for a magazine. He explained that his partner of 40 years, the artist Adrien de Menasce, had died that year. They had lived in this tiny, exquisite apartment together for most of their time together, since the late fifties. Adrien's paintings were hung around the studio, casting a captivating spell on the room. It wasn't this world of elegance and artistry that knocked me for six that afternoon. It was the first time I had heard of a gay relationship lasting longer than the time it takes most young men to change haircuts. Sam and Adrien, a man I never knew, became a template, something to think about that was real, that ended of natural causes.

The relationship between the characters played by Jim Broadbent and Ben Whishaw in the sophisticated BBC drama *London Spy* was the first time I'd seen a proper dissection of this need in younger gay men for older role models, but the script disposed of the opportunity for real insight by adding an unnecessarily sexual element, in which the older man fancied the younger, spoiling what could have been another first for gays and the arts. Not every gay friendship is some catastrophic re-enactment of *Death in Venice*.

I met Sam's twin brother, Wilfred, and his partner, Ray, not long into the friendship. Wilfred and Ray had been together since the sixties, and had devoted a good chunk of their social lives to political change, weathering well their role in the Gay Liberation Front's audacious moves toward equality. They were the protest wing of the family, attending the first Gay Pride march. Wilfred would take great pleasure in playing bad cop to Sam's bon viveur because political change had passed his twin brother by, mostly untroubled. While revelling in its finest details, Sam didn't think of his sexuality as a defining mark of his character.

When it was clear that he was thinking about his own death, when he was in his late eighties, we shared another revelatory afternoon at the studio. He showed me some post-war Super 8 footage of him visiting a friend's house and antique shop on the coast: a young man in a tank top, still discernibly Sam, was drawing freehand a male nude from the rear view, a developing image that looked exactly like the cover of the Smiths' 'Hand in Glove' that I would buy almost 40 years after this was filmed. Sam did not countenance the idea of discrimination. He just got on with living his life as nature intended. He had fallen in love for the first time when posted in India as a soldier during the Second World War and been quite astonished, having written letters to this boyfriend for the last year of his posting, not to find him waiting at the train station on his return. The man had married and was expecting his first child. Unless you had the fortitude and tenacity to follow your heart at the time, that was what you did. It was the road more travelled.

A Party

The first civil-partnership party I attended was that of Elton John and David Furnish. The celebrations happened in three adjoining marquees in the grounds of their home in Windsor on the first day of the legislation passing in England and Wales. It was December 2005. Shayne Ward had triumphed in the ticker-tape finale of *The X Factor* the previous weekend, and the sound of his winner's song, 'That's My Goal', blaring out of the radio as I got ready in a hotel room to attend the evening's festivities took on an oddly appropriate flavour.

For David Furnish, the night before was restless. He and Elton had been scanning the news all day and had no idea what was likely to happen. This was uncharted territory. Their relationship was its patient zero, the marriage that would cement the legislation into the public imagination, for better and for worse, in a manner no legal process could ever match. They were its personal touch. Civil partnerships had been legalised two days earlier in Northern Ireland, and the couple of 11 years had seen a lesbian ceremony egged outside a Belfast registry office on a rolling news bulletin. 'I remember going to bed that night and watching it, Elton turning to me and saying, "Oh God."' David Furnish comforted his partner. 'I said the Windsor police are being really cooperative; they've got an area to put any protestors. We'll go in and just do what we have to do.'

The preparations for the civil partnership of the most famous gay couple on the planet had been, by necessity, put together hastily, not that anyone would have known it on the night. Five weeks before it relocated to Windsor they had a soundstage on hold at Pinewood Studios and cancelled it, instead booking a new party planner to construct the venue in their grounds. The excitement around the ceremony had built to such an extent that the couple had been offered $10 million, a flat fee for exclusive rights to the photos. Instead, they gave one interview and photoshoot, together, to *Attitude* magazine, talking directly to the audience that this momentous occasion would have most resonance with.

The guest list ran like a who's who of contemporary culture. The first marquee had a black interior, with a tower of spot lit white flowers in the middle, casting a gently dramatic, filmic light around the room. In the queue to wish congratulations to the groom and groom I stood behind Hugh Grant and Jemima Khan, and in front of Prince Andrew. Sitting at the top table in the second marquee, a white room arranged in circular fashion so no hierarchies were discernible, were Elton and David, Kate Bush, Donatella Versace and Elton's mum. On my table were Peter Tatchell, Stephen Gately and his boyfriend, Simon Amstell and his, and Victoria Beckham's hairdresser, who was her chaperone for the evening – David was away on a sporting occasion. There was a table of BBC newsreaders from over the years, people you'd never imagine in a room together, all sitting, gossiping. Next to our table was a ludicrous array of fashion luminaries, including Alexander McQueen in a kilt. Figures of legend came and went so frequently you quickly attuned to the idea that you were stuck inside your television set. David Furnish has two favourite photographs of the night: the first, a comedy shot of Gordon Ramsay and Ozzy Osbourne standing next to one another at the urinals, with their heads spun round; the second, one that has developed an enduring poignancy since, of Alexander McQueen laughing, head tossed back on the dance floor.

The third marquee, the curtains of which were pulled back after dinner and speeches, was a purpose-built nightclub, for one night only. These were the days before social-media omnipresence: nobody was stuck on their phone, there was no hashtag to utilise, no Instagram or Twitter feed. Just people. Falling out of a taxi and then into a hotel bed that night, it felt like the last party I would ever need to go to, tidying up with a bow two decades of adventures in gay nightclubs with a slice of wedding cake and the exchange of rings. For all the decadence and glamour, the fact of the matter was that it could have been in a local church hall with a room full of people nobody recognised. The feeling generated from the couple at its centre was of pure, undiminished support and joy. This was the couple to which you could now point and say, Look, it does work after all. This was the pot of gold at the end of the rainbow. The night glistened with the warm sheen of equality.

An Education

At 18 years of age, David Furnish had packed and readied himself to leave his home in the Toronto suburb of Scarborough, in Canada, to take a business degree a couple of hundred kilometres away at the prestigious University of Western Ontario. Scarborough, he says, is a place resembling exactly the environment his schoolmate Mike Myers had built in his film *Wayne's World*: 'Parties in rec rooms with tennis rackets, doing air guitar in flannel shirts and ripped jeans and baseball caps and Kodiak boots. That was Scarborough.' It was Pop-Tarts and McDonald's. 'Remember, this was the eighties,' he says. 'You get a career above all else, because that is what you do. Be a lawyer, be a businessman, be a doctor. That was my parents' version of safe. This is what we know and this is security.' As they filled the trunk, his father was overcome with wistfulness, something David only learned later. 'It's funny how things work on a subconscious level. My dad was very old school, not very vocal about his emotions and feelings, but a loving father who wanted to do the best by his kids. After I got out of his car at my halls of residence my dad sought counselling because he was profoundly depressed. He said he had never felt as upset as he did dropping his son off at university. He knew.'

With the absence of any role models for the person they guessed their son to be, this loving family had directed him towards a life of business success. The night before leaving, David was hospitalised with anxiety pains. 'I knew there was no commercial future in the things I wanted to do and there was no sexual future in the things that I was told to do.' The doctors gave him an antispasmodic and a sedative. 'My dad couldn't verbalise it, and it really, really upset him.' This was not the behaviour of successful fathers in Scarborough. 'Heterosexual men did not go to therapy.'

With some obvious caveats, David Furnish enjoyed his studies. 'It was a great university and I got a great education, and I don't want to denigrate that. I threw myself into it, but it was also just another way of getting approval. My thinking was that a bad rubber stamp is better than no rubber stamp at all. It's a mainstream societal rubber stamp that says you're all right.' On his marketing course, David Furnish and his best friend Jules caused a minor outrage by mentioning to their tutor the incredible viral marketing campaign that had brought Frankie Goes to Hollywood's 'Relax' to global prominence. 'How the whole political message had mixed with the music, the Katharine Hamnett T-shirts, the imagery and the video and the marketing, what genius it all was, how big and bold and beautiful it was. The rest of the class looked at us as though we were freaks.'

Few men have the innate understanding or feeling for how culture affects the inner life as Furnish. 'Elton and I worked,' he says, 'because every single cultural, media, musical, cinematic and photographic reference we shared was all a primer.' David soon learned after they met that Elton sometimes referred to himself as 'Sharon Picket Fence': 'What he wanted, more than anything, was what I came from. It's not what he came from, a broken home, but it was the idea of the picket-fence family. One of the things that really cemented us and what has allowed us to survive through all of our differences and ups and downs is that we fundamentally always believed, because of what I came from, that relationships can survive if you are with your soul mate. If you are with the right person and you work at it.'

For gay men, they understood, there would be challenges. 'If societally, culturally, the winds that blow around you are not supportive, then it is really, really difficult. And it has been difficult at times. A relationship is always really hard work.' Through it all, there was the bold, beautiful certainty of love: 'I never, ever didn't fundamentally believe it couldn't work.' He says a friend of his had been told by her mother on her wedding day that she'd get ten good years out of a man, any man, maximum. 'Imagine saying that to your daughter on her wedding day? I came from the opposite. So, Elton's desire to have it and my belief that it exists was ultimately how our relationship survived. The acceptance of the public has a profound effect on this.'

Elton John has one significant mantra for life, one hard won and repeated by example. 'He's special,' says Furnish of his husband. 'He just is. Elton says that the most positive and uniting influences on our planet are music and sport. They bring people together like nothing else. Because he has that foundation of mainstream acceptance and support, his music breaks boundaries. It is the reason our relationship has reached the acceptance that it has. That is a blessing, and we are so very, very lucky to have it.'

Tell Them Young, It's Going to Be OK

Not long after the civil-partnership party of Elton John and David Furnish, I bumped into an old mentor in the vegetable aisle of Tesco on Bethnal Green Road, east London. I had the fondest memories of this man, tying back to being under his instruction as a confused but bolshy teenager, and a very specific act of kindness he once showed me. At the Manchester Youth Theatre, a summer-long rite of passage for kids with a proclivity towards the arts or bohemia, he'd directed me in a Willy Russell play. I was a useless actor but the play was great. I played the best mate and sidekick of a stupidly handsome lad that the director could see I was obviously a bit in love with. It was unrequited; he was straight. The director would occasionally make knowing little jokes to me about it, kindly, inclusively. I think, in all honesty, he might have been a bit in love with him, too.

Such is life when you're 16 years old that I'd forgotten him a few weeks later, but for that summer it was written all over my blushing face. At the end of the run of the play, the director asked me if he could have a word. I had no idea what it was about but went aside, and he handed me a card. He said, 'Don't open it now, but remember it when you need it.' I got home that night and there written out, in plain letters, was the message: 'Don't worry about it, you're confident, happy, well brought-up and everything's going to be OK.' I knew exactly what 'it' was. So did everyone around me that summer.

In Tesco, by the fruit and veg, 20 years later, it was my turn to dispense the advice, a task I've always floundered at. I asked if he was OK, and his manner turned oblique and disengaged. Then he fell into a tormented monologue of emotional and sexual problems, deeply personal stuff punctuated sometimes by humour but mostly audible distress. Clearly, his honesty was not just about sharing with someone he'd thrown a metaphorical anchor to two decades ago. He was noticeably medicated. Eventually, when I took him outside, there were tears, too. We sat on a park bench for half an hour and talked about everything and nothing. He left saying, 'Don't worry about me.' Two years later I heard he had killed himself.

At the beginning of 2010, I got the kind of phone call every journalist wants – new publication, dream commission. The American website the Daily Beast had launched just over a year earlier, and a fashion editor called to see if I'd like to interview Alexander McQueen for them. The date was arranged for 12 February.

By chance, I bumped into him two weeks before the interview in the Joiners Arms, the spit-and-sawdust Hackney Road gay pub with a well-earned reputation for lawless abandon. I mentioned our upcoming interview to him, said I was looking forward to it. He nodded. McQueen was absolutely the top of my wish-list of interviews, not just because of all that extraordinary talent he executed so purposefully and with such impeccable conviction in his work, but also because I was slightly terrified of him whenever we met in places we both drank or had work ties to. McQueen and Amy Winehouse – the other London cabbie's kid who came from nothing to achieve everything, on exactly her terms – might well be Britain's last rock stars.

On 9 February I got a follow-up call from the Daily Beast saying the interview had been postponed indefinitely, no explanation.

McQueen was the absolute beacon of self-made achievement to me. I knew he was as complicated as he was brilliant. You only get closer to knowing why by asking. Two days later, he was found hanged in his Mayfair bedroom.

Whenever people ask me why gay marriage matters, I think about the designer and the director. The first thing that comes to mind is the card the director gave me, the fact that he could be bothered to go out of his way to write it and the certainty with which I received it. I'm almost at double figures now with gay men I've known over the years who have taken their own lives. I don't believe in happy endings, anyway. I don't think 'It Gets Better', as the gay positivity slogan that captivated America has it. But I do think it gets different and that everyone has the right to be as good as you. I do think happiness should at least look like a possibility and that sexuality should not get in any way of the sometimes futile search for it. I do think about the long haul. Because unlike many others, I had encouragement and an example. I saw it up close.

Someone Saved My Life Tonight

When David Furnish was 21, he told his mother that he was gay. 'She was very emotional,' he says. 'Crying a lot. She sat at the table and kept peppering me with genuine, not bigoted – she is a genuine, all-encompassing, all-loving kind of a person – worries. She said, "I look at your choice and I see nothing but unhappiness." I replied, "How can you say that, Mom?" She said, "You're going to be discriminated against in your job. Name me one successful business person."' He couldn't. 'There was no Lord Browne. There was no David Geffen, really, other than to industry insiders. There was no Tim Cook. There was nobody. She said, "My greatest happiness in life has been being married to your father and having children, growing old with security and society supporting our relationship.

As I age I know that I am going to be supported, legally and societally, with that person for as long as I need them or choose to be with them. That will not be there for you." And so David reverted partially back into the closet, living a double life defined by dating women publicly, throwing himself aggressively into his work at the advertising agency Ogilvy & Mather and investigating the Toronto gay world from under hooded guard, checking his back to make sure nobody from work or home had seen him at play.

David Furnish was a theatre kid at school, too. His three closest friends would congregate at drama class, where they were under the instruction of a teacher working in the grand Canadian tradition of liberalism, one encouraged by prime minister Pierre Trudeau's approach to inclusivity of race, gender and sexuality in the seventies, when Canadian citizens were led by a man who believed in celebrating one another's differences (his son, Justin, the current Canadian prime minister, is doing sterling work in upholding the family tradition). David and his buddies' drama teacher practised yoga and ate organic food. He was a kind man who let them explore their individual possibilities and answer their curiosities. Two of David's high school best friends turned out to be gay. The other, Eric McCormack, would play one of America's most famous fictional gay characters, Will Truman, in the much-loved sitcom *Will & Grace*.

Furnish's fledgling gay identity was emerging in the drama department, but he didn't yet recognise or vocalise it as such, 'because it was too scary.' His core friendship group were the only kids at school who understood the maverick statement he made when he came in with a new copy of Andy Warhol's *Interview* magazine or when he first went to the Toronto branch of Vidal Sassoon and returned with directional hair. David played the lead in a play called *You're Gonna Be Alright, Jamie-Boy*. Eric McCormack performed as a French-Canadian transvestite, in full drag, as a character named

Hosanna. 'You were never judged. We all had the same sensibility. We felt like we fit in. When you're in that environment to study you can almost hide behind it. You can study a play about a gay character and act a person who is a gay character without having to get as close as to say, "Hey, I'm gay."'

David was a music obsessive from a young age. The first record he bought with his own money was Elton John's *Caribou*. 'I remember one of the first crushes I had was him on the album sleeve. He was wearing the fur jacket and he had it unzipped with the hairy chest, and in the seventies I was really into hairy-chested men. My crushes were Burt Reynolds, Lee Majors in *The Six Million Dollar Man*, Paul Michael Glaser in *Starsky & Hutch* and later Tom Selleck in *Magnum, P.I.*'

He became a committed Anglophile after seeing Monty Python's *And Now For Something Completely Different* in a Toronto cinema one afternoon, where he connected to its absurdist, abstract humour. 'There were three people in the audience and I laughed my head off. There was gender play and cross dressing.' He read an interview with gay Python Graham Chapman and was moved at the support he received from his comic clan. 'He described it as being like two trains running along in the same direction. He was on his own track but the others could look over and shout support. Those little things drill into you.' By the time the pictures and stories of the explosive gender-bending new-romantic club culture from London had started filtering over to Canada, he was smitten.

At Ogilvy & Mather, David spent his time working towards a possible move to London. 'I was giving myself cultural and professional reasons to move to Britain and, honestly, it had everything to do with my sexuality.' He spent hours, days even, in the creative department schooling himself in arthouse cinema, art direction and fashion photography. At his first appraisal, his boss told him that his only problem in terms of forging a fantastic career

ahead in advertising was his over-enthusiasm for the job. There were
no gay members of staff at the agency, and through his twenties
David dated women. 'I was leading a double life. I had a girlfriend
and male sex partners. I'd have sex with her, jump in the shower, run
out and have sex with a man. Living your life dishonestly poisons
your soul. It just poisons you with anxiety. And it creates victims.
What was I doing to the women I was dating? It was exhausting.'

He left Canada for the first time in 1985 and holidayed the
next year in London, staying on a nurse's sofa in Harrow. In love
with the British capital, he'd look out for bucket-shop flights on
Canadian airlines to return as frequently as possible. In 1989 he saw
a headhunter at an advertising recruitment agency in London to
talk about whether his professional skills might find a match there.
When word got back to his bosses at Ogilvy & Mather they offered
him a transfer to their London office.

The London he arrived in was bristling with gay possibility, of a
type he hadn't seen in the small square mile of Toronto's gay village.
He'd hear Princess Julia – a woman he'd only read about in the
pages of style magazines – play at Queer Nation on a Sunday and
trip along to Love Muscle at Brixton's Fridge. He'd take in a cheeky
midweeker at Bang on Charing Cross Road. 'Life just changed,' he
says. 'That robust gay culture that existed in London back then was
so different from gay clubs in Canada, where every night would be
the same. What Elton had gone through at the Sombrero and the
Embassy Club in the seventies and eighties, I was going through in
the late eighties and early nineties. There was this incredible sense of
personal liberation. But I was still going to work on a Monday and
lying. People would ask, "How was your weekend?" And I wouldn't
say, "Oh, I was at Queer Nation at the Gardening Club last night
and had three hours' sleep and then came here."'

Through his night-time adventures he built a solid group of
gay friends. When his parents called every week he would talk only

about work. One night he went for dinner with fellow ex-pats shoe-designer Patrick Cox and *Wallpaper* magazine founder Tyler Brûlé, and Madonna's brother, Christopher Ciccone: 'Tyler was so obnoxious during dinner and Patrick was really, really sweet.' With his best friend Ross, he would sit and dissect this thrilling new life over drinks, careful not to mention the gay word too loudly. He says he can trace a direct line of three degrees of separation between Ross and meeting Elton John.

The Seventies Gay Fame Conundrum

In 1973, Paul Gambaccini was sent by *Rolling Stone* magazine to interview Elton John. In an astonishing exchange for the times, the two got to discuss everything on their terms. Elton picked off several sacred cows for robust and hilarious vilification, and only softened to talk with artistic admiration and candour about his love of Liberace. Gambaccini and the artist discussed at length a suicide attempt Elton made after a failed engagement to a woman he couldn't really love. Everything is there, laid out without any clarification of either interviewer or interviewee's sexuality. Gambaccini's favourite moment of the interview was when Elton referred to the producer of *The Sonny & Cher Show* as 'a mincing old queen'. 'He was not holding back,' says Gambaccini. 'Here was a beloved figure just being himself.' Sometimes that is all that it takes.

Gambaccini was in the same predicament as Elton during the seventies, as were Freddie Mercury and Kenny Everett. 'Because of limited information about gay lives, we thought that our gay side was something that you had in addition, not instead of what everybody else had. Before the dissemination of information about how many of us there were, you thought, Well, I can't be a complete freak so how do I address my me-ness with everybody else? I can get married.'

Clearly, Elton John is the marrying type. Several years after his first interview, Gambaccini was back on the artist's trail in Sydney. 'I had been interviewing Elton for television, and the following day I had breakfast in the hotel with the engineer and the tape operator of his album. The engineer was a woman and the tape op was a man who I thought was right up Elton's street.' Gambaccini was back in London when he heard on the radio that Elton had married the engineer, Renate Blauel. 'I was completely floored by this. However, it was sincere on his part. He had told me a couple of times in the late seventies that he wanted a son and heir. And remember, at that time, to do that you had to have a wife. Science has made possible so many wonderful variations in our personal lives.'

Both Freddie Mercury and Kenny Everett married, too. 'Yes, that's right. I don't want to dismiss individual humans as social crutches, but the concept was "I need to have a woman in my life if I'm going to have tenderness, sensitivity and understanding"; however, as we got to know more gay people, those qualities appeared within our own community.'

The suicide attempt Elton had talked of in his *Rolling Stone* profile, says David Furnish, was the reason Bernie Taupin wrote the lyrics to 'Someone Saved My Life Tonight' for Elton. 'Of all the Elton songs, that was the one that always resonated most for me. I have this massive emotional response to that song.'

David Meets Elton

David met Elton on 30 October 1993. He was due to visit a friend for dinner. A mutual acquaintance of both the friend and Elton's was trying to get the singer to socialise more, as he had recently been in an intense recovery programme. The mutual friend suggested they scrap the London dinner party and relocate it to Elton's house in Windsor. The singer was ready to meet new people. Toxic relationships from the past had been left behind. He wanted to start again.

When Elton offered to send his limousine to collect the friendship group for dinner, David said he'd rather drive. As he was the only sober man at the party, he was seated next to Elton. As anybody who has ever met him knows, the idea of Elton John is infinitely more frightening than the cordial actuality. He is a first-class raconteur but a premium question master, too. He likes people. 'Remember,' says David, 'I was still semi-closeted at the time.'

David was in the mood to celebrate, though. The week before, he had won the biggest advertising contract in Ogilvy & Mather's recent history, with the private healthcare contractor BUPA. Into the bargain, he had lost out on a boyfriend he'd been seeing because of it, who had moved to Australia. Furnish was due to visit him when BUPA asked for a second round of pitching and, once again, he chose work over love. That summer, he had enjoyed a brief, *Shirley Valentine*-ish holiday fling with a Greek man named Adonis on the gay party island of Mykonos. 'In Mykonos you feel like the rest of the world doesn't exist. I was kissing in the port, holding hands; it felt like freedom. Then I came back to reality. What that had done, if you can make an analogy with an engine, is open up the valves and let the steam come out. The engine was running. Before that I had been so focused on the career.'

Of dinner that night, despite the exotic new location and starry new host, David Furnish did not have high expectations. 'I thought he'd be interesting and I thought he would sit on his sofa and regale us all with tales of his amazing career and his amazing life, who he'd met and who he knew.' David's preconceptions needed to be left at the door, however. 'He was exactly what I didn't expect. He was wearing a cream-coloured jogging suit and this pointed pair of Versace cowboy boots, the only nod to "Elton". He was warm and welcoming and kind and took our coats and brought us drinks, and he had beautiful skin. All my friends were nervous and so were throwing the champagne back, but I was driving so I didn't drink at all and just talked. He was interested in us, about what we did, our families, where we worked.' They ate spaghetti Bolognese. 'We connected over photography, which Elton was collecting, and he pulled out some books and showed me things, and I remember him putting his arm round me on the sofa and on my shoulder and it felt kind of nice. Then the feeling starts going through your mind: it's Elton John.'

If David had thought about himself in a relationship, it was always with someone like himself, young, urban, professional, with a taste for the night. Elton was 13 years older, in recovery, famous across the globe, the songwriter and singer of a good dozen songs you could comfortably fashion the great British songbook out of, without recourse to anyone else. He was best friends with Gianni Versace and on telephone terms with Princess Diana. He was in the process of suing the *Sunday Mirror* for libel and formed a cornerstone of the national grapevine. He took David for a tour of the house towards the end of the night and stopped midway to make an open confession. There is nothing remotely buttoned up about Elton John. He is a heart-on-sleeve man. 'He said, "You know I'm 46. I just can't keep living my life at this pace. I think it's time I settle down." It was warm and humble, and God, I was really drawn to him.' The picket fence was beckoning. As David, Malcolm and their sozzled friends piled into David's car to drive back to London, Elton asked for David's phone number. Quite out of character, he said, 'Only if I can have yours, too.'

The journey home was quite the do. 'My friends ripped the shit out of me all the way back. There were piano solos on the dashboard and choruses of "Daniel" at the tops of their voices, and I thought, He'll have a million phone numbers and never in a million years call.' When he jumped out of the shower in his Clapham flat on his return, there was a message on the answerphone from Elton, inviting him round to his London house the following week when he was in town for a legal meeting.

Their courtship was short and intense before they started to build a serious life together. Their first meal alone, *à deux*, was a Chinese takeaway ('though this being Elton, it was a takeaway from Mr Chow'). Within six weeks, David had met Elton's mother, at a surreal dinner in Windsor where a surprise guest turned up. 'Elton said, "OK, Michael is going to come down for lunch." I was like, "Michael who?" And Michael Jackson was coming to lunch. I have to meet Michael Jackson and your mother on the same day? Can you just ease me in a little quicker here?' Nonetheless, it was Elton's mother that was the scarier proposition. 'Everyone said to me, "You'd better be on your toes because Elton's mother is formidable, and she will either like you or she will not like you, and if she doesn't like you then she will never like you." Right. No pressure there then, at all. And the first time I met her I got to spend half an hour with her before Michael Jackson floated in the door.'

Michael Jackson was getting help from Elton's medical team, his doctor and therapist, at the time. 'He was just so ill,' says David. 'He was as thin as a pipe cleaner, covered in foundation, and a plaster on his nose with foundation on the plaster as it was curling up. There was weird lipstick that was feathering into the foundation, eyeliner, a hat, skinny, skinny, skinny. When we sat down to lunch he made us close all the curtains in the dining room because he said he was allergic to the sun. The therapist turned to us and said, "You know this is the first time he's sat down with anyone to have a meal in ten years?" That was my first surreal moment.'

Elton and David's favoured dating venue was the central London restaurant Bibendum, the venue of their first public date. 'I remember Elton saying, "I want to protect you and I don't want you being thrown to the wolves."' Rumours had begun circulating and pictures began appearing in the press. The first was of Elton, David, Herb Ritts and his boyfriend emerging from a car at a premiere. Talk began to gather heat at Ogilvy & Mather, and Furnish was called in to see his boss. 'He opened the door and said, "So, I'm not going to beat around the bush here, are you dating Elton John?"' He denied it, before getting a further summons from the CEO. 'Before I sat down he said, "Look, we think you're fantastic and you do wonderful work for us and your private life is your private life, and whether you're dating Elton John or not makes no difference to us. We support you and we stand by you." I was like, "OK, I'm dating Elton John."'

There was a further hurdle to cross. That Christmas he had to come out to his parents a second time, this time with a surprising twist to the tale. This time, David had an example to point to all of his own. When he dropped the words no suburban mother expects to hear in her life, 'I'm gay and I'm dating Elton John', she was ready to embrace her middle son. 'My mother said to me, "We can be a family again," and we were. I got acceptance at work, from the chairman of the agency. He had told me that if any of my clients had a problem with it then he would deal with it personally. OK, wow. So tick the family box, tick the work box. I had that foundation of support in place. As Elton and I stepped into the world honestly and openly, I always had that support system to fall back on.'

Their first official public engagement together was at the 1994 Oscars, when Elton was nominated for three of the five records in the Best Original Song category, for *The Lion King*. Furnish got his *Pretty Woman* moment when his partner took him to shop for his Hollywood outfit at the Versace store on Rue du Faubourg Saint-Honoré in Paris. By day, David had been every inch the advertising executive, in head to toe Armani. Times change. 'Elton put me into a fitting room and said, "Now listen, I know you're beautifully dressed and have a fantastic sense of style, but I'm going to take you to a few places because you might need a few options. And let's pick you out a few things." The assistants came in with suits.' There were the Versace classic silk shirts 'that were just not me. There was an overcoat with big gold buttons, leather trousers, belts, bags. I would say about 70 per cent of what I took I really liked and the other 30 per cent was Elton saying I might like to wear it down the line.' Again, this was new turf for David. 'I actually felt sick to my stomach, actually quite nauseous, and I had to ask him to give me a minute. Just to take a few breaths.' The shopping expedition was rounded off with a visit to Cartier on Place Vendôme.

To calm his nerves and show that it was not just an empty display of wealth, Elton bought the pair matching rings, which they still wear to this day, and have worn through their civil partnership and had reblessed for their eventual marriage. 'We never take them off. You see all these people, 50,000 of them at an Elton concert, and the camera zooms in on his piano playing and it is so nice to see the ring on there. It's such a subtle but obvious public affirmation that we are together and we are a couple.'

For Elton and David there was never a question of hiding away their love. 'No one ever sat us down and said, "Listen, guys, you have to respect that there's a public Elton and a private Elton." It was never an issue and it was never a question. Elton said, "Look, I'm doing this." We came into each other's universe at a time when he was in recovery, which is all about living an honest life, not being ashamed of who you are and refusing to hide away. We never went out and waved banners; we never wrote press releases or had placards. We just quietly got on with it.'

At the Oscars, David Furnish was put in mind of an incident that had affected him as a child. He had been to see a production of *Auntie Mame* in which his French teacher from school was playing the butler. David was 13. 'He played this role as a butler and he really camped it up, and I remember the audience laughing at him, not with him.' The reaction was the beginnings of a lifetime battling with anxiety. 'I panicked. I remember having to get up and leave the theatre and sit on the fire escape in the fresh air, deep breathing, hyperventilating, and my manifestation of that anxiety was thinking, I'm going to be sick. I'm going to throw up. It became my escape device.'

It reminded him of a further incident, even deeper into his childhood, when he saw a man openly scorned at his parents' tennis club for wearing a pink tennis shirt. He says that if you look carefully at the footage of him sitting beside his lifetime's partner at the Oscars that year, at the beginning of their relationship, as the first gay couple celebrated the world over, you can see David Furnish sitting on the aisle seat, just in case a panic attack or a new moment of shame comes upon him and he can make a quick getaway. 'Programmed in my subconscious from very early on was the idea that I'm not safe,' he says. In the event, Elton won the Oscar (and the Golden Globe, let's not deny him), turned to his partner, kissed him and thanked him effusively in his speech. They were less than a year into their relationship. Twenty-four years later, on the verge of their silver anniversary of meeting, they got their picket fence.

Sometimes, when David Furnish is doing the school run with his and Elton's two children, Zachary and Elijah, he will have to gently chastise them for conforming to a lingering hangover of society's ideas of what right and wrong is, what is deemed appropriate behaviour. 'Sometimes my son will see a toy and say, "Oh, pink is for girls." And I will say, "No, it's not. Pink is for anybody who loves pink. It's for boys and girls and everybody is allowed to love pink."'

Good As You

When somebody makes a proper and persuasive argument against gay marriage, one that is not rooted in prejudice, I hear it.

Opposition is not the sole reserve of the religious right. Arguments often appear from within the gay world. When proposals were being put together initially for the bill, the gay pressure group Stonewall was slow to lend its support. More radical figures joined the chorus.

'Gay marriage was not something people were clamouring for in the streets in the UK, unlike the US,' says one-man ideas factory and former *Attitude* columnist Mark Simpson. 'Our history and culture is different. *Top of the Pops* had much more impact on UK attitudes towards gender and sexuality than Stonewall. All the heavy lifting and change had been done already, by Labour governments. Civil partnerships were arguably *better* than marriage, in the sense that they bestowed all the legal protections and privileges of marriage but without any of the historical baggage.' For Simpson, the idea of arguing with cardinals about the meaning of marriage is futile – a hurdle to progress.

'I refuse to use the phrase "marriage equality",' he continues. 'It's propaganda. It's also, like a lot of propaganda, false. Gay and straight marriages are not "equal". And thank fuckery. Gay marriage is a fetish for straight liberals.' I love Mark's mind. He's funny and smart and makes people think. But on this one, something caught me quite off guard, changing my mind forever.

There is an old joke I heard young, from one of the first gay men I ever knew. 'What does a lesbian bring along with her on her second date? Her furniture. What does a gay man bring along on his second date? His second what?' The reason it's so funny is because it isn't just about laughing at a broad stereotype of gay men and women's behaviour; it's because it contains a nugget of recognisable truth.

Yet that nugget is only one piece in the complicated jigsaw puzzle of contemporary British gay life. Since the first civil-partnership celebrations I witnessed, I've seen half a dozen other gay couples I know declare their love in public, with the full weight of statute behind them. The couple who met on the dating app Scruff. The couple who married for visa issues, so they could be together in the country they loved. The friend who thought domestic happiness was the preserve of other people, not him, until he found himself deep in it. The couple whose parents wouldn't come and the ones whose dad made us cry with his speech. It's never not lovely to watch. On all occasions, I think about that universal transition they had each made, from smalltown boy to same-sex marriage, a shared story of confidence built, brick by brick, that seeps generously into communities, equalising my minority.

I gave up on the idea of normalcy years ago. 'Normal' is a false god. Nobody really knows what it is or can claim it as their own. Behind the twitching curtains of suburbia there is as much madness as there is rattling around city centres on a Saturday night. Between the cracks of those who identify at either extreme of the Kinsey scale of sexuality, there is so much space in between, much of it unfactored, undocumented and unsaid. Dab a sponge at the wipe-clean façade of Middle England and its stains show. The moral high ground is no more the rational preserve of one sexuality, religion or cluster of intentioned individuals than it is any other. Science has made parenthood possible for everyone, should that be what they want. Repression is the enemy of everything.

In *Public Speaking*, Martin Scorsese's brilliant 2010 documentary about New York wit and intellect Fran Lebowitz, his subject makes a clever observation when talking about how AIDS decimated her beloved city. She says it wasn't just the deaths of the artists, famous fashion designers, dancers at the New York City Ballet or other celebrated public figures that shook the five boroughs to their core; it was the great swathes of the audience that AIDS depleted, too. Suddenly, there were so many fewer gay men to look at their creations, hear their words and wear their clothes.

I love Lebowitz's democratising idea of gay men as great audience, something I've seen at close quarters. It is not unequal to suggest that, because gay men contemplate long and hard our identity young, in a way that is likely going to marginalise us later, we think about the culture that comes directly into our homes at suggestible ages with magnified personal criteria. We develop extra sensitivities to it. Being gay is not confined to those taking centre stage; it's often about developing in ourselves the ability to bear witness to what is going on there with fresh eyes. Being usefully gay is about validating the minority gaze, affording ourselves the opportunity to look freely at what we choose.

Dave and I were walking home along the South Bank from the filming of *Vicious*. We were reflecting on the passing of the bill through parliament and the funny, charming way we'd been privy to the news of it. We talked about ourselves, together. Pretty early on, we'd said we wanted to get wed, and one day we will. Love, I've found over the years, is not a rational state of mind. It's a kind of ordered madness. So you follow your heart, not your head on these matters. And on that short promenade to the number 26 bus stop over the river, in front of St Paul's, I found out why. He said, 'The thing is, my mum got to marry the man of her dreams, and I want to marry mine.' We stopped for a second. I may even have trembled. Certainly, it was the most romantic thing anyone has ever said to me. Who could argue with that? I had never felt a sensation quite like that before. I was every bit as good as you.

ACKNOWLEDGEMENTS

Thanks to Adam Mattera, Alasdair McLellan, Andrew Goodfellow, Antony Cotton, Antony Dutton, Ben Kelly, Ben Reardon, Beth Harrold, Bill Lyons, Caroline Butler, Caroline McAteer, Carolyn Weinstein, Catherine Russell, Charlie Porter, Chris Payne, Chris Smith, Colin Bell, Daniel Davidson, Danny Bell, Dave Kendrick, David Furnish, David Yelland, Davina McCall, Dawn Shadforth, Diederick Santer, Eugenie Furniss, Gary Hailes, Gert Jonkers, Hanna Hanra, Hattie Collins, Holly Johnson, Holly Shackleton, Isabelle Parkinson, Jeremy Abbott, John Tiffany, Jop Van Bennekom, Judy Blame, Juliet Ace, Katie Grand, Kealey Ridgen, Kylie Minogue, Laura Horsley, Lucie Gonnord, Luke Bainbridge, Luke Day, Luke Howard, Marc Lancaster, Mark Simpson, Matthew Todd, Nick Dear, Paul Burston, Paul Cons, Paul Gambaccini, Paul Osborne, Peter Dalton, Philip Hammond, Polly Hudson, Richard Smith, Rob Gittins, Robbie Rogers, Rupert Whittaker, Russell T Davies, Ruth Drake, Stevie King, Tom Commins, Wendy Rattray, Will Young, William Baker, the librarians at the Hall-Carpenter institute at The London School of Economics and my family